What Is a Mind?

An Integrative Introduction to the Philosophy of Mind

D0145694

What Is a Mind?

An Integrative Introduction to the Philosophy of Mind

Suzanne Cunningham

Hackett Publishing Company, Inc.
Indianapolis/Cambridge

06 05 04 03 02 01 00   1 2 3 4 5 6 7

For further information, please address

> Hackett Publishing Company, Inc.
> P. O. Box 44937
> Indianapolis, Indiana 46244–0937

> www.hackettpublishing.com

Cover and interior designs by Abigail Coyle

Photo: www.comstock.com

Library of Congress Cataloging-in-Publication Data

Cunningham, Suzanne.
    What is a mind? : an integrative introduction to the philosophy
of mind / Suzanne Cunningham.
        p. cm.
    Includes bibliographical references and index.
    ISBN 0-87220-519-3 — ISBN 0-87220-518-5 (pbk.)
    1. Philosophy of mind.   I. Title.

BD418.3 .C79 2000
218'.2—dc21   00-031905

Contents

Introduction   x

Acknowledgments   xii

1   What Sort of Thing Is a Mind?   1

    Theories of Mind   2

      Substance Dualism   2

      Mind Is Not a Thing at All   14

      Behaviorism   17

      Physicalism   21

      Property Dualism   33

      Functionalism   38

    Evaluating Theories   49

      Arguments Pro and Con   50

      Assumptions   50

      Consequences   51

      Explanatory Power   51

      Consistency with Other Well-Founded Theories   52

      Predictive Power   52

      Simplicity   52

2   What Does It Mean to Be Conscious?   54

    What Sorts of Things Are Conscious?   55

    How Can You Tell If Something Is Conscious?   56

    What Are We Conscious Of?   61

    Is Consciousness One Phenomenon or Many?   64

    Theories of Consciousness   69

      Cartesian View   69

      Higher-Order Theories of Consciousness   71

      Consciousness as a Nonphysical Property   79

      Multiple Drafts Theory of Consciousness   82

      Consciousness as Global Workspace   85

Other Approaches to Consciousness   87
   Biological Naturalism   87
   Synchronous Neural Oscillations   88
   The "Mysteria"   89
   Eliminativism   89
What Is the Function of Consciousness?   90

3   Where Do Emotions Fit?   96
   The Rational Animal   96
   Methods of Approach to Emotions   98
   Theories of Emotion   102
      Physiological/Feeling Theories   102
      Behavioral Theories   106
      Cognitive Theories   109
   Can Emotions Be Defined?   120
   What Is the Function of Emotions?   121
   How Do Emotions Relate to Other Aspects
      of the Mental?   123
   Emotions and Theories of Mind   126

4   Did the Mind Evolve?   131
   Evolution by Natural Selection   131
   Arguments Supporting Mental Evolution   134
      Evolution of the Brain   135
      Behavior of Early Hominids   135
      Animal Minds   136
      Natural Selection of the Mental   147
   Arguments against Mental Evolution   148
      Religious Argument   148
      Alfred Russel Wallace   148
      Language   153
   Mental Evolution and Theories of Mind   154

5   What Is a Self?   159
   Theories of Self   159
      Self as a Nonphysical Entity   159

The Psychological Self   162
Bundle Theory of Self   166
Kant's Transcendental Self   170
Self as (at Least) the Body   171
Self as Multidimensional   175
Self as Social Construct   178
Narrative Self   182
Evolution and the Self   184

6   Could a Machine Have a Mind?   189
    Machines and Mechanisms   189
    Symbol-System Theories   191
        Linguistic Model   192
        Computer Capabilities   195
        The Turing Test   197
        "Chinese Room" Response   198
        Skepticism about Symbol-System AI   199
        Computers versus Humans   203
    Connectionism (or Parallel Distributed Processing)   205
        Connectionist Critique of Symbol-System AI   205
        Structure of a Connectionist System   212
        Some Comparisons and Contrasts   214
        Criticisms of Connectionist AI   216
    Tentative Conclusions   218

7   How Do We Link Behavior to Mental States?   222
    Argument from Analogy   223
    Chimps and False Beliefs: Background to
        Alternative Theories   228
    The Theory-Theory of Mental Attribution   232
        Sources of Folk Psychological Theory   235
        Meaning of Mental Concepts   237
        Developmental Data: False Beliefs and Autism   239
    Simulation Theory of Mental Attribution   243
        Meaning of Mental Concepts   251
        Developmental Data: False Beliefs and Autism   252

Some Comparisons and Contrasts   256
Some Tentative Conclusions   256

Some Additional Resources   259
1. Theories of Mind (and closely related topics) 259
2. Consciousness   261
3. Emotions   263
4. Mental Evolution   265
5. Self   267
6. Artificial Intelligence   268
7. Behavior and Mental States   269

Index   271

In loving memory of my mother, Ruth.
Her valuing of education was contagious.

Introduction

Have you ever wondered about your mind—what it is, how it works, where it came from? Mind is one of the most exciting and important areas currently under investigation by researchers in philosophy, psychology, neuroscience, ethology, and a half dozen other disciplines. This text will guide you through some of the insights and many of the puzzles that have emerged from that research.

I have written it for newcomers to the field, even newcomers to philosophy itself, so don't be intimidated by the magnitude of the subject. The book presupposes no background in the area. Like most other texts, this one is full of information—about issues, about theories, and about problems that still plague most of the theories. But I have included two types of information that you won't find in most other texts. The first is information from a number of other fields in addition to philosophy, hence the subtitle "integrative." The text integrates insights from psychology, neuroscience, evolutionary biology, anthropology, computer science, and so forth, into the philosophic framework. Philosophy has come to understand that the mind will yield its secrets only if we approach it from every relevant discipline, integrating the findings of all.

The second type of information I have included comes in the form of **Notes on Terminology**. These explain some of the more technical philosophical terms in ordinary, nontechnical language.

Unlike many philosophy texts, this one is designed not only to inform you about the field, but to *engage* you in the issues discussed. Toward the end of Chapter 1 I suggest a series of steps you can take to help you in **Evaluating Theories**. At the end of each chapter (or, in Chapter 1, at the end of each section), there are **Issues for Discussion**. These will give you a chance to explore some issues during class discussion, to evaluate their respective strengths and weaknesses, to look for alternative viewpoints, and to articulate your own views on the subject. In addition, I have included **Suggested Research Projects**. These are relatively brief projects that target a journal article or a chapter in a book that addresses one or more of the issues discussed in the chapter. They are designed to introduce you to relevant material outside the text and give you an opportunity to develop your skills at writing a paper or making a class presentation.

At the end of the book you will find **Some Additional Resources**. Enjoy your exploration of the world of mind!

Suzanne Cunningham
scunnin@orion.it.luc.edu

Acknowledgments

When I began to write this book, I gave portions of it to students in my undergraduate classes on Philosophy of Mind at Loyola University Chicago. Many of them gave me very useful feedback on what was clear and what was not, what was helpful to them and what was not. As the manuscript came to completion, generous philosophical colleagues read some or all of it and gave me many beneficial suggestions. Although I have not incorporated all the suggestions that were made, the book was greatly improved by including a large number of them. I am enormously grateful to these colleagues for their generosity with their time and their insights. In particular, I want to thank Owen Flanagan, Frank Catania, J. D. Trout, and George Dickie.

Special thanks to Deborah Wilkes, editor at Hackett Publishing Company—an extraordinarily supportive, efficient, and communicative editor—and to Hackett's very capable editorial staff.

1

What Sort of Thing Is a Mind?

A remarkable thing is happening. As you look at this page, you are selecting the black marks against the white background, recognizing them as more than accidental squiggles, registering their meaning, and as a consequence probably thinking about some of the same things that I was thinking when I made them. In a word, your *mind* is functioning. When you think about it, the working of a mind is an astonishing thing.

For centuries philosophers have been fascinated by the mind. What sort of thing is it? Is it a nonphysical thing like a spiritual soul, something quite distinct from the body? Or is it a physical thing like a brain or maybe the whole central nervous system? Is it a *thing* at all? Is it best understood as a *process* or a set of *functions* rather than a thing? These are some of the questions that we explore in this chapter.

As you know if you have taken any other philosophy courses, philosophical questions have no easy and certain answers. Over the centuries, different philosophers have given an affirmative answer to each of the questions I have mentioned above. And today, although some of the proposed views about the mind are less promising than others, there is no universal agreement about which theory of mind is the best. Each has some advantages and some problems. In deciding the case, we cannot simply look and see what the mind is. It does not easily or obviously lend itself to scientific observation. Most philosophical issues are like that. So, how does one decide among competing theories? The first step is to look for reasons or arguments that support a theory, detailing its advantages. The second step is to look for objections to the theory, detailing its disadvantages. (At the end of this chapter there are some suggestions about further steps that can be taken to evaluate competing theories.)

Let's begin by looking at one of the oldest views of the mind—and one that is considered today to be among the most problematic.

Theories of Mind

Substance Dualism

Dualism is the view that the mind and the body are composed of two different things (hence, *Dualism*). The body, quite obviously, is physical—that is to say, it is subject to the physical laws of the universe. But for Substance Dualists, the *mind* is nonphysical. This means that the mind is *not* subject to the laws of the physical universe; it is not governed by the laws of biology, chemistry, or physics.

You probably recognize this view as one that is currently held by people you know, perhaps even by you. It has, in fact, become part of contemporary culture, often through its association with various religious beliefs. But this view is actually quite old. As long ago as the fourth century B.C., some philosophers believed that the mind was best understood as a nonphysical thing. Plato defended such a view. And much more recently, the 17th-century philosopher René Descartes provided a more detailed account of the view, and it has influenced our thinking about the mind right up to the present day. Whether or not one agrees with Descartes's Dualism, he has set up the framework within which issues about the mind are most often addressed in Western philosophy. If one thinks that Dualism is mistaken, one still feels obliged to give reasons for rejecting it. This is one of the many reasons that Descartes is referred to as "the father of modern philosophy." In a number of key areas, he set the terms of the debate. So let us, too, begin our exploration of the mind by considering the view he supported, *Substance Dualism*.

Descartes's version of Dualism claimed that the mind is a nonphysical thing. What does such a claim entail? Among other things, it means that the mind is nonspatial and therefore has none of the properties that we associate with physical things. It has no color, no weight, no mass, no size. That is to say, it is characterized largely in terms of negative properties. But Descartes did say at least two nonnegative things about this nonphysical mind. The first was that this mind/soul must be a *substance*. (See box on page 3.)

When Descartes called the mind a substance, he meant it must be the sort of thing that has its own existence, that does not depend on the body for its existence. This was crucial. If the mind were not a substance, if it did not have its own independent existence, the mind or soul would cease to exist when the body died, and there would be no immortality. Proving that the mind or soul is distinct from the body and therefore capable of surviving the body's death was one of Descartes's

Note on Terminology: When philosophers use the term *substance* it does not have the same meaning as it does in ordinary conversation. We might say in conversation that a child "stepped in a sticky substance" or that someone "has been suffering from substance abuse." In both cases what we mean by "substance" is some specific, observable thing—like gum, drugs, or alcohol. By contrast, the philosophical term 'substance' is more elusive than that. It does not designate an observable thing. It is what we call a "theoretical" notion. That is, some philosophers have postulated 'substance' as the sort of thing that *has* properties like color, shape, weight. It *underlies* those properties, and its existence is distinct from theirs. If you think about it, what we actually observe are simply the properties of things. So philosophical 'substance', if there actually is such a thing, would not be observable. We say that it is a "theoretical" notion because, in addition to not being observable, it appears to be required in order to explain certain things within a particular theory. For example, it can be used to explain how something might remain the same thing in spite of the fact that all its observable properties have changed—like you, from the day of your birth until today. Related to all this, a philosophical 'substance' is the sort of thing that can exist in its own right. It is not dependent on something else (except perhaps, some philosophers would argue, on God).

stated goals for his *Meditations*. As we shall see, this connection between Substance Dualism and immortality became, for some, a reason to accept Descartes's view. So for Descartes, the body and the mind were two distinct substances, one physical and mortal, the other nonphysical and immortal.

The second positive thing Descartes said about the mind was that its defining property is that it *thinks*. But in the notion of "thinking" he included everything that we would consider to be a mental state or event. So on his view, believing, doubting, dreaming, desiring, and so forth, all count as instances of *thinking*. According to the Cartesian view, when you believe something, your believing is a nonphysical property of a nonphysical substance. And this is true for all your other mental states as well.

An important philosophical question is, What reasons can be given for believing that Substance Dualism is correct? To begin with, it seems clear that the most obvious sorts of arguments, which one uses in the empirical sciences, are not available here. One cannot argue that we know the mind is nonphysical because we can *see* that it is or because we have direct empirical evidence that it is. What else might one base one's answers on? In the case of Substance Dualism, there have been several different considerations presented in its support. We'll look at three of them: (1) immortality (which I already mentioned briefly), (2) free will, and (3) differences in our ways of knowing minds and bodies.

Immortality

There is no disagreement about the fact that our bodies die. Most philosophers agree that the reason they die is that they are physical, subject to all the constraints imposed by biology, chemistry, and physics. Physical things normally disintegrate in various ways. Living physical bodies get sick, get old, stop functioning properly, and ultimately die. There is, however, a widespread belief that something about us will live on after our bodies die. If that something is going to survive our bodily death, it must not be physical and it must be a substance—something that can exist in its own right when the body dies. That nonphysical substance is sometimes called a *soul*, sometimes a *mind*. For Descartes, 'soul' and 'mind' were simply different names for the same thing.

> **Note on Terminology:** Although Descartes used the terms 'soul' and 'mind' interchangeably, many earlier philosophers did not do so. Aristotle, for example, used the term 'soul' to indicate the source of *life* in living things. Everything that is alive, on Aristotle's view, has a soul. Different types of souls account for the differences in the activities appropriate to different types of living things. Plants, for example, were thought to have a soul that gives them the capacity to grow and to reproduce. Nonhuman animals were believed to have souls that enabled them to do both of those things as well as to perceive their environment and move around in it. Human beings were thought to have souls that give them all those capacities as well as the ability to think and reason. Notice that on this view what we think of as 'mind' today is not the same thing as 'soul'. It is not even the same thing as a human soul. Rather, it seems to be equivalent to one of the types of activity that a human soul would make possible. In current philosophy of mind, the terms 'mind' and 'soul' are not used interchangeably. In fact, in this context there is virtually no discussion of 'soul' at all.

One obvious question that arises at this point is, How do we know that we are immortal? The answer is that we don't *know* that we are. Nonetheless, many people of different religious backgrounds *believe* and hope that we are. One of the most general reasons for that belief is that life is not fair. Some people live miserable, immoral lives and are never caught and punished for it. Other people live exemplary lives and never seem to be rewarded for it. So it has seemed to some that there must be a time and a place when things will be made right. That place is thought to be heaven (or hell), and that time is after death—hence, the belief in immortality. It is thought to be a matter of justice. Notice that an argument of this sort does not *prove* that we are immortal; it simply provides some support for the belief that we are. It may turn out that life simply isn't fair, and it will not be made fair after death.

So Descartes's Dualism does not guarantee immortality. However, if one already believes in or hopes for immortality, Substance Dualism could provide a framework within which such a belief could make sense. Thus, belief in immortality could become one reason for accepting Substance Dualism.

Free Will

A second reason that some philosophers have had for defending Substance Dualism is that it seems to provide a framework within which one can make sense of freedom of the will. The traditional doctrine of free will is the view that in some situations, but not all, human beings are able to choose between at least two alternative courses of action, and the choice of either of those alternatives is not forced by causal factors beyond the person's control. However, if everything about us is physical and is therefore governed by the laws of biology, chemistry, and physics, then it would seem that everything about us *is* outside our control. If that is the case, then we cannot be held morally responsible for our actions because we are incapable of choosing them ourselves. However, some argue that we *do* feel that we make our own choices and that we are morally responsible for them, so there must be some part of us that is not physical and is not subject to the control of the physical laws of the universe. That part of us, so the argument goes, is the nonphysical mind (or soul).

Again, there is no decisive empirical evidence to show that we do indeed have free will of the sort that the view requires. However, many people feel that in at least some cases we make our own choices relatively unconstrained by physical forces beyond our control. That, of course, is no guarantee that we have a free will. Many of the things that we *feel* to be the case turn out to be false. We may feel that we are thoughtful, considerate people, while everyone else finds us just the opposite. We may feel that we are being persecuted by someone when that person may not have the slightest interest in us. So, feeling that something is the case is not always the best evidence for its being the case. On the other hand, if our feeling about our free will is mistaken, and we are completely determined by physical laws outside our control, then our beliefs about ethics and moral responsibility could also turn out to be mistaken. For many philosophers (and nonphilosophers) that would be problematic and undesirable.

The difficulty with the issue of free will is that it turns out to be problematic on just about any view of the mind that we take. If we are completely physical, there seems to be little room for the traditional notion of free will. But even if we have a nonphysical mind (or soul) that is outside the scope of physical laws, how does it manage to control our behavior? Recall that a nonphysical thing is not spatial and therefore not spatially locatable. It has absolutely no physical properties. If that is the case, how can it cause the physical body to do its bidding? It has none of the properties it would need in order to make anything happen in the physical world. As it turns out, this will be one of the most serious problems for a Substance Dualist account of the mind. If the mind is truly a nonphysical substance, we have no idea how it could possibly interact with the physical body—either to cause its behavior or to receive information from it. So a nonphysical mind does not appear to explain how our behavior could be the outcome of a free (nonphysical) will.

The view that we have a free will that is wholly responsible for our choices presents extraordinary difficulties, and we certainly won't solve them here. But one thing is clear: Postulating a nonphysical mind does not resolve that issue as well as initially hoped.

Note on Terminology: Issues relating to free will, to immortality, to the nature of the mind, to the existence of God, are generally referred to as *metaphysical* issues, meaning that they do not lend themselves to empirical investigation or to the sort of publicly observable evidence that can decide which among various views is correct. Metaphysical views cannot be either confirmed or shown to be false on empirical or experimental grounds. Nonetheless, in spite of their necessarily speculative character, most metaphysical issues are of great importance and interest to us.

Ways of Knowing

The final argument that we will consider for Dualism rests on the different ways we have of knowing our bodies and our minds. An obvious way we have of knowing our own bodies is by looking at them, touching them—that is, perceiving them with our senses. They are publicly observable. We can learn about them not only from our own perceptions of them but also from the observations of other people and from what they tell us about them. With our minds it is different. Even if it turns out that our mental states are actually states of our brains, and therefore physical, we don't experience the two in the same way. When we experience a sensation of red, that sensation doesn't appear to us as an activated neural network. And, although other people can observe our bodies, they don't know our mental states in the same way that we do. They can see how we behave and hear what we say, but our ability to deceive other people leads us and them to think that there is more to our minds than what is observed in our speech and behavior.

This difference, or *asymmetry*, in our ways of knowing our bodies and minds has led some philosophers to argue that these must be two different types of things. Our ways of knowing bodies is a function of the fact that they are physical, and therefore spatial and public. Our way of knowing our minds seems to indicate that they are not spatial or public, and therefore not physical.

Descartes had a special version of this argument. He claimed that we know with certainty that our minds exist. If we try to doubt that they do, the doubting (or even wondering about it) is itself an act of the mind. Any effort to call into question the existence of my own mind becomes self-defeating. However, he claimed that the existence of the body could be subject to doubt. In defense of this counterintuitive claim, Descartes pointed to the phenomenon of the "phantom limb." This is a well-documented phenomenon in which a person who has had an arm or leg amputated will often continue to feel sensations in the missing limb, sometimes even excruciating pain (see box on page 8 for a contemporary explanation of this phenomenon). For Descartes, this was evidence that one could be mistaken about one's body in ways that one was incapable of being mistaken about one's mind. This form of asymmetry he took as evidence of the distinction between mind and body.

One might object that both immortality and free will might well be simply a matter of wishful thinking, and therefore any arguments for Substance Dualism based on them will be highly questionable. After all, there are many people who don't believe we are immortal, and many who don't believe that we have free will. Thus, arguments based on either will be substantively weakened in their appeal. But in the case of the asymmetry in our ways of knowing bodies and minds, there is little dispute that we do seem to know them in distinct ways. For some theorists this fact has continued to suggest support for some version of Dualism.

Phantom Limb: One traditional explanation of phantom limbs suggested that the nerve endings, at the point where the limb had been severed, continued to send (false) messages to the brain about the state of the missing limb. More recently, V. S. Ramachandran, a brain researcher at the University of California at San Diego, has proposed a different theory. He hypothesizes that when, for example, an arm is amputated, the neurons in the brain's "map" of the body rewire themselves in such a way that the portion of the brain map correlated with the face may take over some of the functions formerly carried out by the portion associated with the arm. Stimulation to the face could then affect both the face and the phantom arm. If he is right, then phantom limbs don't raise questions about the existence of the body; they are merely a consequence of the physical rewiring of the brain.[1]

Incidentally, research suggests that there are other types of "phantom" experiences, including taste and smell phantoms.

But other philosophers have raised an objection to this asymmetry argument. The objection asks, What conclusion follows from the fact that we know things in two different ways? Does that automatically tell us anything about the nature of those things? Or does it simply tell us something about variations or limitations in our ways of knowing? Our way of knowing gravity is different from our way of knowing a tree, and both are different from our way of knowing electrons. We know trees by seeing them, planting them, or burning them down; we don't know gravity or electrons in those ways. We know them primarily by their effects and by our theories about them, based on those effects. But what follows from that? Surely it does not follow that some of these things are physical and some are not.

The Dualist will likely respond that the asymmetries involved in the ways we know gravity, electrons, and trees are not comparable to the differences in the way we know bodies and minds. For these Dualists, the asymmetry in our ways of knowing bodies and minds is a special case, unlike all the other asymmetries in our knowledge. Our way of knowing our own mind is by way of *introspection*, a looking inward at our mental states. It is private, not publicly accessible, whereas our way of knowing things like gravity, electrons, and trees is by way of publicly accessible data. So, they argue, the way of knowing the mind is unique and does indeed carry the conclusion that minds are not physical.

1. V. S. Ramachandran and Sandra Blakeslee, *Phantoms in the Brain* (New York: William Morrow, 1998).

One counter to this argument, offered by philosopher Paul Churchland in his book, *Matter and Consciousness*, is that introspection is no more an infallible source of information than is sensory perception. Our perceptions of the world surely do not automatically and infallibly reveal to us the nature of things. If they did, science would never have given us a richer understanding of our world than perception does. To perception, the earth really did *look* flat, and solid objects certainly did not *look* as if they were masses of tiny particles in rapid motion. Our perceptions can indeed be mistaken. Similarly, Churchland argues, there is small reason to assume that introspection simply lays open to us in a clear and infallible way the nature of our mental states. It is every bit as capable of error as perception is. If this is right, then the asymmetry in our ways of knowing minds and bodies—one by introspection, the other by perception—may not entail (i.e., may not lead with logical necessity to) anything specific about the nature of the things we know in these ways.

Strengths and Weaknesses of Substance Dualism

Substance Dualism has several attractive features. If it is true, then we may have a framework within which to understand immortality. It might also explain why we know minds and bodies in different ways. It might even conceivably give some hope of explaining how free will is possible, although such accounts as those now available are not without serious problems. Substance Dualism would also provide some reason for thinking that we are special, unique in the world. Human beings have a long history of believing that we are the crowning glory of the universe, and if we possess a unique substance that no other physical creatures have, that would indeed make us special. Again, this may be little more than wishful thinking.

On the negative side the most serious difficulty for Substance Dualism is that we have no plausible explanation of how a nonphysical mind could cause things to happen in a physical body or how a physical body could bring about changes in a nonphysical mind. By definition, the nonphysical mind is not spatial and so it can have no spatial point of contact with a physical body. And yet we know that mind and body do, in fact, interact. When you drink a couple of beers or take certain medication, it can interfere with your ability to think clearly. When people are depressed, certain medications can relieve the feeling of depression. In other words, we have ample evidence that physical substances like alcohol or medicine can affect the mind. In addition, physical events such as a stroke, brain surgery, or an epileptc seizure can alter mental function. It also seems clear that mental functions can affect the body. When you decide that you want to get up and go into the next room or go get a hamburger, your body gets up and does what your mind has decided to do. A satisfactory theory of the mind cannot leave those causal interactions between mind and body as unexplained mysteries.

Descartes attempted to explain the interaction between mind and body by appeal to *animal spirits*, thought to be tiny bodies circulated by the blood. He suggested that sensory stimuli would cause these bodies to move toward the brain where they would move the pineal gland at the base of the brain. This movement, in turn, would provide information to the mind about the sensory stimuli. Operating in reverse, the animal spirits would carry information passed from the mind to the pineal gland and then to various parts of the body, thereby moving the muscles. The problem with Descartes's solution is that these animal spirits are, by Descartes's own admission, just extremely tiny *bodies*. So the bridge between the physical (even *tiny* bits of the physical) and the nonphysical mind still remains unexplained.

A further difficulty for Substance Dualism arises from evolutionary considerations. If it is the case that human beings are the product of a long evolutionary history—and there is abundant evidence that this is the case—and if evolutionary processes are natural physical processes working on physical entities, it becomes puzzling how a nonphysical substance could come into being. Some religious groups have responded that the soul or mind is a direct creation of God for each individual human being. Such a response, however, is not without its problems. If God exists and is the source of the laws governing evolution, one wonders why the human mind would have to be treated as an exception to the process. Furthermore, many nonhuman animals appear to have some mental states not all that dissimilar to those of human beings, yet no one argues that they must have nonphysical souls or minds. (I should note here that Descartes believed that nonhuman animals do *not* have any mental states at all; he considered them to be purely mechanical physical systems.)

Notice that philosophers have not proved that Substance Dualism is false. Rather, while the view may have some advantages, it presents us with what appears to be an insoluble problem in the case of mind-body interaction. When problems of such magnitude appear, philosophers generally begin to look for alternative views that can avoid such problems.

Recall that the version of Dualism that we have been discussing was a response to the question, What sort of a thing is the mind? Note, too, that the way one formulates a question carries with it certain assumptions and can limit the answers that can be given to the question. If one asks, "When did you stop shoplifting?" the implicit assumption is that one has indeed been stealing things from stores, and the question is asking only about the time when you stopped. If one has never shoplifted, one simply cannot answer the question. The question has been badly framed. For some philosophers, the question, What sort of thing is a mind? is similarly badly framed. It assumes that the mind is some sort of *thing*, physical or nonphysical. The 20th-century British philosopher Gilbert Ryle has argued that making this assumption involves what he calls a "category mistake." We shall turn to his view in the next section.

Issues for Discussion

1. Do you think that the different ways we have of knowing bodies and minds show that minds are nonphysical? Give careful reasons for your answer.

2. Can you think of any arguments other than the "fairness" argument that would support belief in immortality? Or do you think that the belief in immortality is unfounded? Explain your answer.

3. How would you argue in defense of the traditional notion of free will? How would you argue against it? Do you think that either argument is conclusive? Give your reasons.

4. Do you think that biology, chemistry, or physics places any constraints on our behavior? If so, do any consequences follow for freedom of the will?

5. If we are immortal, would you be satisfied to survive as a nonphysical soul/mind ? Do you think that your identity as a female or a male would be lost? If so, do you consider that to be problematic? Give your reasons.

6. One reason that Descartes denied that nonhuman animals have minds was their inability to use language. Can you think of another reason why he would have been reluctant to say that they have minds or souls?

7. If Substance Dualism is right, would that have any consequences for a scientific study of the mind? Explain your answer.

8. Can you think of other arguments that might support Substance Dualism?

9. Can you think of other problems that Substance Dualism faces?

10. Do you think that we should limit our beliefs to those that can be supported by publicly observable evidence? Explain your answer.

Suggested Research Projects

Items marked with * may require more time and effort. *Document all your sources.*

a. Do all religions believe in immortality? If not, can you name some that don't? What view of the mind do those religions have?

*b. What arguments did Plato give, in his dialogue *Phaedo*, for thinking that the soul is immortal? Evaluate his arguments.

c. What is the Hindu view of the soul/mind?

*d. What arguments are *currently* given in support of Dualism? (One well-known source is *The Self and Its Brain*, by Karl Popper and Sir John Eccles, New York: Springer-Verlag, 1977.)

e. What is a *compatibilist* account of freedom? Does it require a nonphysical mind? Do you think that it adequately accounts for moral responsibility?

f. What is *panpsychism*?

g. Read Chapter 7, "Freedom," in Jack Copeland's book, *Artificial Intelligence*. What are some arguments he presents for and against the notion of free will? What two kinds of freedom does Copeland defend?

h. Read Chapter 3, "The Disembodied Lady," in Oliver Sacks's book, *The Man Who Mistook His Wife for a Hat*. Do you think it might make Descartes's willingness to raise doubts about the certainty of the body more plausible? Explain your answer.

*i. Read William Seager's article, "Descartes and the Union of Mind and Body," in *History of Philosophy Quarterly*, vol. 5, no. 2 (April 1988). What arguments does Seager offer in defense of Descartes's interactionism? Do you think Seager is right? Explain your answer.

Some Resource Materials

Some of the *general* research sources for philosophy of mind include:

Encyclopedia of Philosophy (8 vols.). Paul Edwards, ed. (New York: Macmillan, 1967). Topics are listed alphabetically; if you don't find a listing for your topic, check the Index to see if it is included with another topic.

Philosopher's Index (Bowling Green, OH: Philosophy Documentation Center). This is also available on CD. It is a periodical index of journal articles in philosophy.

Blackwell's Companion to the Philosophy of Mind, Samuel Guttenplan, ed. (Oxford: Blackwell, 1994).

The Oxford Companion to the Mind, Richard Gregory, ed. (Oxford: Oxford University Press, 1987).

Some *specialized* books dealing with many of the topics in this chapter include:

Paul Churchland. *Matter and Consciousness*. Rev. ed. 1988.

René Descartes. *Meditations*.

Owen Flanagan. *Science of the Mind*. 2nd ed. 1991.

George Graham. *Philosophy of Mind*. 1993.

Barbara Hannan. *Subjectivity and Reduction. An Introduction to the Mind-Body Problem*. 1994.

John Heil. *Philosophy of Mind*. 1998.

Dale Jacquette. *Philosophy of Mind*. 1994.

Jaegwon Kim. *Philosophy of Mind*. 1996.

Stephen Priest. *Theories of the Mind*. 1991.

Georges Rey. *Contemporary Philosophy of Mind*. 1997.

Peter Smith and O. R. Jones. *The Philosophy of Mind*. 1986.

Mind Is Not a Thing at All

In a very influential book, *The Concept of Mind*, published in 1949, philosopher Gilbert Ryle argued that Descartes's Dualism was based on a profound *category mistake*. Ryle gave several examples of what he meant by a category mistake. Imagine being shown around the local university, and seeing the classrooms, the dormitories, the administration building, the library, and the student union, and then saying, "Yes, I see all this, but where is the university?" One has mistakenly supposed that "the university" is one more building on equal footing with the others that one has seen. But "university" is a collective name for the whole entity. That is, it does not belong to the same *category* as the library, the dorms, and so on. It belongs to a more general category that can refer to whole collections. Similarly, imagine looking at a large number of soldiers in uniform marching by and saying, "Well, I see all these soldiers in formation, but where is the military division?" Again, this is a category mistake. A "division" is not something in addition to the soldiers. It is a collective term, belonging to a more general category.

For Ryle, Descartes's Dualism had made a category mistake when it claimed that the mind was a substance, a *thing*, placing it in the same category as the body but giving it a puzzling set of nonphysical characteristics. On Ryle's view, the concept 'mind' does not designate a thing of any sort, nonphysical or physical. It is a collective name we use to designate *patterns of behaviors*. Notice that the fact that 'mind' is a noun does not mean that it must name some *thing* (in spite of your fourth grade lessons in grammar). Many nouns do name things, but many don't. "Happiness" doesn't name a *thing*; neither does "democracy" or "the future." Similarly, from Ryle's point of view, 'mind' does not name a thing. It is a general word we use to refer to patterns of behavior, dispositions, or tendencies to behave in certain ways.

In spite of Ryle's protests to the contrary, his characterization of 'mind' in terms of behaviors has led most other philosophers to classify his view as Behaviorist. His Behaviorism was not, however, of the standard psychological sort. He was concerned with *language*, not with metaphysics. Instead of arguing about the nature of a supposed thing called the mind, he wanted to show that all mental *concepts*, or mental *words*, including 'mind', could be translated into descriptions of actual or potential behavior. For example, to say that someone *believes* that dogs make good pets simply means that if asked, he will nod his head or say, "Yes, dogs make good pets." The concept of belief is to be understood in terms of a bit of behavior. Ryle's view is sometimes referred to as Linguistic (or Logical) Behaviorism.

Perhaps because of Ryle's influence, many philosophers today speak less of *the mind* and more often of *mental states*, like the state of believing something, or the state of desiring something, or the state of remembering something. As you will see in later chapters, there are additional good reasons to stop thinking of 'mind' as if it were one unified, all-or-nothing thing and, rather, to think in terms of collections of mental states or mental capabilities. This will become especially apparent in our discussion of mental evolution.

> **Mental Dissociations:** One of the reasons for thinking of mind as a collection of capabilities rather than as a unified, all-or-nothing thing is that neuroscience and psychology have provided us with abundant evidence of various types of *mental dissociations*. It is possible for a person to lose one mental ability while retaining all or most of the others. One can lose an aspect of memory and yet retain the capacity for beliefs, desires, language use, and so forth. Alternatively, one can lose the ability to articulate what one sees in part of one's visual field but maintain all other normal cognitive functions. Mental dissociations include such phenomena as amnesic syndrome, blindsight, hemi-neglect, split-brain syndrome, aphasia, prosopagnosia. I shall have more to say about them as we go on in the text.

If Ryle is right, then the question, What sort of thing is the mind? is a misleading question that will encourage mistaken answers. If so, then the mind is not a nonphysical substance or even a physical one; it is not a *thing* at all.

Strengths and Weaknesses of Ryle's View

One of the advantages of Ryle's view is that, if he is right, he avoids the most significant problem associated with Substance Dualism. If issues associated with the mind are transformed into questions about behavior, then one is no longer concerned with the issue of how a nonphysical *thing* can interact with physical things. Clearly, body and behavior "interact" in apparently obvious ways. And, if his view is right, then the apparent asymmetry in our ways of knowing would disappear. If 'mind' really refers to patterns of behavior, then we know minds in the same way we know bodies, by publicly observable data.

Ryle's view, however, is not without its own problems. When a mental concept like 'desire' is translated into a description of behavior, one gets some unexpected results. For example, "Sally desires some coffee" would translate into something like, "If coffee is present, Sally will try to get some." The problem is that there is a hidden premise here—one that includes a second mental state. Sally will try to get some coffee only if she *believes* that it is present. In other words, the translation of one mental concept, 'desire', into a behavioral pattern requires a tacit commitment to another mental concept, 'belief'. Furthermore, it turns out that efforts to translate 'belief' will require an analogous (and tacit) commitment to 'desire'. When one translates, "Charlie believes that his brother is a great ballplayer," into "When asked if his brother is a great ballplayer, Charlie will nod his head or say that he is," the translation will be adequate only if one assumes that Charlie desires to tell the truth. In the end, it doesn't seem to be possible to get a purely Behavioral translation of mental concepts. Some other mental concept always lurks in the background and apparently cannot be eliminated.

Issues for Discussion

1. Can you explain the concept 'belief' in language of actual or possible *behavior* without making tacit assumptions about any other mental concepts? Do you think that the explanation gives an adequate account of what the term 'belief' means?

2. Can you give another example of a category mistake?

3. Do you think that Ryle was right when he claimed that the concept 'mind' does not designate a *thing* of any sort? Give careful reasons for your answer.

4. How do we decide when something counts as a *thing*? What sorts of characteristics must it have?

5. Can you think of examples, other than category mistakes, in which language can mislead us?

6. Why would the meaning of *words* and *concepts* like 'mind' be relevant to a philosophy of mind?

Suggested Research Projects

a. What was the "linguistic turn" in 20th-century philosophy? (Richard Rorty's edited collection, *The Linguistic Turn* [Chicago: University of Chicago, 1967], should be some help

here. Also, most histories of 20th-century philosophy should
have an account of this.)

*b. What were some of the reasons that motivated 20th-century
philosophers to become so concerned with language?

c. What was "Ordinary Language Philosophy"? Who were
some of its most famous practitioners?

Behaviorism

Next, consider some different approaches to Behaviorism (that is, other
than Ryle's Linguistic Behaviorism) that were proposed early in the
20th century. Some versions took the form of *Metaphysical Behaviorism*; other, more cautious versions, are sometimes referred to as *Methodological* (or *Psychological*) *Behaviorism*. A bit of background will help
to highlight how these views became so influential during the first half
of the 20th century.

During the past four hundred years, natural science has made
remarkable progress. With the theories of people like Newton, Galileo,
Darwin, and Einstein, our understanding of the physical universe has
increased enormously. But it was not until relatively recently, in the
19th century, that the social sciences—including psychology—began to
make significant progress of their own. To some extent, their progress
was enhanced by their efforts to imitate the methods of the natural sciences. People like the philosopher and psychologist William James
made important contributions to an increasingly scientific approach to
psychology. James was especially important in bringing attention to the
experimental method in American psychology. Before the 19th century, psychology was a part of philosophy and involved virtually no
experimental work. By the early 20th century observation and experimentation in psychology were becoming more commonplace.

One other psychologist at the forefront of the effort to make psychology more scientific was John Watson. He was the founder of Psychological Behaviorism. Until the late 19th and early 20th centuries the mind
had been studied primarily by way of *introspection*, simply looking in on
one's own mind to see what was going on there. Recall that one argument that Substance Dualists used in support of their view was that we
know our minds in a different way from the way we know our bodies.
Introspection was thought to be the only way we know anything about
the mind. And since one can introspect only one's own mind, it was
thought that there are no publicly observable data about mental states.
As a consequence, psychological data based solely on introspection had

been problematic from a scientific point of view. Such data could be gathered only by asking individuals to look in on their own minds and report what was happening. If different individuals gave inconsistent reports about how a given mental state functioned, there was literally no "court of appeal." The psychologist could not introspect the two minds to see what was really happening. He or she could only introspect his or her own mind and perhaps produce a third account.

Watson found this method unacceptable for a scientific psychology. If psychology was going to make any progress as a science it would have to deal with publicly observable data. The obvious candidate for such data was *behavior*. More broadly, Watson believed that psychology should concern itself with environmental stimuli and the organism's responses to such stimuli. B. F. Skinner, following in Watson's footsteps, urged that psychology become the science of behavioral responses to stimuli.

Behaviorism took two somewhat different forms. In its most radical version, mental states were simply *identified* with behavior. It was thought that there was nothing more to it, nothing internal or hidden. This view is sometimes referred to as *Metaphysical Behaviorism* since it makes a metaphysical claim about the nature of mind or mental states, namely, that they are just publicly observable behavior. The more moderate version, called *Methodological Behaviorism*, made no claims about the nature of the mental but held that if there were an internal mind or mental states, it was for all practical purposes inaccessible to scientific observation and should on that account be disregarded. This more moderate view did not deny the existence of mental states that might be accessible only to their owner, but it argued that behavior could give an adequate indication of whatever mental states there might be. On the other hand, it did not make any commitment to the existence of such internal mental states either.

Strengths and Weaknesses of Behaviorism

The advantages of Behaviorism were obvious. One could study the mental (or "psychological") using the methods of the natural sciences — observation and experimentation. One no longer had to argue for the existence of a mysterious private entity, the mind. All the relevant items were public and verifiable. This was, after all, the sort of method that was used in studying the psychology of nonhuman animals. Given evolutionary considerations, it seemed plausible to suppose that similar methods would be adequate for the related but more advanced psychology of human beings. Of course, a Behaviorist account of the mental

Hemi-Neglect: Hemi-neglect is a deficit that highlights an abnormal link between brain and behavior. Hemi-neglect usually occurs with damage to the parietal lobe in the right hemisphere of the brain. It results in the patient ignoring or neglecting the left side of her visual field. As Patricia Churchland notes, "They may dress and clean only the right side of [the] body, eat only food on the right side of the plate, read only the right side of a page, and draw only the right side of a figure."[2] She further notes that even if the relevant material is completely in the patient's right visual field, she will still generally neglect its left half. It seems, then, that the problem is not with vision but with neglect. For some reason, this particular type of damage to the brain results in a peculiar behavioral syndrome.

also resolved Descartes's interaction problem. Mental states were construed as behavioral states (or dispositions to such states), so there was no problem of trying to link anything nonphysical to the physical body. Behavior is simply an activity of the physical body itself. To this extent, at least, it appeared to be an improvement over Substance Dualism.

From the point of view of Watson and Skinner, perhaps the most important practical strength of Behaviorism was the possibility that one might learn how to predict and control behavior by controlling stimuli and rewarding appropriate responses to them. If the latter were possible, it would have enormous social and political consequences. But it is likely that the most lasting positive legacy of Behaviorism was its insistence that the mental be understood within the context of an organism's interaction with its environment. This was a significant implication of its emphasis on stimulus and response.

The difficulties with Behaviorism were slower to come to the fore. I noted one of these difficulties in connection with Ryle's Linguistic Behaviorism. Where a Rylean account of *translating* concepts like belief and desire appears unable to eliminate implicit reference to some residual mental state, so Psychological Behaviorism suffered an analogous problem in its efforts to *explain* belief and desire. Consider the same sort of example that I discussed in connection with Ryle. One might be said to *desire* ice cream if, in the presence of ice cream, one made efforts to get some. Notice that there is no reference to any internal state of the organism. The explanation of desire is entirely in terms of stimulus (ice cream is present) and response (one tries to get it). But again, this expla-

2. Patricia Churchland, *Neurophilosophy* (Cambridge, MA: MIT/Bradford, 1986), p. 230.

nation seems to require an assumption that the individual *believes* that ice cream is present and has no other countervailing *desires*. Neither that belief nor the other possible desires is simply an observable behavior. That is, it looks as if one can give a Behavioral account of one psychological state only by assuming other *non*behavioral psychological states like relevant beliefs and such. In a word, it appears that one cannot give a completely Behavioral account of the mental that requires absolutely nothing more than stimuli and responses. As philosophers Ned Block and Jerry Fodor expressed it, "The fundamental argument against behaviorism is simply that what an organism does or is disposed to do at a given time is a very complicated function of its beliefs and desires together with its current sensory inputs and memories."[3]

Other difficulties gradually became apparent. A Behavioral account of mental states ignores any qualitative content they may have. A pain, for example, is not simply a response to a certain type of stimuli; it also has a certain *feel* to it. Relatedly, Behaviorism has nothing to say about consciousness, a fact that more recent theories of the mental are working to remedy. Finally, as any professional actor or even any liar can attest, it is possible to behave in ways that bear little relation to one's actual mental state. Deception depends on the ability to conceal one's mental state by behaving in ways that suggest a quite different state.

It is widely agreed by most philosophers today that although Behaviorism made some important contributions to our psychological understanding, it is not adequate as a complete theory of the mental.

Issues for Discussion

1. Can you give some examples of behavior in nonhuman animals that we take to indicate to us their psychological state?

2. In what way might the performance of an actress on stage present a difficulty for Behaviorism?

3. Give some examples of ways in which we try to control one another's behavior by using certain stimuli.

4. Are there any limits to predicting someone else's behavior in the presence of some stimulus? Explain your answer.

3. "What Psychological States Are Not," *Philosophical Review*, 81, no. 2 (April 1972); reprinted in vol. 1 of *Readings in Philosophy of Psychology*, Ned Block, ed. (Cambridge, MA: Harvard University Press, 1980).

5. Do we have access to other people's minds in ways other than by observing their behavior?

6. What are some of the most significant differences between Behaviorism and Substance Dualism? Which of the two theories seems most plausible to you at this point? Explain your answer.

Suggested Research Projects

a. What account of free will did B. F. Skinner give in his book, *Beyond Freedom and Dignity* (New York: Knopf, 1971)? Why would a Behaviorist hold such a view?

b. What behavioral account of *thinking* was credited to John Watson? (Note that he later denied that he really intended to defend that view.)

*c. What was Noam Chomsky's criticism of B. F. Skinner's theory about how children learn language? (See Chomsky's 1959 review of Skinner's book, *Verbal Behavior*, reprinted in vol. 1 of *Readings in Philosophy of Psychology*, edited by Ned Block.)

d. What are "innate ideas"? If there are such things, do they present any problem for Behaviorism? Explain your answer.

Physicalism

I pointed out earlier that Substance Dualism is a very old theory of the mind. Its chief competitor, Physicalism, is at least as old. Like Dualism, it too had its adherents among the ancient Greeks. For example, Democritus and Epicurus believed that everything consists of material atoms. Unlike Dualism, Physicalism locates the mind within the natural physical world and considers it to be subject to all the laws that govern that world. The early versions of the view were called *materialism*. That simply indicated that the mind, like the body, was taken to be a material thing, most commonly the brain. One of Descartes's contemporaries, Thomas Hobbes, was a Materialist. He believed that everthing in this world could be explained in terms of matter in motion.

Physicalist philosophers have been motivated partly by the difficulties they see in Dualism (and later, Behaviorism) and partly by some of the more positive aspects of a physical account of mental states. Postulating a nonphysical substance that had none of the characteristics

Note on Terminology: The term 'materialism' as it is used here does not mean the same as it sometimes does in ordinary conversation. It does not mean that one is crassly devoted to accumulating material things. It is nothing more than a name for the view that everything that exists in this world, including the mind, is material — that is, *matter*. In recent years, given our increased understanding of physics, many philosophers have substituted the term 'physicalism' for the traditional 'materialism'. The reason is that the physical world contains not only matter but also energy. A term like 'physicalism' broadens the claim to say that everything that exists in this world, including the mind, belongs to the realm of the physical.

associated with ordinary objects appeared to some Physicalists to be little more than unfounded speculation. There was no direct evidence for the existence of such a thing. Furthermore, a Dualistic account of the mind put it forever beyond the reach of scientific investigation, and, as we noted earlier, there is abundant evidence of a very close association between mental states and the physical state of the brain and body. It seemed to Physicalist philosophers that the *simplest* account of the mind would be in terms of the familiar objects and laws of the physical world rather than in terms of a second reality that was inaccessible to science or to empirical evidence.

The most obvious candidate for identification with the mind was, of course, the brain, or some subset of brain states. Damage to the brain clearly alters mental function. So it seemed plausible to argue that the mind is located in the brain. A Physicalist account of the mind could also explain why things like drugs and alcohol could affect one's moods, one's ability to think clearly, one's ability to remember things.

Physicalism could also explain how the sensory systems of the body (visual, auditory, etc.) could transmit information to the mind. Physicalism solved the "interaction problem" that Substance Dualism faced, by simply explaining an organism's mental states in terms of its brain states. According to Physicalism there is no metaphysical divide that has to be crossed to a nonphysical mind. On this view, everything will ultimately be explained within the context of the physical sciences.

Unlike Substance Dualism, which maintained one basic form over the years, Physicalism has taken a number of different forms. The early versions were general, arguing simply that the world was composed of physical atoms or that everything could be explained in terms of the motions of those bits of matter. By the 20th century the views became

Prosopagnosia: Prosopagnosia is a deficit usually caused by damage to the right hemisphere of the brain. Although the patient can recognize a face as a face, he loses the ability to recognize *familiar* faces. In some cases, the person is no longer able to recognize even his own face. The deficit is sometimes overcome to some degree by using other clues about the identity of people—for example, by paying attention to the voice or the presence of glasses. Nonetheless, in spite of the inability to consciously recognize familiar faces, certain aspects of the (unconscious) autonomic nervous system react differently in the presence of familiar faces.[4] Deficits like this one highlight the very close connection between brain function and mental function.

more specific, and a number of different versions of Physicalism have developed. While all versions are committed to the view that everything in this world is physical, they differ in the precise accounts they give of mental states. We will look at five varieties: *Type Physicalism, Token Physicalism, Reductive Physicalism, Nonreductive Physicalism,* and *Eliminative Physicalism.* In fact, they are not all mutually exclusive. One might, for example, hold some version of both Token and Reductive Physicalism. But to get clear about the differences we shall simply look at them as distinct versions of Physicalist theory.

In this century one of the early progenitors of a full-blown Physicalism was called the "Central State Identity Theory." It emerged in the mid-1950s partly as a reaction to an all-encompassing Behaviorism. The theory agreed with Behaviorism that mental states like beliefs and desires were perhaps adequately explained behaviorally, but it argued that at least a few mental states required something more than simple stimulus and response accounts. The name "Central State Identity Theory" indicated a commitment to two things. First, its proponents, philosophers J. J. C. Smart and U. T. Place, insisted that in addition to the stimulus and response advocated by Behaviorist explanations of the mental, there were at least some mental states that occurred *internal to* the organism. Behavioral stimuli and responses were *peripheral,* that is, they occurred outside (or at the periphery) of the organism. Central State theorists argued that some states, particularly sensations and consciousness, occurred *centrally* or internal to the organism and could not be fully explained simply in terms of behavior.

4. See Lawrence Weiskrantz, *Consciousness Lost and Found* (Oxford: Oxford University Press, 1997), p. 26; Steven Pinker, *How the Mind Works* (New York: Norton, 1997), p. 272.

The second reason for the name was that its proponents argued that these centrally occurring states were *identical* to brain states. Like the earlier Physicalists, they insisted that all mental states are physical states—but in this case they allowed that some are behavioral while others are brain states.

The Central State Identity Theory (or, more simply, the Identity Theory) allows for two variations, *Type Physicalism* and *Token Physicalism*. The differences between the two rely, not surprisingly, on the distinction between *types* and *tokens*.

Note on Terminology: A *token* is just an individual example, or "instantiation," of a general group or *type*. For example, Fido, Spot, and Lady are all *tokens* of the *type* dog. Red, yellow, and blue are *tokens* of the *type* color.

Type Physicalism

In the case of *Type Physicalism*, specific *types* of mental states were postulated to be identical with particular *types* of brain states (hence the name). For example, sensations (a type that would include tokens, like a particular headache or a particular experience of red) were said to be identical with some particular type of brain state. It was not known exactly which brain states were identical with which mental states, but there was a conviction that a mature neuroscience would be able to specify that. For example, to have a visual sensation was thought to be identical with being in one type of brain state, and any organism having a visual sensation would be in that same type of brain state, call it "brain state VS." Having a belief would be identical with being in a different type of brain state, call it "brain state BF," and any organism having a belief would have to be in that same BF state.

Type Physicalism was soon shown to be problematic. Among other things, it became clear that different types of brains might be capable of the same types of mental states. The first and most obvious example of this disparity is among different species. For example, certain species of nonhuman animals, whose brains are somewhat different from ours, still appear to be capable of sensations, memory states, desires, fears, and the like. As some philosophers put it, Type Physicalism was *chauvinistic*—that is, the theory seemed to be based on human mental states, on the assumption that all mental states would have to be of the same type as ours. But while my believing something might be identical with my brain state BF, my dog's believing something might be identical with its brain state DF. Furthermore, the brain states of different human beings might be relevantly different. Therefore, it has seemed to many philosophers that Type Physicalism was too strong.

Some philosophers have suggested that one can minimize the objection of chauvinism by making Type Physicalist claims that are *domain specific*.[5] That is, one can limit the types to particular domains like "human brain," "dog brain," and so forth. However, that may leave unanswered one further problem: It could be the case that even different individuals of the same species have slight differences in brain structure. In fact, some recent experimental work suggests that that may indeed be true for humans.[6]

However, there is one area of ambiguity in discussions of Type Physicalism that might provide some room for response to these concerns. It surrounds the notion of a brain-state *type*. "Brain-state type" might refer to a number of different things. It could mean neural activation in one particular structure of the brain (say, the visual cortex) or it might mean activation of one particular neural network; again it might mean activation of a collection of one particular type of neuron (the cortex has a variety of types of neurons—e.g., "chandelier," "basket," "pyramidal," which generally have different levels of connection with other neurons[7]); yet again it might be some particular level of activation of neurons (e.g., 40 Hertz, 100 Hertz, etc.). The first alternative, and possibly the second, would seem to require relevantly similar brain structures for identity of brain states; the third and fourth would seem to allow for considerable variation in *structure* as long as the brains had similar types of neurons or were capable of similar levels of neural activation.

Token Physicalism

Still, many philosophers moved to a more liberal version of Physicalism, *Token Physicalism*. On this view, every mental state is identical with *some* physical state, but instances of the same type of mental state (e.g., believing or desiring) might occur as different types of physical states. For example, the brain state that might be a desire in a chimpanzee could dif-

5. See Patricia Churchland, *Neurophilosophy*, pp. 356–62.

6. See William Calvin and George Ojemann, "How the Brain Subdivides Language," Chapter 14 in their book, *Conversations with Neil's Brain* (Reading, MA: Addison-Wesley, 1994); also George Ojemann, "Individual Variability in Cortical Localization of Language," *Journal of Neurosurgery*, 50 (1979).

7. Cf. A. G. Cairns-Smith, *Evolving the Mind* (Cambridge: Cambridge University Press, 1996), pp. 135–7.

fer from the brain state that would constitute a desire in a human being. Or, a desire in you could involve a different brain state from a desire in your mother. In other words, for two organisms to be in the same type of mental state, their two brains would not have to be in the same type of state. Desiring would be a physical state of the brain, but it need not be the same physical state in every brain that had a desire.

It might seem obvious that Token Physicalism is preferable to Type Physicalism. After all, it eliminates the sort of chauvinism that would try to explain all mental states simply in terms of *human* mental states. But even Token Physicalism is not without its problems. If *different* physical states can all be instances of the same mental state (e.g., a belief), what is it that they all have in common that makes them all beliefs? Or, to put it somewhat differently, how can one have a *general Physicalist theory* about beliefs or about mental states as a group, if they don't necessarily have anything physical in common?

There are several ways one might approach this problem. The first approach, closely related to the domain-specific approach of Patricia Churchland, suggests that one might construct theories that are species specific. That is to say, there would not be a completely general theory of mental states, but there could be distinct theories for each species. On this view, there would be a theory of mental states for humans (and for any other species whose brain states are sufficiently similar to human brain states), and a slightly different theory for each other species that has relevantly different brain states that instantiate its mental states, and so forth. If one were to ask why these mental states all go by the same names—'belief', 'desire', and so on—in spite of the fact that they can be different physical states with different theories, one might say that the names simply indicate some overlapping similarities. A completely general theory would appear to be unattainable. Notice that the species-specific approach would need to assume a good deal of relevant similarity among the brain states of all the members of a species.

A second approach could argue that what all these mental states have in common is that they all have the same *function* in the system. So, a belief—whatever physical state instantiates it—might have the function of guiding the behavior of the system, based on available information. We'll consider this view in greater detail when we turn to Functionalist theories of the mental.

Eliminative Physicalism

A third, and more radical, way to solve the problems associated with Token Physicalism involves a departure from the Identity Theory. It is called *Eliminative Physicalism*. As the name suggests, this view *eliminates* all reference to mental states. But that is not simply because it claims that they have been reduced to and are identical with brain states. The view is much stronger than that. It argues that there are no such things as mental states like beliefs, desires, and so forth. From the point of view of the Eliminativist, terms like 'belief' or 'desire' refer to nothing at all. They are elements in an outdated, no longer plausible, theory called "Folk Psychology." They should be dropped completely in favor of straightforward neuroscience. The idea is that when neuroscience is completed it will turn out that there are no states of the brain that correspond with what we have been calling beliefs, desires, and so on. The "geography" of brain states just will not link up with such things. Clearly, if this view is correct, then there is no need for a general theory of mental states because there are no such states.

To see that the Eliminativist view, while perhaps counterintuitive, is not entirely without plausible motivation, consider the case of the "four humors." At least four centuries before the present era, the Greeks theorized that disease and health were caused by the relative mix of the four humors—blood, phlegm, black bile, and yellow bile. The balance among these four was later thought to control one's temperament as well. The theory of the four humors, in both medicine and personality theory, continued into the 19th century, when it was finally discredited. Notice that it was widely held to be true for over two thousand years. The moral of the story for an Eliminativist is that the simple fact that a theory has been believed and used for a very long time is, by itself, no guarantee that the theory is correct. The elements in a theory may, in fact, name nothing and have no genuine explanatory value at all. For the Eliminativist, this is the case with Folk Psychology and with the elements it refers to as 'beliefs', 'desires', and so on. Hence, a general theory of mental states is not only not required, it is not desirable. It would be a theory of fictional entities, like the theory of the four humors or a theory of leprechauns. Paul Churchland and Patricia Churchland have on occasion defended Eliminativism.

Reductive Physicalism

Reductive Physicalism is the view that theories about mental states can be completely reduced to theories about physical brain states. Notice that Reductive Physicalism is a version of the Identity Theory and thus is quite consistent with either Type or Token Physicalism. When a theory *identifies* mental states with physical states (usually brain states), that theory is normally committed to the view that theories about the mental can be reduced to or replaced by physical theories. So a general theory of mental states will turn out to be a general theory of certain brain states (or perhaps a series of domain-specific theories). Notice that this theory differs from Eliminative Physicalism in that it does not deny the existence of mental states. Rather, it maps them onto physical states. So on this view, there really are beliefs, desires, and such; and they are identical with certain physical states of the brain.

Nonreductive Physicalism

On the other hand, *Nonreductive Physicalism* is the view that although everything that exists is physical (hence, Physicalism), nevertheless, some theories about portions of that physical reality cannot be reduced to theories in physics or neuroscience. The reason for the irreducibility is generally thought to be the fact that theories at one level (e.g., theories about mental states) capture levels of organizational complexity that are omitted in theories at a lower level (e.g., theories about brain states). Theories about brain states are couched in terms of neurons, networks of neurons, neurotransmitters, and so forth, while theories about mental states need to be couched in terms of beliefs and desires. According to the Nonreductionist, there is no obvious way that the latter elements can be reduced to or simply replaced by the former. A great deal of relevant information would be missed, the Nonreductionist claims.

To see the sort of point the Nonreductive theorist is making, consider a situation in the economic sphere. Suppose you wanted to explain what factors cause the stock market to rise or fall. Whatever theory you propose—perhaps in terms of consumer demand, national debt, possible fluctuations in inflation and interest rates, and so forth—it seems implausible that such a theory could be completely reduced to a theory in physics about the movement of electrons, and so forth. Theories about electrons fail to pick up the complexities involved in such phenomena as inflation—in spite of the fact that inflation is a phenomenon with completely physical causes. The Nonreductive Physicalist in philosophy of mind is making an analogous claim. She argues that just as physics cannot provide the level of complex generalizations required for theories in economics, so too, neuroscience cannot provide the level of complex generalizations required for theories about mental states.

The Reductivist response here generally argues that a *mature* neuroscience (which we don't yet have) will be able to account for all the complexity involved. Patricia Churchland has argued that what is required before a complete reduction will be possible is the "co-evolution" of theories in both psychology and neuroscience. She notes that both sciences are still in their infancy. "For psychology, one major difficulty is that it is still far from clear what the macro-capacities and macro-properties are which need, ultimately, to be explained neurobiologically; for neurobiology, one major difficulty is that it lacks theories of higher levels of organization—theories which specify the representational and computational properties of cell assemblies and, in turn, of collections of cell assemblies."[8]

Physicalism, in one form or another, is probably the dominant view of the mental among philosophers today. That, of course, does not mean that they all agree about which form of Physicalism is correct. It merely means that many philosophers of mind believe that the mental is best understood as belonging to the natural physical world. Whether that means that mental states are identical with types or with tokens of brain states, that theories about them are reducible or not reducible to theories about those brain states, or that reference to them should be discarded altogether—these issues continue to be very much a matter of debate.

From the Dualist point of view, of course, the Physicalist is giving up on any effort to explain immortality or free will. But the Physicalist would respond that both of these are themselves speculative notions. We have no direct evidence for either one of them, so we have little reason to base our theories of mind on them. The third argument of the Dualist—the argument from different ways of knowing bodies and minds—is still a matter of considerable debate. Philosophers Frank Jackson and Thomas Nagel have defended the asymmetry in our knowledge apparently as a basis for some version of Dualism (although Nagel's later work suggests a more flexible view), and philosophers like Patricia and Paul Churchland continue to argue that different ways of knowing things do not entail anything about the nature of those things.

Strengths and Weaknesses of Physicalism

Physicalism has several advantages. It avoids the most serious problem faced by Dualism—the inability to explain just how a nonphysical mind can interact with a physical body. If the mind is physical, for example, some subset of brain states, then there is no mystery about how it could cause other states and behaviors in the physical body. That is precisely the sort of thing that neuroscience deals with. So Physicalism places the mind squarely within the scope of science, making it the sort of thing that can be investigated and treated in the way other natural phenomena

8. Patricia Churchland, "The Neurobiological Basis of Consciousness," in *Consciousness in Contemporary Science*, A. J. Marcel and E. Bisiach, eds. (Oxford: Clarendon, 1988), p. 278.

are. Furthermore, it can locate mental states within the context of evolution. As natural selection led to changes and developments in physical bodies or organisms, one would expect it to lead to developments in the structure and function of the brains of those organisms. Human mental states could thus be seen as a completely natural development from earlier brain functions in nonhuman animals.

But like all other theories of the mental, Physicalism is not without its problems. One of these has already been mentioned. It still lacks a widely accepted explanation of the asymmetry in our knowledge of bodies and minds. If mental states are just physical, then one needs an account of why they are known in apparently private, introspective ways while the rest of the physical realm is not. Another difficulty for the Physicalist arises from the need to explain how the physical brain is able to cause *consciousness*. At this point in history, that remains an exceedingly puzzling issue, one to which we shall return in the next chapter.

Finally, there are two types of mental states that some philosophers see as defying a completely physical account. One of these is *intentional* states, states like beliefs, desires, and fears. For some philosophers *intentionality* cannot be realized in a purely physical system. Other philosophers believe that intentionality is indeed a characteristic of some physical systems, like human beings, and perhaps some sophisticated computers.

> **Note on Terminology:** When philosophers speak of *intentionality* or say that a mental state has an *intentional* structure, they do not use the term 'intentional' in its ordinary sense. They do not mean that it is deliberate. Rather, they are using the term that originated in Medieval philosophy and that was brought into modern discussions of the mental by the philosopher Franz Brentano. Brentano argued that it is *intentionality* that distinguishes the mental from the physical. Mental states are *intentional* in that they are *about something*; they are states that are *directed toward something*; they are states that *represent something*. The peculiar thing about that is that what they are about, directed toward, or represent does not need to exist. One can believe in Santa Claus, wish for a unicorn, or hope that the Easter Bunny will bring candy. Each of these mental states is about a nonexistent thing, but each is a genuine mental state.

What makes intentional states problematic is that physical things normally can be related only to things that actually exist. You can't sit on a nonexistent chair; you can't eat a nonexistent hamburger. But you can think about them, believe in them, desire them, imagine them, and so forth. This peculiarity of intentional states has made it seem that they are not physical. In Chapter 3 on emotions we shall explore this issue further and suggest that there may indeed be a way for Physicalism to handle this problem.

The second aspect of mental states that has caused problems for Physicalism is called *qualia*. These involve the way things look to you or the way they taste or smell. When scientists study the brain, they can perhaps see the activation of networks of neurons when you see a pumpkin, but they cannot see how the pumpkin looks to you. There is no place in your brain that turns orange. They might be able to see an activation of neurons when you smell hot coffee. But again, they don't know how it smells to you; they don't find the smell of coffee somewhere in your brain. Opponents of Physicalism have argued that qualia cannot be physical—on the grounds that they do not behave like physical objects. Qualia are not publicly observable; they don't appear to play any role in physical science; and if they were different from one individual to another we would have no sure way of knowing that fact. Nevertheless, for most Physicalists, a mature neuroscience will show that qualia are indeed physical, in spite of the fact that we don't simply observe them in the brains of other people.

Issues for Discussion

1. Some religions believe in the resurrection of the *body*. Do you think that a Physicalist could use this view to argue that Physicalism need not deny immortality—it can simply claim that immortality involves the eventual continuation of the body, not the continued existence of a nonphysical soul? Would you find such an account of immortality satisfactory? Give reasons for your answers.

2. Some people have thought that Physicalism denies our value as human beings. Why might someone think that? Do you agree?

3. Do you think that the mind ought to be subject to scientific investigation? Give careful reasons for your answer.

4. If the mind is physical, why can't we observe someone's thoughts or their qualia when we observe their brain?

5. How might the investigation of brain damage and brain disease help us to better understand the relationship between

brain states and mental states? Do you think that such investigations would lend support to a Physicalist view of the mind? Explain your answer.

6. Do you think that it is plausible to suppose that our commonsense Folk Psychology might be false, that references to mental states like beliefs and desires need to be eliminated in favor of neuroscience? Explain your answer.

7. What are some of the most significant differences between Physicalism and Substance Dualism? Between Physicalism and Behaviorism? Which of the three theories strikes you as the most plausible? Give reasons for your answer.

8. Which version (or versions) of Physicalism do you find most plausible? Give reasons for your answer.

9. Can you think of any additional arguments that would support Physicalism?

10. Can you think of any other problems with a Physicalist view of the mind?

Suggested Research Projects

Document all your sources.

a. Why did some of the ancient Greek philosophers believe that matter was imperfect? Do you think that they were right? What are your reasons? How has this attitude affected our views of human beings? Of God?

*b. George Berkeley, an 18th-century bishop and philosopher, defended a view called "immaterialism." What, exactly, was the view? What arguments did he give in support of it? Do you find his view plausible? What are your reasons?

c. What is *psychopharmacology*, and how might it be relevant to a Physicalist view of mind?

d. What is a PET scan? How does it relate to our knowledge of mental functions?

e. If you are currently taking a course in psychology, look carefully at your psychology text book and see if you can determine if the text favors a Dualist, Behaviorist, or Physicalist view of the mental. Cite specific evidence from the text to support your claim.

Property Dualism

Lest you think that Physicalism is the only view that has more than one permutation, we will take a look at a variation on Dualism. Substance Dualism has retained its basic form over the years, but a more recent version of Dualism, *Property Dualism*, recognizes the difficulties attaching to the claim that humans are composed of two distinct *substances*, which are required to interact with one another. The Property Dualist argues, instead, that human beings are *physical* entities but they have two distinct sets of *properties*, physical properties and *mental properties*.

The theory claims that the brain has physical properties like its shape, weight, color, and so forth. In addition, it has mental properties like consciousness, beliefs, desires, and so on. These mental properties are *caused* by processes in the brain (hence, they don't have an independent existence of the sort that Descartes's 'mental substance' has). On one common account, these mental properties *emerge* from certain structures or processes in the brain when the latter reaches a certain level of complexity. To understand what the Property Dualist means when claiming that mental properties emerge from the brain, consider an example of an emergent physical property. Water is composed of two gases, hydrogen (which burns) and oxygen (which supports burning). But when the two gases are combined in a certain way, new properties emerge: H_2O is not a gas, and it doesn't burn or support burning; it is a drinkable liquid that extinguishes fire. That is to say, the properties of water *emerge* from a particular combination of two other things that have none of the properties that water has.

Other common examples of apparently emergent properties are color (atoms have no color) and solidity (solidity arises from structured clusters of moving atomic particles). When Property Dualists claim that mental properties emerge from the physical brain when it reaches a certain level of complex organization, they mean something analogous to these examples of the emergence of physical properties. According to this theory, when brain structure and function are at a certain level of complexity, they give rise to a new and different set of properties, namely, consciousness, beliefs, desires, and so on.

The interpretation and evaluation of this view depends to a considerable extent on what one means by the term 'mental' in the phrase 'mental properties'. There are at least two interpretions. First, if mental properties are emergent in the same sense that color, solidity, and the properties of water are emergent, then they can be completely accounted for by physical theories. They are a special, complex version of physical properties, and their difference is captured by theories at a higher level of generalization than theories about atoms or electrons or neurons. On this interpretation, 'mental' properties still belong within the framework of the natural physical world and might be seen on analogy with economic properties or aesthetic properties. Notice that this sort of Property Dualism is a version of Nonreductive Physicalism. The 'Dualism' is really a dualism of *theories* rather than a dualism of ontology or metaphysics. One might term this view *weak* Property Dualism, where the second set of properties is treated only in the higher-level theories.

John Searle, in his book *The Rediscovery of the Mind*, appears to defend a view of this sort in connection with consciousness. There has been considerable debate about Searle's view, and it is possible that it does not fit neatly into any one of the standard classifications we have been discussing. But some of his claims sound reasonably close to the version of weak Property Dualism (or Nonreductive Physicalism) that I have described. Searle says, "What I want to insist on, ceaselessly, is that one can accept the obvious facts of physics—for example, that the world is made up entirely of physical particles in fields of force—without at the same time denying the obvious facts about our own experiences—for example, that we are all conscious and that our conscious states have quite specific *irreducible* phenomenological properties."[9] He goes on to say that his view is "emphatically not a form of dualism." But it does seem that he comes close to what I have called weak Property Dualism.

A second interpretation of emergent mental properties is possible. On this view, 'mental' indicates something nonphysical, a set of metaphysically unique properties sharing many of the characteristics that Descartes attributed to the mental. This constitutes the *strong* version of Property Dualism. This sort of view has been defended by Frank Jackson in several of his papers[10] and by David Chalmers in his book *The Conscious Mind* (about which I'll have more to say in Chapter 2, on consciousness).

9. John Searle, *The Rediscovery of Mind* (Cambridge, MA: MIT/Bradford, 1992), p. 28.

10. See Frank Jackson, "Epiphenomenal Qualia," *Philosophical Quarterly*, 32 (1982), and "What Mary Didn't Know," in *The Nature of Mind*, David Rosenthal, ed. (New York: Oxford, 1991).

Strengths and Weaknesses of Property Dualism

On either interpretation, Property Dualism has several advantages. First, it can account for the very different status that properties like consciousness, beliefs, and desires have, as compared with publicly observable properties of the brain like its shape and color. As Dualists of any sort have argued, we know mental states or properties in a different way from the way we know bodies and their properties and states, and this suggests that there is something importantly different about the two. Secondly, Property Dualism takes very seriously the admittedly close relationship that exists between the brain and mental states, since it sees the brain as causing mental states. Third, it avoids postulating a substance that has no causal history in the natural world. And fourth, it emphasizes mental states as a series of properties rather than theorizing about mind as if it were one unified, all-or-nothing sort of thing (as Descartes's mental substance was). This feature will become important when we come to consider the evolution of the mental in Chapter 4.

There are, however, some difficulties with Property Dualism. The weaker version shares all the problems that accrue to Physicalist theories in general. These include an inability to explain consciousness as a physical property and an inability to account for the asymmetry in our ways of knowing physical and mental properties. But the stronger interpretation of the theory also has problems. First, one needs to know the relationship between the nonphysical mental properties and the brain states that cause them. There appear to be two possibilities: (1) Either the mental properties in turn cause things to happen in the brain, or (2) they don't. In the first case, one seems to have a new version of the problem that plagues Substance Dualism, namely, how can something that is genuinely nonphysical exert a causal influence in the physical world? Nonphysical things, whether substances or properties, seem to be incapable of inserting themselves into the physical world, causing things to happen there.

But the second alternative is not better. If mental properties, construed as nonphysical, have no causal powers in the physical world, they turn out to be *epiphenomenal* (see box on page 36).

Epiphenomenalism here would mean that one's mental properties—like consciousness, beliefs, desires, and so forth—play no role at all in causing one's behavior. On such a view, our behavior would be the outcome of purely physical processes and laws, while our conscious beliefs and desires would be the quite useless and irrelevant offshoots of those processes. They would amount to little more than mental shadows that can appear but that have no function whatsoever.

> **Note on Terminology:** An *epiphenomenon* is something that has no
> causal powers of its own. For example, your shadow is generally
> thought to be an epiphenomenon. Your body, standing at a certain
> position in relation to a light source, causes your shadow. But your
> shadow by itself is incapable of causing anything else to happen. Pro-
> viding shade for a flower, for example, is not done by the shadow
> alone but by the positioning of your body. In the philosophy of mind,
> *Epiphenomenalism* is the view that mental properties, although
> caused by something physical, have no causal powers of their own.

It may, of course, turn out that Epiphenomenalism is true. But there
are at least two reasons that speak against it. One is that our mental
properties and states would turn out to be completely gratuitous. Such
a status does not seem especially troubling with something as simple as
a shadow. Shadows play virtually no explanatory role in our understanding of the world. But with a complex system of interrelated mental
states that normally appear to play a critical explanatory role in our
behavior, it seems far less plausible to suppose that they are in fact
entirely ineffectual. The other reason that speaks against Epiphenomenalism is that it is difficult to see how the process of natural selection
would have contrived to produce such an elaborate system of states and
properties that play absolutely no role in our efforts to deal with our
environment. We shall explore this idea further when, in Chapter 2, we
consider some of the possible functions of consciousness. The one sav-
ing grace of Epiphenomenalism is that it helps to avoid the vexing issue
of how nonphysical properties can interact causally with physical properties. But that issue may be the unavoidable inheritance of any form of
metaphysical Dualism.

Issues for Discussion

1. Do you think that Property Dualism is an improvement over
   Substance Dualism? Do you think that Descartes would
   have accepted it? Give reasons for your answer.

2. Would Property Dualism provide an explanation of how
   immortality and free will might be possible? Explain your
   answer.

3. Would a Property Dualist need to claim that some nonhuman animals also have mental properties? Explain your
   answer.

4. How do you think that the mental properties of Property Dualism are best interpreted—by the weak theory, or by the strong theory? Explain your answer.

5. What other properties—besides consciousness, beliefs, and desires—would a Property Dualist be likely to count as mental properties?

6. Is there any difficulty in understanding how physical processes in the brain could cause genuinely nonphysical properties to come into existence?

7. Can you think of any further arguments that support Property Dualism?

8. Can you think of any further difficulties with the theory?

9. Do you think that either version of Property Dualism is more plausible than Reductive Physicalism? More plausible than Eliminative Physicalism? Explain your answer.

10. Do you think that Epiphenomenalism is plausible?

11. How might an epiphenomenalist reply to the objection that evolutionary processes would not have selected for mental states if they were completely useless?

Suggested Research Projects

a. Thomas Henry Huxley, a defender of Darwin's theory of evolution, was a supporter of Epiphenomenalism. How did he defend the view? Did he reconcile it with the theory of evolution? (See his *Methods and Results: Essays*, chap. 5, New York: Appleton, 1898.)

b. In his book, *Consciousness Reconsidered*, Owen Flanagan offers several arguments that support Epiphenomenalism and several arguments against it. What are his arguments, and which ones do you find most convincing?

*c. What is *supervenience*? How does it relate to Property Dualism?

d. Read R. W. Sperry's "Mental Phenomena as Causal Determinants" in *Consciousness and the Brain*, G. Globus, G. Maxwell, and I. Savodnik, eds. (New York: Plenum Press,

1976). Do you think that Sperry's view is a version of Nonreductive Physicalism or a strong version of Property Dualism, which sees mental properties as nonphysical? Cite material from the article to support your claim. Why is his view not epiphenomenalist?

Functionalism

Background for Functionalism

In order to understand *Functionalism*, it helps to know some of the other events that helped to motivate its development. During the 1940s and 1950s a number of things happened that inspired some profound changes in our thinking about the mental. For one thing, serious exploration of outer space began when the government of Soviet Russia launched its satellite *Sputnik* in 1957. The ensuing program of space exploration focused our attention on the possibility that there might be other forms of intelligent life "out there" (extraterrestrial intelligences or ETIs, as they are called). If there were such beings, there was little reason to think that they would look just like us, as the movie *E.T.* amply demonstrated. And there was equally little reason to think that their brains, if they had such things, would be just like ours. Considerations like these led philosophers to question the assumption that mental states were simply identical with brain states, let alone that they were identical with *human* brain states, as early versions of Type Physicalism seemed to assume. If ETIs were intelligent, then they would have mental states of some sort, but if they lacked brains like ours, or lacked brains altogether, then their mental states could not be identical with brain states like ours, and perhaps not with brain states at all.

Another development that began during World War II and has continued to the present time is the effort to teach language to various types of nonhuman animals, in particular to other primates like the chimpanzee. In addition, there have been efforts to train animals like dolphins and whales to carry out various behaviors on command. The results in all these cases have suggested that these animals have some degree of intelligence. They can learn to understand and to remember commands; some of them appear able to make limited use of a symbol system like American Sign Language; and some have shown a limited ability at problem solving. All of this strengthened philosophers' suspicions that we were indeed being chauvinistic in assuming that mental states were a function of human brains alone. Experiments with other primates and the dolphins strongly suggested that they, too, have some form of mental states, but their brains are not identical with ours. Once again, it seemed that mental states could not simply be identified with human brain states.

Finally and perhaps most significantly, World War II also led to the development of the modern computer. First used to decode intercepted messages, it rapidly became apparent that it would be capable of a great deal more than that. We now have computers that play champion-level chess, diagnose illnesses, guide airplanes, and much more. We speak of the computer's *memory*; we note its ability to *solve problems* in mathematics and logic faster and more accurately than we can; and we communicate with it by way of *languages*. These capabilities were previously thought to be the exclusive prerogative of human minds.

The possibility of ETIs, increasing evidence of some mental capacities in nonhuman animals, and the apparently intelligent capabilities of some computers suggested to philosophers that mental states are capable of *multiple realizations*. That is, they appear to be realized in a number of different types of systems.

These developments motivated philosophers of mind to broaden the framework within which to think about the mental. Until this time, one of the primary questions that had been addressed by philosophers concerned the *composition* of minds or mental states. Were they nonphysical substances (human souls/minds)? Were they human brain states? Were they special properties of brain states? Were they patterns of human behavior? Once again, the way the questions were framed limited the answers that could be given. A new question was introduced—one that could allow the answer to include intelligent ETIs, intelligent nonhuman animals, and even intelligent computers and robots. The new question was roughly this: What does a system have to be able to *do* in order to qualify as being intelligent or as having mental states? The answer to this new question was that an intelligent system has to be able to *function* in certain predictable ways. It has to be able to take in information, process that information, and produce a reasonable response based on that information. All these relations—between input, internal processing, and output—were taken to be *causal* relations.

Notice two things about this new theory. First, concern has turned away from what intelligent systems are *composed of* and has turned toward the issue of what intelligent systems *can do*. If I were to ask you to define table salt, you would probably respond that it is sodium chloride. Similarly, if I ask for a definition of water, you would say H_2O. That is, you would define them in terms of what they are composed of; you would give them what I call a *compositional* definition. But if I were to ask for a definition of a boat, you would not tell me that it is something composed of wood (or fiberglass or metal). A boat is not defined by what it is made of but by what it does, what functions it can carry out. You would probably tell me something about a boat being a vehicle that can carry cargo of some sort while it floats on water; you would give me a *functional* definition. In philosophy of mind, the turn to Functionalism is a move away from compositional accounts of the mental and a move toward functional accounts. On this view, minds, mental states, or intelligent systems can be made of many different sorts of things (maybe nonphysical as well as physical), but whatever they are made of they have to be able to carry out certain sorts of functions.

A second thing to notice about Functionalism is that it combines partial but important aspects of both Behaviorism and the Identity Theory. Like the Behaviorist, the Functionalist insists on the importance of environmental input ("stimuli") and plausible or predictable output ("response"), but like the Identity Theorists, the Functionalist also insists that something essential goes on *within* the system. Of course, Functionalism also disagrees partially with both Behaviorism and the Identity Theory. Against the Identity Theory, it denies that mental states are *identical* to brain states, arguing that there are many different types of internal states in a system that could process incoming information. Brain states are not the only possibility. Against Behaviorism, it insists that externally observable stimuli and responses are not enough to explain the mental. The internal process is crucial.

The early proponents of Functionalism include philosophers David Armstrong (who called his theory the Causal Theory of Mind), David Lewis, Hilary Putnam, and Jerry Fodor. Let's begin with an early version of Armstrong's Causal Theory of mental states. It provides a rather neat transition between Identity Theories and Functionalism.

Causal Theory of Mind

Recall that the Identity Theorists argued, against Behaviorism, that at least some mental states are identical with brain states. At first they had in mind only states like consciousness, sensations, and the like. David Armstrong begins within the context of the Identity Theory: "But suppose that the physico-chemical view of the working of the brain is correct, as I take it to be. It will be very natural to conclude that mental states are not simply *determined* by corresponding states of the brain, but that they are actually *identical* with with these brain-states, brain-states that involve nothing but physical properties." He then expands on this view by arguing that "the concept of a mental state . . . [is] the concept of a state that is *apt to be the cause of certain effects or apt to be the effect of certain causes.*"[11]

What this early version of the Causal Theory meant to defend was the identification of mental states with brain states in virtue of their identical *causal* roles. If what appear to be two distinct things are really apt to be caused by the same causes and are apt to have the same effects, then that fact provides some evidence that they are in reality just one and the same thing. Theorists agreed that the argument did not show that mental states were *necessarily* identical with brain states, but it did show that it was not *impossible* that they are identical. As it turned out, although a Causal analysis did not prove the Identity Theory, it did pave the way for a successor theory, Functionalism. A few years later, Armstrong made this connection quite explicit: "If the essence of the mental is purely relational, purely a matter of what causal role is played, then the logical possibility remains that whatever in fact plays the causal role is not material."[12] Although Armstrong goes on to defend a Physicalist theory of the mental, his point is that the composition of the system is not the essential factor; rather, its network of causal relations determines its status as mental. And later in the same book he states, "A central consideration for the materialist here is that for him there is no particular reason to think that the only physically possible minds have a neurophysiological nature" (p. 160). In other words, even from a Physicalist point of view, something other than brain states might play that causal role. Armstrong's Causal Theory of mental states became *Functionalism*.

Machine Functionalism

Like Dualism and Physicalism, Functionalism also comes in a couple of varieties. The oldest and perhaps the best known version is *Machine Functionalism*. The "machine" that dominates this type of Functionalism is the Turing Machine. Named after its "author," the mathematician Alan Turing, the Turing Machine is not a physical machine at all (hence I refer to its "author" rather than its "inventor"). It is actually an abstract model for any computational device that can take an input,

11. David Armstrong, *The Nature of Mind and Other Essays* (Ithaca, NY: Cornell, 1981), p. 19; p. 20; reprinted in *Mind and Cognition*, W. Lycan, ed. (Cambridge, MA: Blackwell, 1990).

12. Armstrong, "In Defence of the Casual Theory of Mind," in D. M. Armstrong and N. Malcolm, *Consciousness and Causality* (Oxford: Blackwell, 1984), p. 157.

process that input in relation to its own internal state, and produce an appropriate output. The serial computer is a concrete example of a Turing Machine.

What the Machine Functionalists claim is that what characterizes mental or psychological systems is that they are best understood on the model of *Turing Machines*. Whatever they are made of, such systems function in a rule-governed way to process the information that they receive. How is this related to the causal relations mentioned earlier as the defining relations in a Functionalist account of the mental? In order to see the connection, it might help to consider the notion of a mathematical function. Recall from your high school algebra class that a problem like the following, $x = 2y$ can be read as: "x is a *function* of twice y." Or, the value of x is a function of (that is, will be determined by) multiplying y by 2. So, if $y = 3$ then x must $= 2(3)$ or 6. Whatever one puts in the place of y will determine (one might say "cause") the value of x. Carrying the analogy into a Functionalist theory of mind, one could say that the current internal state of a computational system is a function of (is determined or caused by) its past internal state and any input it receives; its output is a function of (is determined or caused by) its current internal state and any input it receives.

One of the first things to notice about this version of Functionalism is that it provides a theory of mental or psychological states for *any* system that can execute the appropriate sorts of computations. There is no longer any talk about mental substances or brain states. The whole story is told at a much higher level of abstraction. And because the theory operates at this level it is able to offer a solution to the problem that we noted in connection with Token Physicalism: How can one provide a general theory of mental states when those states need have nothing in common except the fact that they are physical? The Functionalist argues that what all the physical tokens that count as beliefs have in common is that they all have the same function for the system—that is, they are caused by the same sorts of input and they have the same sorts of causal relations with other internal states of the system, and in turn cause the same sorts of effects or output. Notice, too, that although this responds to the difficulty faced by Token Physicalism, the Functionalist theory of mental states is not committed to Token Physicalism. It can be made consistent with any ontology. Nonetheless, versions of Functionalism that limit their ontology to Physicalism (and currently that is most of them) are often versions of Nonreductive Physicalism. That is, these theories characterize the mental in terms of its *functional* properties and do not see those theories as reducible to theories in physics or neuroscience. Philosopher Jerry Fodor has defended a version of the

Nonreductive view in his book, *The Language of Thought*. The view is sometimes characterized in terms of the "autonomy of psychology" because it claims that psychological theories, theories of the mental, are not reducible to theories in the physical sciences.

David Armstrong gives an example of what it is that might be common to all cases of belief, in spite of the fact that they might be instantiated in different physical tokens: "what does seem to mark off belief, or at least the central cases of belief, from mere thought is that a belief is something on which we are prepared to act. Beliefs feed in causally to our purposes, and it is their so feeding in which constitutes their being beliefs."[13]

The ability to provide a perfectly general theory of mental states that is independent of their physical composition is one of the strengths of Machine Functionalism. At the very least, it offers this advantage over both Type and Token Physicalism. But it is not without its own problems. And these problems arise from one of the very strengths we just noted—the level of abstraction at which the theory is pitched. The theory has little to say about the *qualitative* character (or the qualia I spoke of earlier) of states like sensations. While this qualitative character seems to be an intuitively obvious aspect of some of our experiences, it plays no role in the Machine Functionalist theory. Some Functionalists have offered two arguments to show that qualia are in fact functionally irrelevant: the Inverted Spectrum argument and the Absent Qualia argument, both discussed by philosopher Ned Block.[14]

The Inverted Spectrum argument is perhaps best introduced with a thought experiment. Consider the possibility that one of your friends experiences what you think of as red each time she looks at the sky. And she experiences what you would call blue whenever she sees a ripe tomato. That is, her *qualia* are "inverted" in relation to yours. But since she has had these experiences from birth, and has been taught to use the word "blue" when she refers to the color of the sky, and "red" when referring to tomato color, you have no way of knowing that the color she actually experiences differs from what you see. Functionally, she appears to be indistinguishable from you. You both receive the same inputs, and can produce the same linguistic outputs in their presence. Your internal processing is likely to be somewhat different, but Functionalism allows for that; computers don't process inputs in just the same way that we do. Thus, it looks as if the qualitative character of

13. "In Defence of the Causal Theory of Mind," in *Consciousness and Causality*, p. 154.
14. See his "Troubles with Functionalism," in his *Readings in Philosophy of Psychology*, vol. 1.

some of our mental states is simply irrelevant to a Functionalist theory of the mental. A qualitative difference in the states of the two systems does not show up as a *functional* difference.

Several responses to the problems of inverted qualia have been suggested. On the one hand, one might claim that inverted qualia are not verifiable and therefore may not even be possible. If they are not possible, that would leave the argument based on them without a foundation. On the other hand, if they are possible, they may be simply irrelevant from a Functional point of view and therefore not an essential part of a theory of the mental. Or they may eventually be functionally characterizable. None of these responses has been universally accepted, so the issue of the status of the qualitative content of mental states continues to be a problem for Functionalism.

> **Blindsight:** Blindsight is a visual deficit that can occur with damage to certain portions of the visual cortex. The blindsighted individual claims to see nothing in a certain portion of his visual field. But when asked to *guess* what is there (e.g., an X or an O), he will often respond at better-than-chance levels. The usual explanation for that is that although the patient has no awareness of visual qualia, his brain is still receiving some information about what is in that portion of the visual field. And that information allows him to make a reasonably good guess in spite of his apparent inability to consciously see what is there.[15]

An analogous point can be made with the Absent Qualia argument. It is possible to conceive of a system that functions in a normal way but has no qualitative content at all. One example of such a system is referred to as a "zombie." The thought experiment goes like this: You can conceive of a system that is functionally identical to you—same inputs, same outputs, and even the same internal processing—but it has no qualia at all. The claim is not that there are such zombies, just that they are conceivable. And if they are even conceivable, then it is at least *logically possible* to have a system with the relevant functional organization but no qualia at all. In other words, perhaps qualia are epiphenomenal.

Arguments like this one involving zombies may seem far-fetched, and in one sense they are. But the point of such thought experiments is

---

15. See Weiskrantz, *Consciousness Lost and Found*, p. 16 ff.

not to pose actual possibilities. Rather, their point is to consider the limits of conceivability, the limits of what is logically possible. What that does, from a practical point of view, is to highlight whether or not some phenomenon is *absolutely* or *logically impossible*. If it isn't, then there is no logical necessity that things be as they seem to be. The zombie argument is meant to show that there is no conceptual or logical necessity that any system that functions in just the way that we do must also have all the qualia that we have. We shall return to the issue of zombies in Chapter 2, on consciousness.

In addition to failing to account for qualia, Machine Functionalism also says nothing about the role played by physiology in psychological states like fear and anger. One obvious reason for these omissions is precisely the fact that the theory has abstracted from the composition of the systems. Therefore, anything associated with human (or some nonhuman animal) psychology that requires physiology will not figure in the Functionalist account of the mental. The very generality that allows the theory to combat chauvinism and to be inclusive of nonliving systems like computers and robots seems to leave it unable to fully account for mental states like emotions, which are tied into the physiology of living systems.

Homuncular Functionalism

Another version of the theory is sometimes referred to as *Homuncular Functionalism*. This version has been defended by philosophers Daniel Dennett and William Lycan.[16] The Homuncular approach to Functionalism tries to disarm the concern that psychology must account for the notion of an inner Self or *homunculus* (literally, "little man") that observes its mental operations and performs all the intelligent activities associated with human mental activity. The theory claims that one needs to see the operations of intelligent systems in terms of a hierarchy of units ("homunculi" of sorts) within the system, cooperating to produce some result. But this theory claims that these units are *not* little men at all; they are simple elements that can carry out one operation at a time and can pass on the results of that operation to other units in the system. As one descends in the system, the units appear to be more and more "stupid" until one reaches levels where the operations could be carried out by completely simple mechanical units. The units at the

16. See Daniel Dennett, "Introduction," in *Brainstorms*, and "Why the Law of Effect Will Not Go Away"; and Lycan, "The Continuity of Levels of Nature," the latter two in Lycan's *Mind and Cognition*.

"top" of the hierarchy will appear to be intelligent because they carry out operations that depend on all the lower operations that have been fed upward to it. The idea is that the functions of a system that appear to be intelligent may ultimately be explainable in terms of a descending hierarchy of units, none of which are genuinely intelligent but some of which can carry out fairly sophisticated operations simply because they work on the results of many stupid units below them. Notice that Homuncular Functionalism, like Machine Functionalism, provides a theory that can explain how computers and robots might be capable of having apparently intelligent mental functions.

Teleological Functionalism

A further variation on the Functionalist theme has been proposed by philosopher Elliott Sober.[17] His proposal is to use a notion of "function" that is more closely related to *biological* function rather than to mathematical function. Recall that mathematical functions rely primarily on the fact that the value of one variable can be determined by the values of other variables. Its use in philosophy of mind relies on the claim that the nature of a mental state is determined by the nature of the inputs, outputs, and other mental states to which it is causally related. That notion of function carries no implications of purpose or goals for the system. Sober's *Teleological Functionalism*, on the other hand, argues that the proper notion of function for a theory of mental states is closer to the biological notion. The biological function of the heart is to pump blood. That is to say, the function of the heart is seen in relation to what it contributes to the larger system, the body. As Sober puts it (taking his cue from a definition proposed by philosopher Robert Cummins), "The function of a part [e.g., heart] of a containing system [e.g., body] is whatever that part does [pump blood] to contribute to the containing system's having whatever properties it has [life?]" (p. 104).

Obviously, Homuncular Functionalism is compatible with Teleological Functionalism—that is to say, masses of unintelligent homunculi could carry out the functions that a system or organism requires. William Lycan combines versions of the two.[18] However, the proper way to understand the notion of function—whether in its mathematical or biological sense—continues to be a matter of considerable debate.

17. See his article, "Putting the Function Back into Functionalism," in Lycan's *Mind and Cognition.*

18. See his article, "Form, Function, and Feel," *Journal of Philosophy*, 78 (1981):24–50.

Strengths and Weaknesses of Functionalism

One apparent strength of Functionalism in any of its forms is that it does an "end run" around the long-standing debate about the composition of the mind or mental states. The argument between Dualists and Physicalists has continued, without resolution, for centuries. When there seems to be little progress on a problem, it is sometimes wise to try a completely different approach to it, which is what Functionalism does. In addition, it expands our notion of what sorts of systems might plausibly be said to have mental states. The claim that we had been too chauvinistic in our efforts to characterize mental states entirely in terms of human brain states is surely right. The Cartesian framework encouraged an unfortunate habit of seeing ourselves as the pinnacle of the natural world and as the paradigm case of intelligent, minded creatures. Functionalism relieves us of that conceit.

On the other hand, Functionalist accounts of mental states have been thought by some philosophers to be too liberal. For some, the idea that a computer or a robot could have mental states in the same sense that a human being has them has seemed profoundly mistaken. These philosophers have argued that computers are incapable of conscious states with qualitative content and are incapable of genuine emotions. When some versions of Functionalism omit any account of qualia, of emotions, or of consciousness, this might be part of an effort to include some nonliving systems as possible candidates for mental states. But certain critics of Functionalism argue that an adequate theory of mental states in *living* systems requires that an account of qualia, consciousness, and emotions be included.

A further objection is that nonliving systems like computers do not use incoming information on behalf of their own survival and well-being, as do human beings and nonhuman animals. Nonliving systems have no need to do so since they are not systems for whom survival is an issue; they have no interests of their own. These considerations, objectors argue, suggest the need for further refinements in Functionalist theories—possibly refinements that offer domain-specific theories, distinguishing at the very least between living and nonliving systems.

Might some of the objections to Functionalism be answered if one were to stop thinking of the mind as if it were one, unified, all-or-nothing thing? Might one instead look simply at individual mental states, and take seriously the possibility that some systems are capable of having a few of these states but not all of them, (e.g., memory and problem solving, but not emotions or qualia) while other more complex systems are capable of having a greater number and variety of such states? On such a view, one would no longer speak of the computer, for example, as having or not having a mind. Rather, one would speak simply of its capacity for memory, for problem solving within limited contexts, and so on. And one would not ask if the chimpanzee has a mind, but rather would ask about its capacity for memory, for generalization, for language use, for deception, and so on. Furthermore, might such a view be more compatible with an evolutionary view of how individual mental abilities developed gradually in a variety of different species until the collection of such abilities reached the complex form found in human beings?

In spite of the objections that have been raised against Functionalist accounts, however, Functionalism in one form or another is among the leading contenders today for a satisfactory philosophical theory of mental states. Recall that I said earlier that most philosophers of mind today are Physicalists. But notice that one can be both a Physicalist and a Functionalist. For certain forms of Physicalism, it is not crucial that mental states be brain states. What is essential to them is that mental states be *physical*. And while the early Functionalists said that a system that was capable of the relevant functions could be made of *anything*, including nonphysical substance, the vast majority of Functionalists are committed to the view that the relevant systems are indeed physical.

Issues for Discussion

1. How would you define each of the following, compositionally or functionally? (a) a pen (b) a sheet of paper (c) alcohol (d) a computer (e) sugar (f) blood.

2. Do you think that some things lend themselves to both compositional and functional definitions? Do you think that mental states lend themselves to (or require?) both types of definitions? Explain your answers.

3. Do you think that it is plausible to believe that ETIs would have mental states? Dolphins or chimpanzees? Computers? Robots?

4. Do you think that evolution theory could support a Functionalist account of mental states? What are your reasons?

5. Does it seem plausible to you that we should replace our talk of 'the mind' with talk about 'collections of mental capacities', and that one type of system might have only a few such

capacities while another type of system might have many of them?

6. Can you think of any further arguments that would support Functionalism?

7. Can you see any other difficulties with a Functionalist account of mental states?

8. Do you think that Homuncular Functionalism succeeds in eliminating the need to posit an inner Self that is the source of all intelligent activity?

9. How do Machine Functionalism and Teleological Function- alism differ? Which one seems more plausible to you? Give careful reasons for your answer.

10. Does Functionalism seem to you to be a more plausible the- ory of the mental than Substance Dualism? Explain your answer.

Suggested Research Projects

*a. Prepare a brief summary of Marvin Minsky's book, *The Soci- ety of Mind*. Which version of Functionalism do you think he would support? Give reasons for your answer.

b. What is Functionalism in psychology? What are the similari- ties and differences with its philosophical counterpart?

Evaluating Theories

We have considered a number of different theories about the mind and about mental states. The question now is, How is one to decide among them? Which theory is the best? Which one (or ones) ought to be discarded? This section suggests a number of steps that you can take that should help you to decide which of the above theories is the most plausible one from your point of view. Notice that the issue is one of *plausibility*, not of *truth* or *falsehood*. At this point in history, it would be virtually impossible to give adequate support to the claim that one particular theory of mind is either completely true or com- pletely false. Plausible (or not plausible) is a much more reasonable claim to defend.

In suggesting these steps for evaluation, I am giving priority to the characteristics of theories that are widely assumed to be important. They are the sorts of characteristics that one looks for in plausible, well-tested, scientific theories. These are the types of theories that have the greatest possibility of being widely understood and accepted as reasonable explanations of the phenomena under consideration. In contrast, theories that are merely the product of individual whim or wishful thinking are not likely to contribute much to our understanding of the world or of ourselves. The following subsections detail some of the things to consider when evaluating a theory.

Arguments Pro and Con

In our discussion of each of the theories, we noted some of the reasons or arguments that could be given for each, some of its advantages. We also cited some of the objections, problems, or disadvantages that attach to each. One of the first steps to take in evaluating theories is to look carefully at all the arguments *for* and all the arguments *against* the theory (including any arguments that you may have added). Try to decide which set of arguments carries the most weight for you. When the arguments against a theory far outweigh those in its favor, it is probably wise to discard it as having little promise. This step alone may help you to discard a theory, but it often is not quite enough to allow you to single out the one theory that is the most promising.

Assumptions

A second step is to look at the *assumptions* that a theory makes. When you look for the assumptions behind a theory of mind (see box on page 51), you want to consider only those that are relevant to the sorts of conclusions that the theory wants to draw. For example, one of the assumptions that the Substance Dualist must make is that it is possible for a type of reality to exist that has none of the properties of the physical world, a reality that is, in principle, beyond the scope of science. Ask yourself if this is a plausible assumption to make, or should it be rejected? (Note that the issue is not whether you can *prove* the assumption to be true or false. That is generally quite difficult to do and sometimes impossible. The question here is whether the assumption is plausible or implausible.) The Physicalist, by contrast, assumes that everything that exists is natural and should eventually fall within the scope of scientific investigation. Again, do you find this a plausible or an implausible assumption? After you make explicit the relevant and significant assumptions of each theory, ask yourself if you are willing to accept those assumptions. If you are not, then you may have at least one good reason to put the theory aside. If you do accept the assumptions, then move on to the next step in evaluation.

Note on Terminology: An 'assumption' is a belief that is relevant to a theory, is essential to a theory's being correct, is taken for granted by the proponent of the theory, but remains *unstated*. For example, when I am speaking to you, some of the many assumptions that I will be making are that you are conscious, that you are rational, that you speak English, that you are not hearing impaired. I won't *state* any of this. I will simply take it all for granted. However, if I am mistaken in any of my assumptions, my speaking to you will not be successful. Philosophical theories are always backed by some set of assumptions. When trying to evaluate those theories, it is important to ferret out relevant assumptions and evaluate them. Are they reasonable? Plausible? Debatable? Highly questionable? And so forth.

Consequences

A third thing to look at is the sort of *consequences* or implications that follow from a given theory. If the theory is true, what follows from that? If Machine Functionalism is true, then there are no significant theoretical differences between mental states in living systems and mental states in nonliving systems. If Metaphysical Behaviorism is true, then neuroscience is irrelevant to psychology. Again, if you don't find the consequences of a theory to be acceptable, that may be a reason to discard it or at least put it aside. If the consequences seem acceptable, move to the next step.

Notice that if you find neither the assumptions nor the consequences of a theory to be plausible, you probably have good reason to put it aside. Of course, you also want to consider the possibility that your reasons for rejecting certain assumptions or consequences may not be very good. You should not, for example, reject them because they are new to you or different from what you have always thought. In the process of examining the assumptions and consequences of various theories, it is important to be clear about, and critical of, your own reasons for evaluating them as you do.

Explanatory Power

A fourth area to consider is whether or not a given theory is able to account for all the elements that you think that an adequate theory of mind should be able to account for. That is to say, how strong is its *explanatory power*? Some of the questions you might ask of it are as follows: Can it account for the presence of consciousness? Can it account for the relationship between cognition and emotions? Can it account for the possibility of some mental states in nonhuman animals? Can it explain some of the brain/mind deficits that we have discussed? (Add your own list of requirements that you believe an adequate theory of mind should meet.)

Consistency with Other Well-Founded Theories

Fifth, consider whether or not the theory is *consistent* with all the other things that you have good reason to believe. Is it consistent with scientific theories that you take to be well supported? This might be further specified in a number of ways: Is it consistent with the most recent versions of evolution theory? Is it consistent with our best current neuroscience? Is it consistent with our most reliable experiments in psychology? Or perhaps it is important to you that it be consistent with your particular ethical view. Another aspect of this consistency criterion is whether or not the theory of mind is itself internally consistent. Does it make any claims that are mutually incompatible?

Predictive Power

A sixth step to take in evaluating theories is to consider the *predictive power* of the theory. Does it make testable predictions? Does it offer a reasonable research program? In the case of a theory of the mental, does it offer any clues as to how one might prevent, alleviate, or cure a mental disorder?

Simplicity

One final test that is often urged in connection with scientific theories and that is perhaps appropriate here as well is: Is the theory as simple as it can be while still explaining everything that needs to be explained? The notion of *simplicity* here has nothing to do with the theory being easy to understand. Rather, the idea is that a good theory won't appeal to five elements if everything can be completely explained by using three. A simple theory is one that has dropped any "bells and whistles" when they don't really contribute to the explanation of the phenomena. For example, a theory that can explain some disease by appeal to virus and/or bacteria, won't add an appeal to evil demons.

Now assess the overall strength of each of the theories we have considered on the basis of these seven factors. Your final decision about a theory is, of course, not guaranteed to be correct. But at the very least it should be a careful, informed, rational assessment of the current possibilities for a satisfactory theory of mind.

Issues for Discussion

1. Can you construct a theory of mind that would be more satisfactory than any of the ones discussed in this chapter? Explain your answer.

2. How would you now define 'mind' or 'mental states'? Give reasons for your answer.

3. Are there other steps that you have found useful in evaluating theories?

4. Using the evaluative steps we have discussed, which of the theories of the mental do you find most plausible? Explain the outcome of each of your evaluative steps.

Suggested Research Project

*a. Donald Davidson has proposed a theory of the mental that he calls 'Anomalous Monism'. What does the name mean?

2

What Does It Mean to Be Conscious?

There are few things more familiar to us than our conscious experience. Paradoxically, providing a satisfactory theory about its nature and function is proving remarkably difficult. Philosophical disagreements about consciousness are even more profound than the ones concerning the nature of mind. That may surprise you; you might have assumed that theories of mind, of the mental, would automatically include theories of consciousness. And in some very general sense they do: Physicalists will take consciousness to be something physical; Functionalists will try to provide a Functionalist account of it, and so forth. But that is about as far as theories of mind take it. The reason is quite simple. Recent research provides compelling evidence that not all mental states and processes are conscious. For example, the processes involved in hearing and interpreting a piece of language, and then selecting words for your response, are largely unconscious. As a consequence, a theory of the nature of mental states and processes won't automatically include a theory of consciousness. Something more is needed. And specifying the nature of that "something more" has proven unexpectedly difficult.

A possible first step toward solving the problem might be to look for a characterization of consciousness that makes clear just exactly what the phenomenon is that is in need of a theory. Suppose I were to ask you to give me such a characterization. What would you say? One possible answer might be that consciousness is awareness. But how much would that really tell me? You would be giving me another word for consciousness, but if I were having difficulty understanding consciousness, simply giving me a different word for it wouldn't necessarily shed much light on things. Real explanations generally require something more than a synonym for what is being explained. That becomes clear if I then ask you to explain what awareness is. You might be tempted to respond that it is consciousness, and then we would be going in a circle that will get us nowhere.

Might you say that being conscious means being awake? Alert? Attentive? Do all these terms have the same meaning? Although we sometimes use these words interchangeably in everyday conversation, there are reasons to think that they may bear somewhat different relations to consciousness. For example, when I am asleep and dreaming, I am aware of images in my dreams. If consciousness and awareness are the same, then I am conscious when I dream, but I am not awake. Of course, if one insists that to be conscious one must be aware of one's *external* environment, then maybe being conscious is the same as being awake, but then it would not simply be the same as being aware. As for being alert and attentive, I think that most people would agree that if you are alert and attentive you are conscious, but the converse may not always be true. It may be possible to sit quietly, staring into space, thinking about nothing, and still be conscious; it just isn't focused consciousness. Being alert and attentive seem to be strong senses of the notion of being conscious, not simply interchangeable with it in all cases. So it seems that the apparent synonyms for consciousness point us in the direction of further distinctions among instances of consciousness, rather than providing us with a clear characterization of one phenomenon.

The fact that consciousness is familiar to us, then, does not mean that theories about it will come easily. Many centuries ago Augustine of Hippo commented that we all know perfectly well what *time* is—until we are asked to explain it. Consciousness can look a good deal like that. We all know perfectly well what it is from our firsthand experience of it, but it eludes easy explanations. Nonetheless, a number of different theories of consciousness have been proposed, but before considering them I want to explore briefly several questions that might highlight the complexity of some of the relevant issues. This, in turn, may help you to evaluate the various theories of consciousness when we discuss them. You may want to consider how well each theory can deal with some of the puzzles I shall mention.

What Sorts of Things Are Conscious?

Whatever consciousness is, it appears that rocks don't have it. At least they don't give us the slightest reason for thinking that they do. So one characteristic of conscious things appears, at least at first sight, to be that they are *living* organisms rather than nonliving things. But even that claim is not without its opponents. Supporters of *panpsychism*, for example, claim that everything, including nonliving systems, has some degree of consciousness. And many supporters of "strong" Artificial Intelligence (AI) would argue that computers could someday be conscious. It is difficult to prove that either view is mistaken unless we have a clear and comprehensive theory about the nature of consciousness. With such a theory, we might then be in a position to say which systems could be conscious and which could not.

Whatever the merits of panpsychism and strong AI, for now let's focus on the consciousness that appears to be present in living systems. (In Chapter 6 we shall return to the question of whether or not a non-living system like a computer or robot could be conscious.) But even with living systems things are not simple. For example, would you want to say that *all* living systems are conscious? One might be able to make a fairly convincing case that chimpanzees possess some degree of consciousness. In making such a claim, we would operate on the same sort of indirect evidence that we use in the case of other human beings: they have an anatomy and physiology similar to ours; much of their behavior is similar to ours in the presence of relevantly similar stimuli, and so forth. What would you say about your dog or cat? Their anatomy is somewhat different from ours, but they surely behave as if they are conscious. What about a fish? Or what would you say about the spider spinning its web outside your window or the fruit flies in the lab? In none of these latter cases is the answer obvious. We do seem to be more inclined to attribute consciousness to nonhuman species whose brains and behaviors are reasonably like ours. But that may be a bit of vanity on our part. All of this leads to a related question.

How Can You Tell If Something Is Conscious?

In deciding whether or not something is conscious, one needs to consider what sorts of criteria should be used. Should one rely on the organism's ability to *report* what it has seen or heard? Its ability to control its bodily behavior? Its reasonable and predictable behavior? Its ability to react *nonverbally* to what it sees or hears? Its ability to *remember* what it saw, heard, tasted, smelled, or touched? Its *self-awareness*? Its expression of *emotions*? Its ability to *introspect* its mental states? Something else? As you will see, even criteria like these, that we normally use in attributing consciousness to others, are not without their problems.

Let's start with the most familiar case. How do you know when *you* are conscious? Once again, consider the case of dreaming. Are you conscious when you dream? At some level you seem to be aware of what happens in your dreams, and you sometimes feel emotions in them. Notice that occasionally you even seem to recall bits of them when you wake up. Still, in most cases in the morning you have scant memory of your dreams. Furthermore, you seem to have little or no control over the content of your dreams and generally no control over your bodily movements during them. Some theorists have argued that short-term memory is the seat of consciousness. If that is right, such a view might suggest that we are indeed conscious when we dream, but the contents of the dreams rarely make it to long-term memory. Hence, we have forgotten them by morning. However, that view says nothing about our lack of control over dream contents or bodily movements.

So, even in your own case, you get a split decision when you try to apply a standard set of criteria for the presence of consciousness. Must *all* the criteria be satisfied before one attributes consciousness, or will a few be adequate? Would just *one* be enough? If so, which ones would be adequate by themselves?

Suppose you decide that *behavior* is the best clue to the presence of consciousness. On such a view, reasonable or predictable behavior might then be taken to indicate that it is guided by consciousness. Would you say that you are conscious or unconscious when you sleepwalk? You are clearly carrying out some degree of ordered behavior, and witnesses often describe the sleepwalker as behaving in reasonable and apparently purposeful ways—that is, avoiding obstacles, opening doors, and the like. (And notice that even when people are awake, their behavior is not always entirely reasonable.) Yet most sleepwalkers claim that they were not conscious of their behavior and have no memory of it.

If you are not sure about whether the behavior exhibited in sleepwalking is sufficiently controlled to constitute conscious behavior, would you perhaps suggest that feeling one is in control of one's own behavior is the mark of being conscious? If that seems more plausible to you, would you say that you are conscious or unconscious when you are under hypnosis? There is an important sense in which one wants to say that people under hypnosis are conscious, and yet there is another sense in which they may not be fully in control of their own behavior. And what is one to say about possible behaviors guided by posthypnotic suggestion?

This was supposed to be the easy case—decisions about how you know when you are conscious. It is obviously not as easy as one might hope. Our knowledge about our own consciousness seems at first glance to be clear and unproblematic. But just a bit of reflection on phenomena like dreams and sleepwalking highlights some of the puzzles. The consciousness that is most familiar to each one of us does not always carry with it unmistakable signs of its presence or its nature.

One conclusion we can draw here is that introspection alone does not seem to provide unambiguous answers about consciousness. This conclusion is important from a methodological point of view. Given the obvious familiarity of our conscious experience, some earlier philosophers believed that it is transparent and clearly known to us simply by introspection. Descartes was one of the most explicit defenders of such a view. It appears that he was unduly optimistic.

If even the apparently easy cases—those involving our own experience of consciousness—leave us with questions, what can we say about the more difficult cases? How can you tell if another organism is conscious? How do you know that your roommate or brother is conscious? In the case of other humans we tend to assume that if they are sufficiently like us in their behavior, then they are conscious: "If it looks like a duck, walks like a duck, and talks like a duck. . . ." Of course, when you think carefully about it, there really aren't any guarantees. Would it be possible for an organism to be living, to have a complex nervous system, to look human, to behave as you would in various circumstances, and yet not be a conscious being—be incapable of consciousness? Some philosophers have argued that such beings are logically possible (that is, their existence would not involve a contradiction). I mentioned such logically possible beings in Chapter 1—zombies. It isn't that anyone is arguing that such zombies actually exist. One point that these philosophers want to make is that we cannot be absolutely certain about the consciousness of *any* other system. The consciousness of another organism is not itself publicly accessible to you, so you must rely on indicators of its presence—any one of which could conceivably be mistaken. None of the "commonsense" indicators that I mentioned—being alive, having a complex nervous system, looking human, behaving in reasonable ways—*guarantees* the presence of consciousness.

In the strongest version of the zombie thought experiment, you are asked to imagine an organism that is physically *identical* to you, but is not conscious. One important consequence that some philosophers have drawn from this logical possibility is that consciousness is not a physical phenomenon. That is to say, if it is even conceivable that a system could be *physically identical* to us and still not be conscious, then that would indicate that consciousness is not a *physical* property. So the zombie thought experiment is sometimes used to support some form of Dualism.

In spite of the fact that views based on zombies strike many people as little more than science fiction, there are two considerations that seem to motivate them. First, we do not yet have a satisfactory account of what it is that causes consciousness. A complex nervous system surely appears to have some critical role to play. Note that we use anesthesia to induce an unconscious state in a person by affecting neural circuits in the brain. But so far we have no idea how to get from neurons in the brain, operating with electrical impulses and chemical neurotransmitters, to conscious experience. The "explanatory gap" between neurophysiology and consciousness is still huge. The second factor that motivates the zombie argument is that there is no universal agreement about the *function* of consciousness. Some defenders of the logical possibility of zombies argue that consciousness may have no function at all. They are suggesting that it could be the case that consciousness is *epiphenomenal*—that it does not do anything. Hence, they argue, it would be possible for another organism to look and act exactly like you, but not need (and not have) consciousness. Again, the point is not that these philosophers believe that there really are zombies. Rather, they argue that the physical and behavioral aspects of other organisms do not guarantee the presence of consciousness (in spite of the fact that those are precisely the sorts of evidence that we use every day when we attribute consciousness to others).

Earlier I spoke with some confidence that we could probably make a good case that chimpanzees are conscious. On what grounds would we do so? What is it about chimps that assures us that they are conscious? Obviously, if the zombie argument has any force in connection with our knowledge of the consciousness of other human beings, it should have equal force in the case of nonhuman species. And when we move away from species like chimps, which are somewhat like us, the case becomes murkier. How would you know if an amoeba is conscious? How about an extraterrestrial being with very different anatomy and physiology from that of humans? And we haven't even considered the case of nonliving systems like robots.

One fairly safe conclusion that we can draw is that it may not be possible to be *absolutely certain* that any other organism is conscious. But from a practical point of view, we rarely have any doubts about the consciousness of other human beings at least. We operate on the basis of what we take to be reasonably good evidence when we attribute consciousness to them. And we generally take behavior of a certain sort to be a pretty reliable indicator. Nonetheless, we have already noted that there are some unusual cases in which even the behavior of a person can be puzzling—for example, in the case of sleepwalking. The behavior of the sleepwalker can appear fairly normal, and yet the person on awakening can deny being conscious of any of it. But there are still more puzzling cases. Consider the *split-brain* syndrome.

During the 1960s, a new medical procedure was tried on some patients suffering from particularly severe forms of epilepsy that did not respond to conventional medication. The new procedure involved surgically cutting some fibers (the corpus callosum) in the central part of the brain, fibers that connect the two hemispheres of the brain. The operation is called a *commissurotomy*. The surgery generally did alleviate the epileptic seizures, but it also had an unexpected side effect. Under very carefully controlled experimental conditions, the patients behaved in ways that indicated that one hemisphere of the brain literally did not know what the other hemisphere knew. (See accompanying box, which describes the experiment.) This phenomenon is commonly referred to as *split-brain syndrome* because the two hemispheres of the patients' brains can function quite independently of one another. In order to understand what happens here, it is important to recall that most of the functions on the right side of the body (e.g., hand, foot, etc.) are controlled by the *left* hemisphere, and the functions on the left side of the body are controlled by the *right* hemisphere.

Split-Brain Syndrome: "When the patient stared at a dot at the centre of a projection screen, so that words (names of objects) flashed briefly to the left and right of the dot were transmitted respectively to the right and left occipital lobes [areas of the brain that deal with visual data], he could verbally report only the word on the right. This in itself was not surprising, as it was known that in most people the organization of speech requires use of the left hemisphere, which in these patients was presumably cut off from the information in the other. . . . [I]n some cases, although unable to speak the word flashed to the left of the dot, the patient could use his left hand correctly to retrieve the object it named, from a collection accessible behind a curtain. This implies that the right hemisphere, though unable to organize speech, can recognize at least some words and use the information to determine movements of the left hand. Further tests showed that with a so-called 'split brain' it is possible for a human being to pursue disparate and even conflicting goals with the left and right halves of his body, while vocally denying all knowledge of what the left half (regulated by the right hemisphere) is doing."[1]

What is fascinating about split-brain experiments is that they suggest the possibility that a person with a split brain might have two different centers of consciousness, each of which can be unaware of what the other one knows. For example, when a picture is directed only to the left side of the brain, the person can say what she has seen. When a picture is directed only to the right side of the brain, she cannot say what

---

1. Donald MacKay, "Divided Brains—Divided Minds?" in *Mindwaves*, Colin Blakemore and Susan Greenfield, eds. (Blackwell, 1987), pp. 6–8.

she has seen and may indeed say that she has seen nothing, but she will be able to draw what she has seen or pick it out of a collection of things with her left hand. Paradoxically, when asked why she drew what she did or selected the object she did, she will often construct a plausible but irrelevant story about why she did it, apparently because she is genuinely unaware (in the speaking half of her brain) of what caused her hand to do what it did. (I should note that outside of experimental circumstances, when both of the patient's eyes are allowed to see the full visual field, these split-brain patients function quite normally.)

All of this has raised a series of perplexing questions about consciousness. Is there any center of consciousness in the brain? Should we say that only the left, language-using, hemisphere of the brain is capable of consciousness? Is there some necessary connection between consciousness and language use? Or are there different and potentially separable types of consciousness, one verbal and the other largely nonverbal? What can be said about the apparent absence of one unified "overseer" of the consciousness in the two hemispheres of the split-brain cases under experimental conditions?

Returning to our earlier point—that from a practical point of view we normally use the behavior of another person as an indicator of his or her consciousness—one can see that the split-brain syndrome complicates this a bit. The behavior of the patient, when only her right hemisphere receives a piece of information, is puzzling. She can behave in entirely reasonable and predictable ways, drawing what she has seen or selecting it from a collection of things. But she (i.e., her "speaking" left hemisphere) speaks as if she (i.e., her generally nonspeaking right hemisphere) is unaware that she has seen the object. That is to say, there seems to be some degree of dissociation between her behavior and her own verbal account of what motivated it. Not only do we find some reason to be cautious about the reliability of the criteria that we routinely use to assure us of another person's consciousness, but we have further reason to wonder about just what we mean by consciousness. But let's look at one more piece of the puzzle.

What Are We Conscious Of?

In order to count as a conscious being, what sorts of things must an organism be capable of having access to? Is awareness of one's environment enough? Must one also be aware of oneself? Must one be able to introspect one's thoughts or be aware of the phenomenal character of one's experiences? When we attribute consciousness to an organism, do we mean that it is able to access all these sorts of things? Or would it be adequate if an organism has the ability to access just one or two of them?

Visual Agnosia: Psychologist Nicholas Humphrey refers to this deficit also as "mind-blindness." It generally arises from damage to the association cortex in the brain, and it appears in a variety of forms. An individual may claim that everything looks the way it did before, but he is unable to recognize a certain class of objects. Humphrey sees *visual agnosia* as leaving sensation intact, but damaging higher, perceptual/recognition capacities. In some cases the deficit is quite general. Humphrey describes a man who could not recognize most large objects in spite of the fact that he seemed cognitively normal in other respects. Sometimes the deficit is more limited. "Patients have been described who are unable to perceive shape, or movement, or spatial location, or color; or unable to recognize particular classes of objects, such as faces, or vegetables, or musical instruments. But all the time they will say that their sensation is quite normal—and that nothing looks any different to the way it did before."[2] In general, the term 'agnosia' indicates an absence of some form of knowledge. *Prosopagnosia*, described in Chapter 1, is a very special type of agnosia.

I suggested in Chapter 1 that it is probably wise not to think about the mind as one simple, unified thing that one either has or lacks. One might better speak of various mental capacities, where an organism might have some of these and not others. That is, one should perhaps think about 'the mental' as a collection of capacities rather than being an all-or-nothing sort of thing. Might something similar be true for consciousness? Could one say that there are different types of consciousness, different conscious capacities—perhaps one directed toward the environment, one toward the self, one toward thoughts, one toward qualia? Let's explore that possibility.

If we look at consciousness as being a variable collection of capacities determined by the type of objects with which each capacity could deal, we make sense of some of the differences between human consciousness and the consciousness attributable to some nonhuman species. Normal adult human beings clearly seem to be capable of consciousness at all the levels we mentioned. We can be conscious of our

2. Nicholas Humphrey, *A History of the Mind* (New York: HarperCollins, 1992), p. 83.

Note on Terminology: Recall from Chapter 1 that the term 'qualia' refers to the qualitative or phenomenal character of some of our experiences. For example, when you smell a cup of coffee, the way the coffee smells to you is its qualitative or phenomenal character. Qualia present a particular problem for theories of mind — especially Physicalist theories — because we don't seem to have a good theory about how they fit in with everything else that we know. They do not seem to be publicly observable. And if one cuts into the brain, one does not find the smell of coffee or the sound of train whistles, or the color of the lemon.

In this last connection, however, one point is worth noting: A system can transmit data by transducing it into a different form. As Stephen Pinker notes, "When you telephone your mother in another city, the message stays the same as it goes from your lips to her ears even as it physically changes its form, from vibrating air, to electricity in a wire, to charges in silicon, to flickering light in a fiber optic cable, to electromagnetic waves, and then back again in reverse order."[3] So the fact that neurons might carry information about color or smell in an electrical and chemical form without themselves being colored may not be as mysterious as it first seems.

environment, of ourselves, of our thoughts, of our qualia. And many nonhuman species surely seem to be capable of at least the first of these. When your dog or cat goes to its food dish to eat, the most plausible explanation of its behavior is that it is conscious of that dish and what is in it. While we have no guarantees of this consciousness, the consistently plausible behavior of animals like your dog in relation to their environment provides some indirect evidence that they are conscious of it. Keep in mind that we use the same sort of indirect, behavioral evidence in the case of other human beings. In the absence of compelling evidence to the contrary, it is reasonable to believe that many nonhuman organisms are indeed conscious of their environment. It is likely, too, that they are conscious of qualia. They are aware of pain, of smells, of sounds. Indeed, these would be among their best guides to their environment and to their own bodily needs.

On the other hand, it is commonly believed that we don't have even indirect evidence that most nonhuman animals are conscious of their thoughts. But should it follow from that that we should not attribute *any* consciousness at all to nonhuman animals?

3. Steven Pinker, *How the Mind Works*, p. 24.

As for consciousness of Self, in what does that consist? Is awareness of one's body sufficient? Most animals must have some consciousness of their own bodies in order to feed them, protect them, perhaps groom them, and so forth. Experimental evidence suggests that chimps (and apparently only chimps among nonhumans) have the further capability of recognizing their own bodies in a mirror. If awareness of one's body is adequate for "self-consciousness," perhaps self-consciousness is more prevalent than we might think. If, in addition, the notion of Self includes awareness of one's place in a network of social relations, then a number of species show evidence of this, behaving in ways that indicate awareness of their place in the social hierarchy or in their relations to parents or offspring. If, however, 'Self' is more than one's body and/or one's social relationships—for example, if it means awareness of oneself as a moral agent—then maybe only humans are capable of such a level of consciousness.

However one chooses to answer these difficult questions, it does seem plausible to suppose that an organism could have one or more of these levels of consciousness without having all of them. But that brings us to the question of whether there is something common to each level that constitutes it as an instance of *consciousness*, or is each level sufficiently different that we should think of three or four (or more) distinct phenomena that are only loosely related but are all labeled 'consciousness'? Is language perhaps misleading us (as Ryle suggested in connection with 'mind')—sending us in search of one theory when we are perhaps dealing with a series of distinguishable phenomena?

Is Consciousness One Phenomenon or Many?

Before constructing a theory about something, it is helpful to specify as clearly as possible just what phenomenon one is theorizing about. If, for example, you were going to propose a theory of culture, you would begin by specifying just what you mean by the term "culture." If it turns out that "culture" designates a multitude of distinguishable phenomena, then there is a question about whether one unified theory of culture will be satisfactory or whether you may need a series of more limited theories—one for each of the distinguishable components.

Similar concerns arise when one is looking for a theory of consciousness. For some theorists, consciousness is one unified phenomenon for which a single comprehensive theory can be provided. Other theorists argue that the term 'consciousness' is currently applied to a variety of distinct phenomena, each of which is likely to require its own explanation. One might ask, for example, if a theory of visual awareness would need to be different from a theory that explains introspective awareness.

Deciding which of these two approaches is to be preferred is both important and difficult. If one's theory simply assumes that the term 'consciousness' designates one unified phenomenon, one's theory may ignore significant elements of conscious experience that don't fit the mold. On the other hand, if one assumes a multiplicity of distinct capacities, and provides separate theories for each, one could overlook what they might have in common.

Consider three approaches that one might take in trying to specify what a term like 'consciousness' might mean. The first approach favors a simple, unified meaning for the term. It specifies a set of *necessary and sufficient conditions* that must be met in order for the term to apply. A common example of a term whose application can be specified by a set of necessary and sufficient conditions is 'water'. In spite of the variations in its appearance as liquid, steam, or ice, for a substance to be called water, it must always consist of H_2O.

Note on Terminology: The notion of *necessary and sufficient conditions* can be very important when you are trying to define or explain something. A condition is *necessary* for something if it is impossible for that thing or event to be present without that condition being fulfilled. For example, it is a necessary condition for the presence of water that the liquid contain oxygen. You cannot have water without oxygen. However, oxygen alone, while a necessary condition, is not *sufficient* for the presence of water. Something more is needed; there must be hydrogen as well, and it must be combined with the oxygen in a precise ratio. A *sufficient condition* for something, on the other hand, is a condition that guarantees the presence of the thing or event. So, for example, rain is a sufficient condition for the presence of water. Note, however, that it is not necessary to have rain in order to have water but if you do have rain, that is sufficient to guarantee the presence of water. So, it is possible that a condition can be necessary without being sufficient, or it can be sufficient without being necessary. Obviously, the strongest set of conditions, the set that will offer a full definition or explanation of the thing you are trying to understand, is the set of *necessary and sufficient conditions*. These will specify both what is required for the thing to be what it is and what is adequate so that nothing else is required. In the case of water, hydrogen plus oxygen (in proper relation) are necessary *and* sufficient.

Can consciousness be defined in terms of necessary and sufficient conditions (see box on page 65)? Consider some of the criteria for attributing consciousness that we discussed earlier. Would any of them constitute *necessary* conditions for consciousness? Is the ability to respond appropriately to certain stimuli required? If so, would that entail that some persons who are deaf and blind, or paralyzed, are not conscious? How about 'being awake'? One sometimes finds this specified as a necessary condition for consciousness, but that automatically (and perhaps arbitrarily) eliminates the cases of dreaming. Another possibility might be the ability to report on the information one has received. But the case of the split-brain patient calls that into question. Note that when information was directed only to her right hemisphere she was unable to report it. If her ability to draw the object counts as a case of being conscious of it, then the ability to report on the information would not count as a necessary condition for consciousness. If self-awareness, or the ability to introspect, or the ability to control one's bodily behavior were necessary conditions for consciousness, then it would seem that young infants would not count as conscious. If the ability to recall what has happened recently is necessary, then patients with amnesic syndrome would not qualify as conscious, nor would infants. It seems, then, that specifying necessary conditions for attributing consciousness is difficult.

Should any of the above conditions count as *sufficient* conditions for consciousness? If one *is* able to respond to a stimulus, is that sufficient to guarantee the presence of consciousness? If that is right, would that mean that your car is conscious when it responds to the stimulus of having its accelerator depressed? Is being awake enough? Would that mean that a mosquito that is not sleeping must count as conscious? Is the ability to recall or to report on received information enough? Would that make your computer conscious? If one includes only *living* systems as possible candidates for consciousness, then of course some of these counterexamples vanish. Are there any good reasons for insisting that only living organisms can be conscious?

The answers here are not easy or obvious. And some philosophers and psychologists have argued explicitly against assuming that consciousness can be defined by a set of necessary and sufficient conditions. Patricia Churchland notes that "what we now lump together as 'consciousness' may be not so much a unitary phenomenon admitting of a unitary explanation, but a rag-bag of sundry effects requiring a set of quite different explanations."[4] David Armstrong, whose theory of

---

4. "Neurological Basis of Consciousness," in *Consciousness in Contemporary Science*, A. J. Marcel and E. Bisiach eds., p. 281.

consciousness we will consider shortly, notes, "It is not even clear that the word 'consciousness' stands for just one sort of entity, quality, process, or whatever."[5] Additionally, the psychologist Alan Allport says, "My own view is that there *are* no such (general) criteria [for identifying instances of consciousness], because *there is no such phenomenon*. That is, there is no unitary entity of 'phenomenal awareness'—no unique process or state, no *one* coherently conceptualizable phenomenon for which there could be a single, conceptually coherent theory."[6]

These concerns lead us to consider two other approaches to specifying the meaning of terms like 'consciousness': *Family Resemblances* and *Prototype Theory.*

Early in the 20th century, philosopher Ludwig Wittgenstein cautioned that we should not insist on finding a set of necessary and sufficient conditions for all our concepts. He used the example of 'games', and noted that there is a wide variety of activities that go by the name 'game'—one can think of football, solitaire, charades, ring-around-the-rosy, Trivial Pursuit, psychological games, and so forth—that do not all satisfy one set of necessary and sufficient conditions. Rather, they share what Wittgenstein called "family resemblances," that is, some overlapping similarities. Some games require teams and some don't; some need special equipment and some don't; some keep score and some don't; and so on. The term 'game' is simply a convenient label for a family of things that are somewhat alike and somewhat different.

It is possible that consciousness ought to be understood this way, as a family name for a series of capacities that have some overlapping similarities as well as some significant differences. On such a view, dreaming and hallucinating would involve awareness of internally generated images but not necessarily awareness of the external environment; memory sometimes involves awareness of images but can also involve accessing factual information, reconstructing past experiences, or calling up bodily skills; conscious perception is normally generated by external stimuli; introspective awareness might involve some internal scanning mechanism. Some of these states and processes might have qualitative content and some might not. In other words, the causes, the contents, the effects of these different mental states and processes might have some overlapping similarities as well as some differences in the consciousness associated with them. Patricia Churchland suggests that

5. "What Is Consciousness?" in Armstrong's *The Nature of Mind*, p. 55; reprinted in *The Nature of Consciousness*, N. Block, O. Flanagan, G. Guzeldere, eds. (Cambridge, MA: MIT/Bradford, 1997), p. 721.

6. "What Concept of Consciousness?" in Marcel and Bisiach, p. 161.

the differences among conscious states like these may be best accounted for by somewhat distinct neurobiological theories.

A third way to approach the issue of specifying the meaning of the
term 'consciousness' is by way of *Prototype* theory. In the 1970s and early
1980s, psychologist Eleanor Rosch did a series of experiments to show
that when we categorize things—birds, for example—we don't do it by
checking off a set of necessary and sufficient conditions that have been
met. Rather, we settle on a paradigm example of the category, a "prototype" (in the bird case, probably a robin or sparrow) and then include
other cases insofar as they are more or less like this prototypical case.
What that gives us is not a perfectly neat category with all the boundaries
clearly established by necessary and sufficient conditions, but something
like a set of concentric circles. The prototype, maybe a robin, is at the
"center"; reasonably similar things like pigeons and eagles are close by,
and somewhat less similar cases like penguins and emu are near the
outer edges. In a case like birds, even the fringe cases can be decided on
reasonable scientific grounds to "really" belong to the category. However, in cases like "writing instrument," where the prototypes would
probably be pens and pencils, the fringe cases may fade into things like
lipstick (it can be used to write, but . . .), a telegraph machine, or a
bloody finger. Here it is a matter of convention whether we decide that a
particular fringe case belongs to the category or does not.

Using Prototype theory to characterize the notion of consciousness
might involve taking something like visual awareness of one's external
environment as the central or prototypical case. Other examples of conscious states might shade off gradually toward some fringe cases like
dreaming, or right-hemisphere awareness in the split-brain person.
Questions would remain, however, whether or not those fringe cases
genuinely belong to the category or are simply included by linguistic
convention. In fact, the very outside cases might well shade off into
semiconscious and eventually unconscious states. This kind of continuum from unconsciousness to focused conscious states might allow one
to make sense of some of the differences between conscious states in
humans and possibly more limited or slightly different occurrences of
conscious states in some nonhuman animals. Furthermore, a continuum of that sort would be what one would expect within an evolutionary framework.

So is 'consciousness' best understood as one phenomenon with certain essential characteristics, no matter what its object or behavioral manifestations, or is it best understood as designating a series of more loosely
related phenomena? In deciding which of these approaches is likely to be
more satisfactory, some theorists have urged that we use empirical investigations of the rich variety of conscious states to explore their differences

while keeping an eye open for possible commonalities. Philosopher Owen Flanagan notes that getting at the complex structure of consciousness, "requires coordination of phenomenological, psychological, and neural analysis."[7] Alan Allport advises, "Like 'understanding,' like 'life,' our everyday concept of 'phenomenal awareness' denotes . . . a great range of different states of affairs. The important and exacting task that confronts us, therefore, if we are to make any scientific headway with the concept of 'consciousness,' is to describe, to characterize in functional detail (including, of course, to provide behavioural and/or physiological *criteria* for the identification of), these different phenomena. Only then may we hope to ascertain whether there is, in fact, any identifiable property or properties in common between them."[8]

So, before one constructs a theory of consciousness, one needs to be clear about precisely what phenomenon or phenomena one is theorizing about. One needs, first of all, to decide whether there is just one simple unified phenomenon definable by some set of necessary and sufficient conditions or whether one is theorizing about a collection of related phenomena that may not share any one set of defining properties. One needs to decide if one's theory is to apply equally to cases of dreaming, sensory perception, remembering, imagining, introspecting, making decisions, feeling emotions—or whether many of these will require a somewhat distinct account. Once again, answers to these questions are neither easy nor obvious. And as you will see, in proposing theories of consciousness theorists don't always make explicit their assumptions on these issues. Many of them appear to assume that there is one phenomenon for which one general theory will be adequate.

Having considered a number of the puzzles that face the theorist, let us turn to consider some of the leading theories of consciousness that have been proposed.

Theories of Consciousness

Cartesian View

Given the difficulties and paradoxes that surround our notions of consciousness, you should not be surprised by the fact that the theories that have emerged are somewhat removed from our everyday notions about

7. *Consciousness Reconsidered* (Cambridge, MA: MIT/Bradford, 1992), p. 220.

8. Alan Allport, "What Concept of Consciousness?" in Marcel and Bisiach, p. 162.

consciousness. I begin with a brief look at one of the oldest and simplest views of consciousness, that suggested by Descartes. He does not provide what we would now consider a full-blown theory of consciousness, but his views were influential for a long time and will provide helpful background for the more recent theories that we will discuss.

Recall that Descartes proposed a Substance Dualist account of mind and body. He didn't offer a separate theory of consciousness. Rather, he took consciousness to simply be a characteristic of all mental states. He says:

> Now as to the doctrine that there can be nothing in the mind, insofar as it is a thing that thinks, of which it is not aware, this appears to me self-evident, because we understand that nothing is in the mind, so viewed, that is not a thought or is not dependent upon thought. For otherwise it would not belong to the mind insofar as it is a thing that thinks. Nor can there exist in us any thought of which we are not aware at the very same moment it is in us. For this reason I have no doubt that the mind begins to think immediately upon its being infused into the body of an infant, and at the same time is aware of its thought, even if later on it does not recall what it was thinking of, because the images [*species*] of these thoughts do not inhere in the memory.[9]

So it seems safe to conclude that when Descartes characterizes himself as a "thing that thinks," he means a *conscious* thinking thing. Furthermore, he claims that he (as a mental substance) exists just so long as he is thinking. So on his view as long as he exists he must be conscious. That would mean that he would count at least some of the various puzzling cases that we discussed earlier—especially dreaming and sleepwalking—as instances of consciousness.

For Descartes, consciousness appears to be a necessary, nonphysical property of all mental states. One of the important differences between this view and the ones currently held by most philosophers of mind is that it is now no longer common to identify consciousness with mind or with the mental. As I noted earlier, there is substantial evidence that many mental functions are unconscious. For example, you have probably had the experience of working on a difficult problem, perhaps in math or logic, and—unable to work out the answer—you went to bed. When you woke up you found that you knew just what you needed to do to solve the

9. René Descartes, "Reply to the Fourth Set of Objections," in Descartes, *Philosophical Essays and Correspondence*, Roger Ariew, ed. (Indianapolis: Hackett, 2000), p. 190.

problem. One very plausible explanation of such an experience is that your mental processes were working at it while you slept, without your being aware of it. More commonly, when you are trying to remember a name and can't, have you sometimes gone on to do something else, and later the name suddenly pops into your head when you weren't even looking for it? Unconscious mental processing is likely at work.

Given the fact that Descartes implicitly characterized all mental states as conscious, his theory of mind no longer seems to be very helpful in providing an account of consciousness. The latter is a property of some, but not all, mental states. A useful theory will need to explain what distinguishes conscious mental states from unconscious ones.

In recent decades a number of diverse theories of consciousness have appeared. We will consider several of the more prominent ones: Higher-Order theories, a Property Dualist theory, the Multiple Drafts theory, and the Global Workspace theory.

Higher-Order Theories of Consciousness

A second approach to consciousness, one that is currently very influential among philosophers, involves Higher-Order (HO) theories of consciousness. Although there are several versions of the view, the basic idea in Higher-Order theories is that a mental state is conscious (or an organism has a conscious mental state) when that mental state is the object of a second ("higher-order") mental state.

Note on Terminology: A higher-order mental state is one that is *about* or *directed toward* another, lower-order or first-order, mental state. For example, my thought about my belief in God would be a higher-order thought. My desire to change my desire for a cigarette would be a second-order—that is, higher-order—desire.

In their simplest form, these theories argue that consciousness is not a property of a single mental state; rather, consciousness arises from a relation between two mental states. Notice that on Descartes's view, consciousness is just a property of each individual mental state—much as color or spatiality is a property of each visible physical object. But for Higher-Order theorists, consciousness should be understood as a *relational* property. Other more common examples of relational properties include being a brother or being a daughter or being taller than one's roommate. These sorts of properties arise only when one is in a certain relation to someone or something else.

There are two basic versions of HO theories of consciousness. According to one, proposed by philosopher David Rosenthal, an organism has a conscious mental state when it has a higher-order *thought* about that state. According to a second version, proposed by William Lycan, a mental state is conscious when it is the object of some mental *process* like a mental *scanner* (but not of a *thought* as such). Both versions of the theory have their roots in a proposal made by David Armstrong, so let's begin with a brief look at Armstrong's view.

Armstrong: An Early View

In 1981, David Armstrong published an influential essay, "What Is Consciousness?"[10] In it he noted that the term 'consciousness' can have at least three senses. The first he termed "minimal consciousness," and said that it occurs when there is *some* mental activity occurring in the mind. He called the second "perceptual consciousness," in which we are aware of aspects of our perceptual field. This entails "minimal consciousness" but is not entailed by it. The third sense that he notes is "introspective consciousness." He likens this to a kind of "perception" of the mental, or what we would simply call "introspection."

To illustrate the differences among these three senses, he uses an example that will seem familiar to anyone who drives a car. Armstrong describes a long-distance driver who has been driving for some time without apparently being aware of what he was doing. Armstrong argues that the driver had to have the first two levels of consciousness — minimal and perceptual — or he would not have seen the road or stayed on it. What he lacks, says Armstrong, is the third level, introspective consciousness. That is, he is not conscious of his own mental states.

Let's look more closely at Armstrong's three senses of consciousness and his use of them to explain the experience of the long-distance driver. He equates minimal consciousness with the state in which anything mental is going on. To avoid Descartes's problem, where consciousness is simply equated with the mental, let us assume that all that Armstrong means here is that in minimal consciousness the individual is at least awake, not that every mental event is necessarily consciousness. This notion of consciousness has received little explicit attention in later theories, but the other two, perceptual and introspective, have been the focus of a good deal of attention.

Perceptual consciousness has been taken by some theorists to be the paradigm case (the prototype so to speak), the case most common

10. Armstrong, *The Nature of Mind*, Chapter 4.

among humans of all ages and probably among many nonhuman species. In the case of the long-distance driver, Armstrong is surely right in his claim that there must be some perceptual consciousness in the driver or he would not be able to keep the vehicle on the road, out of the path of other vehicles, and so on. Were the driver blind, he surely couldn't do all those things. What the example suggests, of course, is that there are *degrees* of perceptual consciousness—some very focused and attentive, some marginally focused, and some hardly focused at all.

The question, then, is what might account for these differences of degree? Although Armstrong does not frame the issue in these terms, his explanation is that the driver lacks *introspective* consciousness. What he means is that the driver is not introspectively conscious of his perceptions of the road.

There is an old philosophical distinction that lies in the background here. The point has been raised by philosopher Fred Dretske.[11] The distinction is between a mental *act* (like perceiving) and the *object* of a mental act (like the road, the cars). On Armstrong's account, it seems that when perception of something is inattentive, it is because one is not introspectively conscious of one's *act* of perceiving. That assumes that attentive perception requires attention not merely to the perceived *objects*, but attention to the *act* of perceiving. Put another way, for Armstrong, perceptual consciousness is not attentive unless there is a second (higher-order), introspective act of consciousness that is aware of it. Armstrong's model provided the background for the Higher-Order (HO) theories. We will consider two of these: William Lycan's Internal Sense theory, and David Rosenthal's Higher-Order Thought (HOT) theory.

Lycan: Internal Sense Theory

Notice that Armstrong characterized introspective consciousness as "perception" of the mental. William Lycan's theory builds on this analogy. He sees consciousness in terms of a system of internal "scanners" that take mental states as their objects. For Lycan, introspective consciousness does not simply account for attentive perception; it provides the theory of all conscious states: "if one is wholly unaware of some mental state, that state is not a conscious state."[12]

---

11. See "Consciousness," in *Naturalizing the Mind* (Cambridge, MA: MIT/Bradford, 1995).

12. "Consciousness as Internal Monitoring," in *The Nature of Consciousness*, ftn. 18 (quoting Rosenthal), p. 769.

Lycan is explicit in his disagreement with both Armstrong and Dretske about perceptual consciousness. Appealing to the distinction between an act and an object of perception, Dretske argued that one can be perceptually conscious of an *object* without being conscious of the *act* of perceiving. Armstrong implicitly agrees with this when he says that the long-distance driver has some minimal degree of perceptual consciousness even when he is not aware of his perceiving (otherwise he would crash). However, Lycan's theory is about what makes conscious *states* (or acts) conscious. He grants that there might be *some* sense of 'conscious' in which one could be conscious when one is focused on a perceived object and is unaware of the state/act of perceiving. But, he says, his Inner Sense theory of consciousness "is not and never has pretended to be a theory of 'perceptual consciousness' in Dretske's and Armstrong's sense. It is a theory of conscious awareness, of 'conscious states' in my original sense of: states one is conscious of being in" (p. 759). One is conscious in the sense he intends only if one has a higher-order awareness of one's mental state. As Lycan puts it, "The Inner Sense theory has it that conscious awareness is the successful operation of an internal scanner or monitor that outputs second-order representations of first-order psychological states" (p. 762).

Lycan's response to Dretske illustrates the fact that the precise meaning of the term 'consciousness' is still open to significant debate, a point Lycan himself acknowledges.

Lycan anticipates and responds to some possible objections to his view. First of all, an internal scanning device might seem to require a Self of some sort to "read" it. But Lycan suggests that a conscious system can have many scanners, probably each of which contributes information to the control of some aspect of the system's behavior, but none of which would constitute a "primary" scanner, or Self.

Lycan's theory of consciousness should be understood within the larger context of his Homuncular/Teleological Functionalism. Recall that on this view, a system with mental states is one that has a large collection of "homunculi" organized in a hierarchy ranging from those that are utterly simple (and stupid) on/off mechanisms to the more complex ones that receive and act on input from the simpler levels. For Lycan, consciousness might emerge at any level in the system, hence, he notes the possibility of "many consciousnesses" in "a single human body" (p. 765).

A second possible objection to Lycan's account is that it is likely that an organism has many internal scanners that have nothing to do with consciousness. For example, there might well be scanners keeping track of blood pressure, hormone levels, and so on. And yet these scanners don't generate consciousness. He replies: "The operation of an internal monitor does not *eo ipso* constitute consciousness. . . . the outputs might go unheard, or they might be received only by devices that do nothing but turn patches of the creature's skin different colors. For consciousness constituting, we must require that monitor output contribute—specifically to the integration of information in a way conducive to making the system's behavior appropriate to its input and circumstances" (p. 762). Lycan acknowledges that this formulation is vague: What sorts of integration? How much? What kinds of behavior are relevant?

Lycan believes that consciousness comes in *degrees*, so perhaps there can be different degrees of integration leading to different degrees of consciousness. His theory, however, does not seem to lend itself to a Family Resemblance account of these different degrees of consciousness, or even to Prototype theory. Notice that on his account, *every* conscious state requires higher-order representations, apparently as a necessary and sufficient condition.

Finally, notice that what will make a given state conscious is *not* that it has a particular qualitative *feel*. The *function* of the state is decisive: integrating information with a view to guiding behavior. So Lycan offers a Functionalist theory of consciousness that is both Physicalist and, on his view, consistent with evolution theory.

Rosenthal: Higher-Order Thought (HOT) Theory

David Rosenthal has proposed a somewhat different and more comprehensive version of a Higher-Order account, called the Higher-Order Thought (HOT) theory of consciousness. Like Armstrong and Lycan, he locates his theory within the framework of Naturalism, Physicalism, and evolutionary considerations, but he proposes more than a theory about attentive perceptual consciousness. His Higher-Order representations are not modeled on perception; they are *thoughts*.

Rosenthal begins by arguing that a satisfactory Physicalist theory of consciousness cannot treat it as a *simple intrinsic* property of mental states (as Descartes did). One reason for this is that we have no idea what *intrinsic* physical property consciousness could be identified with. Furthermore, if it were a *simple* property, consciousness could not be analyzed into its constituents (since simple properties don't have constituent parts). Without an analysis of its constituent parts, he argues that no theory would be possible. Rosenthal concludes that consciousness must therefore be a *relational* property. And the relation he proposes is that between a mental state and a higher-order thought about that mental state. A perceptual state is conscious just in case it has a higher-order thought (HOT) related to it. And one has introspective consciousness just in case there is a still-higher-order thought related to it. As he put it, "a state's being conscious is its being accompanied by a roughly simultaneous higher-order thought that one is in the target mental state. So being conscious is an extrinsic property of those mental states which are conscious."[13]

It is both necessary and paradoxical that Rosenthal must argue that the relevant higher-order thoughts are not themselves conscious. The necessity arises from the threat of an infinite regress: if the HOT were conscious, then one would need an account of what makes it conscious, and so on. One needs to come to an element that does not itself possess consciousness in order to explain consciousness in a noncircular way. Rosenthal specifies this element as the higher-order thought. In order for that HOT to become conscious there needs to be a still-higher-level thought that relates to it but is itself unconscious.

The paradoxical appearance arises from the claim that we have unconscious thoughts that play an essential role in making us conscious. For Rosenthal, this is one of the strengths of his theory. He notes, first, the widely accepted view that not all mental states are conscious. So the notion of an unconscious thought is not self-contradictory. In addition, Rosenthal sees a positive advantage to such a formulation. To explain consciousness in terms of unconscious mental states is to "bridge the intuitive gulf between consciousness and matter." He goes on to explain: "If we can explain consciousness by appeal to states that are mental but not conscious, perhaps we can in turn explain those nonconscious mental states in nonmental terms. This tiered picture would sustain naturalism."[14] He later elaborates on the evolutionary plausibility of such a view: "creatures with the capacity to be in conscious states could have evolved from nonmental organisms. One might speculate that this capacity relied on the intermediate capacity to be in nonconscious mental states" (p. 749, ftn. 22).

Rosenthal distinguishes between conscious creatures and conscious states. One possible motivation for making such a distinction is that a creature is conscious if it is capable of being conscious in spite of the fact that sometimes it is unconscious. A conscious state, by contrast, cannot sometimes be unconscious. However, Rosenthal has a more

13. "The Independence of Consciousness and Sensory Quality," *Philosophical Issues*, 1, 1991, p. 16.

14. David Rosenthal, "A Theory of Consciousness," in *The Nature of Consciousness*, p. 735.

substantive reason for making the distinction. He argues that states by themselves can never be conscious of anything; only creatures can. He explains his claim in terms of "transitive" consciousness. "Being transitively conscious of something is a relation that a person or other creature bears to that thing. So only creatures can be transitively conscious of things. A mental state may well be that state in virtue of which somebody is conscious of a thing, but the state cannot itself literally be conscious of anything" (p. 738).

So, on Rosenthal's view, a creature has a conscious mental state when it is conscious, by means of an unconscious higher-order thought, that it is itself in that state. More concretely, I am conscious of that chair in front of me when I have an unconscious thought that I am perceiving a chair.

Strengths and Weaknesses of Higher-Order Theories

Notice that HO theories (both Rosenthal's and Lycan's) are not constructed as a result of empirical investigations. Rather, they are constructed to satisfy certain conceptual or theoretical requirements: to avoid an infinite regress, to provide a bridge between consciousness and the physical, to construct a theory that is consistent with what we know about evolution, and so on.

HO theories of consciousness have a number of attractive features. For Physicalists, they offer the promise of explaining consciousness in terms of physical states of the brain, like scanners or unconscious mental representations of some sort. And as the theorists point out, this feature makes consciousness amenable to an evolutionary explanation. Most versions of the theory also hold out the possibility of a plausible account of consciousness in nonhuman organisms. Moreover, they attempt to explain consciousness in terms that don't presuppose it. Additionally, they highlight the important role that unconscious mental states can play in our understanding of the mind. Finally, by treating consciousness as a relational property, they offer the possibility of explaining its emergence with the development of certain types of complex structures within a system.

But HO theories are not without their problems. One objection, raised by Dretske, asks how it is that having a higher-order thought or having internal scanners makes a state conscious, whereas HO thoughts and scanners don't make all of their objects conscious?

One reply, from Lycan, is that the object of the higher-order state must be a *mental* or representational state. It seems clear, however, that for Lycan's response to be acceptable he must insist that the representation that is the object of the higher-order scanning must be a *mental* representation, not simply any representational state. One might, after all, have mechanisms in an airplane that would scan representations of the plane's altitude, its angle of flight, and so forth, without thereby making those representations conscious. That raises a question about what it is about *mental* representations that makes them candidates for consciousness. Do they possess some set of properties that make consciousness possible, and if so, might that set of properties itself be responsible for the emergence of consciousness without the addition of some higher-order state? On the other hand, even in the case of mental representations, is it not possible to have scanners of mental representations, which integrate information and guide behavior, without generating consciousness—as, perhaps, in subliminal perception?

Rosenthal's reply to Dretske's objection is a bit different. He argues that the higher-order thought does not *cause* the first-order state to be conscious; rather, its being conscious just consists in its relation with the HOT. According to Rosenthal, the objection assumes that consciousness is an intrinsic property, whereas he argues that it is relational. And the relation is one of transitive consciousness, not of causality. This response is a bit elusive. It is difficult to find relevant examples of properties that emerge in relations, but in which causality plays no role at all. The case of consciousness is not like the case of a pen and a pencil sitting on a desk. Admittedly, the pen and pencil are in some sort of relation (a spatial one) without one causing something in the other. Since there are no changes in either the pen or pencil, there is no need to explain what caused a change. But when a HOT relates to a lower-order mental state, it seems that a change does occur in the latter. Something must be responsible for that change. One would normally look to some causal factor. It is not entirely clear why this case should be different.

A second objection, also raised by Dretske, concerns the apparent disregard of the distinction between a mental *act* and its *object* (a concern we discussed earlier). HO theories (with the probable exception of Armstrong's) seem to argue that a mental state's being conscious consists in one's being aware of being in that state, rather than in one's being aware of some object of that state. One response might, of course, be that being aware that one is in that state includes being aware of the object (or objects) of that state. But that may not completely address the problem. While it surely seems to be *sufficient* for consciousness that one is aware of being in some mental state, is it *necessary*? If I am not aware of whether I am remembering something or imagining it, whether I am perceiving or dreaming—but I am aware of some content or object other than my mental state, would it follow that I am not conscious? Or is the higher-order unconscious thought not required to have information about which *type* of mental state it is, in order for that state to be conscious? But then it isn't clear just what the content of that HOT must be.

An objection aimed primarily at Lycan's version of the theory, by philosopher Alex Byrne, is that if perception is the model on which to understand the internal scanners, we should find them fallible (as we do with external perception). Byrne argues that we can't. I suggested earlier that it is indeed possible to be uncertain or even mistaken about what state we are in and even to correct our judgment about it in light of later evidence. However, Byrne's objection can be understood as asking whether or not it is possible to be mistaken about whether or not I am *conscious* (not about which particular conscious state I am in). But even here, perhaps some of our earlier examples of unusual cases like hypnosis or split-brain syndrome might provide cases where one might be mistaken about whether or not one is conscious of something.

In spite of some objections to Higher-Order theories of consciousness, they remain widely discussed candidates for a promising theory.

Consciousness as a Nonphysical Property

In his 1996 book, *The Conscious Mind*, philosopher David Chalmers offered a very different account of consciousness. Like the Higher-Order theories, Chalmers's approach is conceptual rather than empirical; unlike them, however, it is not a Physicalist theory.

Recall the zombies that I described earlier—hypothetical beings that are physically identical to us, function just like us, but lack consciousness. Chalmers makes use of the zombie thought experiment to argue that it is logically or conceptually possible for an organism to be physically identical with a human being and not be conscious. As I noted earlier, the logical possibility of such zombies is intended to show that consciousness is not identical with any physical property of human beings. So as a start, Chalmers argues that consciousness is a nonphysical property. "The dualism implied here is . . . a kind of *property* dualism: conscious experience involves properties of an individual that are not entailed by [i.e., not logically necessary consequences of] the physical properties of that individual, although they may depend lawfully ["supervene"] on those properties. Consciousness is a feature of the world over and above the physical features of the world."[15]

15. *The Conscious Mind* (New York: Oxford University Press, 1996), p. 125.

So Chalmers's view is a version of Property Dualism. It is not, how-ever, the version in which *theories* about consciousness are not reduc-ible to physical theories because of the complex structures involved. Rather, his view is the stronger version of Property Dualism, which "involves fundamentally new features of the world" (p. 125). He argues that consciousness, like "space-time, mass-energy, charge, spin, etc." is one of the "fundamental properties" of the world (p. 126).

This highlights one of his other differences from the HO theorists. Whereas they argued that consciousness must be seen as a *relational* property, arising in the presence of certain higher-order mental states, Chalmers sees it as an intrinsic property of the world, unanalyzable into any simpler components.

As I have described it so far, his view has two rather unappealing con-sequences. First, it raises the real possibility of *panpsychism*—a possibil-ity that Chalmers accepts. If consciousness is a fundamental feature of the world, on a par with features like space-time, it looks as if it could be present everywhere. That, of course, is possible. But a theory that leads to panpsychism seems to lose contact with the notion of consciousness that we find most intriguing and puzzling—the conscious awareness that certain organisms seem to exhibit and rocks seem to lack. And it was this very aspect of consciousness—"phenomenal" or "qualitative" consciousness—that Chalmers had set out to explain. The distinction between us and rocks vanishes into simple matters of degree with panpsychism, and the really interesting issues surrounding conscious-ness seem to dissolve. In spite of its lack of intuitive appeal, however, we have no conclusive argument to show that panpsychism must be false.

A second consequence of Chalmers's view, again recognized and tentatively accepted by him, is *Epiphenomenalism*. Recall that in the discussion of the strong form of Property Dualism in Chapter 1, I noted that we have no plausible account of how nonphysical properties could causally interact with the physical world. If consciousness is a nonphys-ical property, then it looks as if it can exert no causal force on the physi-cal. That is to say, it would be causally inefficacious in relation to the behaviors of the organisms that have it. That is Epiphenomenalism. What makes such a consequence undesirable, of course, is our intu-ition that our conscious states do guide our behavior. But, as in the case of panpsychism, we lack conclusive evidence or argument that Epiphe-nomenalism is false. Counterintuitive, yes; but not proven to be false.

Although Chalmers argues that consciousness is not *logically* entailed by the physical (it is *conceivable* that one could have a physical world just like ours but without consciousness), still he believes that con-sciousness is, as a matter of fact, part of the natural world. It is natural but not physical. He calls this "naturalistic dualism." What then is the relationship between these two disparate aspects of the natural world? Chalmers says that nonphysical consciousness *supervenes* on the physical—that is, consciousness varies lawfully as the physical, on which it depends, varies. Since the two don't interact causally, one needs a different kind of relation to explain their lawful dependence. One needs "bridge laws" that regulate the supervenience (or lawful dependence) relation between consciousness and the physical. Chalmers suggests the possibility that *information* might play a role in these psychophysical bridge laws (that is, laws governing the relations between the psychological or nonphysical consciousness and the physical on which it depends). But when Chalmers speaks of "information" he is not referring to what we ordinarily mean by that term when we use it in conversation. He is referring to the *mathematical* notion of information.

Note on Terminology: The *mathematical* notion of information intended by Chalmers is based on the 1948 view of Claude Shannon: "[Shannon] focused on a formal or syntactic notion of information, where the key is the concept of a state selected from an ensemble of possibilities" (Chalmers, p. 278). In a computer, for example, the binary system consists of 0s and 1s. Each selection of a 0 or a 1 exemplifies an information state. How the 0s and 1s are interpreted is not the issue. The "information space" has either a 0 or a 1 in it, and that very fact constitutes its information. It could have had either, and once the selection is made, the uncertainty ends: there is information.

Chalmers suggests that information of this sort can be found in both the physical and phenomenal realms. Any changes in the information states of one could be linked nomologically (that is, lawfully) with corresponding changes in the other. For example, "Any given simple color experience corresponds to a specific location within this [phenomenal] space [of color experiences]. A specific red experience is one phenomenally realized information state; a specific green experience is another." He continues, "whenever we find an information space realized phenomenally, we find the same information space realized physically [e.g., by changes in brain states]" (p. 284). He concludes, "We might put this by suggesting as a basic principle that information (in the actual world) has two aspects, a physical and a phenomenal aspect. Whenever there is a phenomenal state, it realizes an information state, an information state that is also realized in the cognitive system of the brain. Conversely, for at least some physically realized information spaces, whenever an information state in that space is realized physically, it is also realized phenomenally" (p. 286).

Strengths and Weaknesses of the Property Dualist Approach

A good deal of Chalmers's theory rests on the plausibility of the zombie argument, and not all philosophers of mind accept that argument as plausible, including Daniel Dennett and Owen Flanagan. Some have argued that logical or conceptual possibility proves nothing, except perhaps the poverty of our concepts or the limitations of our powers of imagination. Others have argued that the real issue concerns *empirical*, not logical, possibility, and they conclude that zombies are not empirical possibilities. Still others have offered parallel examples intended to provide a *reductio ad absurdum* argument (literally, one that tries to reduce the view to absurdity). Imagine, one might say, an organism that is physically and functionally identical to you, but is not alive. Is such a thing logically possible? If one felt that it was not self-contradictory, would that validate the conclusion that life must be a nonphysical property? How is one to decide what is logically possible? This is where the poverty of our concepts may lead to conflicting intuitions.

One of the virtues of Chalmers's theory is that consciousness surely seems to have an important relation to information (probably in both its mathematical and its conversational sense). However, as Chalmers himself admits, he has not yet worked out the details of that relationship to the point where they are clear.

Multiple Drafts Theory of Consciousness

From Daniel Dennett we get a series of developing theories about consciousness that end in what might be called a "deconstruction" of consciousness. In one of his earlier books, *Content and Consciousness* (London: Routledge, 1969), Dennett distinguishes two senses of 'aware'. The first sense requires that the content of the input reaches the "speech center" of the individual; the second sense only requires that the content of the input direct the individual's current behavior. The first type of awareness requires the ability to report what was experienced; the second only that one be guided by it. Notice that both cases are analyzed in terms of the possible *behavior* of the individual, linguistic or otherwise, and not in terms of anything like "how it feels to be conscious." Both of these descriptions of awareness are intended to move the discussion of consciousness away from the personal, experiential level to what he calls the "subpersonal" level.

Recall from our earlier discussion of Dennett in connection with

Homuncular Functionalism, that he believes that mental states and processes need to be explained in terms of armies of progressively more stupid homunculi. This move to the "subpersonal" level is a move away from global personal feelings of consciousness to the work of the many subsystems of homunculi.

In awareness of the type that requires an ability to *report*, the move is to the networks of neural homunculi responsible for language output. In the second type of awareness that Dennett mentions, the move is to the networks responsible for controlling other behavior. A few years later, in *Brainstorms* (1978), Dennett focuses primarily on the connection between consciousness and linguistic behavior: "we are speaking creatures (we have a sort of print-out faculty), and—at least to a first approximation—that of which we are conscious is that of which we can tell, introspectively or retrospectively."[16] According to this account, consciousness is intimately tied up with the ability to speak. Such a view seems to entail that prelinguistic children and nonhuman animals could not be conscious. Dennett is skeptical about their status, but thinks the issue deserves more study.

Aphasia: Aphasia is a loss of language competence caused by brain damage, most often to the left hemisphere. It is generally not the case that the individual cannot articulate words. Often he is able to repeat what is said but his ability to actively use the language correctly is impaired. Psychologists have described several forms of aphasia. In *Broca's* or *nonfluent aphasia*, the individual has a problem finding the appropriate words and arranging them in correct grammatical order. People with Broca's aphasia are often aware of their deficit, but are unable to control it. In another form, sometimes called *fluent aphasia*, the individual speaks with great ease, but the words he uses make no sense together. And this person is generally unaware of the problem. In yet another form, sometimes called *Wernicke's* (or *sensory*) *aphasia*, the individual is unable to understand language. There are, in addition, a number of other variations: *transcortical aphasia*, in which the individual tends to repeat everything that is said to him; and *motor aphasia*, in which the individual loses spontaneous speech but retains his understanding of language.[17] Aphasia clearly affects linguistic competence. Its effect on consciousness is less clear.

---

16. *Brainstorms* (Cambridge, MA: MIT/Bradford, 1978), p. 152.

17. See Weiskrantz, *Consciousness Lost and Found*, p. 27 *ff.*; Michael Corballis, *The Lopsided Ape* (New York: Oxford, 1991), p. 170 *ff.*

Consciousness, on Dennett's view, should not be understood by its phenomenal "feel" but by the behavior it controls—linguistic or otherwise. This is clearly a Functionalist and Physicalist approach to consciousness, and its early versions arise largely out of conceptual and theoretical considerations.

In his 1991 book, *Consciousness Explained,* Dennett expands on his homuncular view, drawing on numerous experimental data, particularly in psychology. Additionally, in more recent articles he emphasizes a modular view of the mental—a view in which the mind consists of semiautonomous modules (networks of neurons organized to carry out specific functions). Unlike his early view—in which there appeared to be two dominant modules relating to consciousness, one for speech and one for behavior—his more recent account allows for numerous competing modules, none of which is *the* "stream of consciousness." As he put it in 1997, "The 'stream of consciousness' is not a single, definitive narrative. It is a parallel stream of conflicting and continuously revised contents, no one narrative thread of which can be singled out as canonical—as the true version of conscious experience."[18]

Given this Multiple Drafts theory of consciousness, as he calls it, what gives it the semblance of unity that we seem to find in consciousness? He says in the 1991 book, "What would make this sequence the stream of consciousness? There is no one inside, looking at the widescreen show displayed all over the cortex. . . . What matters is the way those contents get utilized by or incorporated into the process of ongoing control of behavior" (p. 166).

Strengths and Weaknesses of Multiple Drafts Theory

The important relationship between consciousness and behavior is, then, an enduring theme for Dennett. This constitutes one strength of his approach, in contrast to some of the other theories we have discussed.

On the other hand, it remains to be seen whether or not Dennett's homuncular approach will prove satisfactory. He has said, "if you don't begin breaking them [the phenomenal aspects of conscious experience] down into their functional components from the outset, and distributing them throughout your model, you create a monster—an imaginary dazzle in the eye of a Cartesian homunculus."[19] One major

18. Dennett and Kinsbourne, "Time and the Observer," in *The Nature of Consciousness,* p. 145.

19. "Facing Backwards on the Problem of Consciousness," in *Explaining Consciousness—The Hard Problem,* Jonathan Shear, ed. (Cambridge, MA: MIT/Bradford, 1995–97), p. 34.

issue for Dennett's homuncular approach to consciousness is whether or not armies of *unconscious* neurons can account for the emergence of consciousness. Marvin Minsky has offered a little story that speaks to a similar concern:

> I'll prove that no box can hold a mouse. A box is made by nailing six boards together. But no box can hold a mouse unless it has some 'containment.' No single board contains any containment, since the mouse can walk away from it. And if there is no containment in one board, there can't be any in six boards. So the box can have no containment at all, and the mouse can escape.[20]

Minsky's suggestion, of course, is that sometimes properties emerge from *collections* of elements, where the elements themselves lack those properties. Science provides many examples of such emergent properties. Whether or not consciousness will prove to be a property that emerges from the activities of collections of unconscious neurons remains to be seen.

A second issue is whether or not the phenomenal, subjective "feel" of consciousness can be adequately accounted for by an appeal simply to Functional connections with behavior. The answer to that concern is also yet to be found. On some views, a purely Functional account of consciousness simply ignores its phenomenal aspects and is, to that extent, inadequate.

There is a concern, too, with Dennett's emphasis on the close link between consciousness and language use. What consequences does this have for the severely aphasic individual or a person with split-brain syndrome? And what is one to say about consciousness in prelinguistic children and certain nonhuman animals?

One attraction of Dennett's method is his concern to make his theory consistent with what we know from neuroscience, evolution theory, and psychology.

Consciousness as Global Workspace

Psychologist Bernard Baars has recently offered a widely discussed theory of consciousness that bears some resemblance to Dennett's view. Baars sees the mind as a series of mental processors that compete for access to what he calls a "global workspace." For Baars, conscious experience occurs when one or more mental processors are able to access the global workspace, and are thereby able to broadcast information

20. Marvin Minsky, *The Society of Mind* (New York: Simon & Schuster, 1985), p. 28.

widely to other processors or systems. Hence, the term 'global' work-space. Baars puts it this way:

> we develop only a single theoretical metaphor: a *publicity meta-phor* of consciousness, suggesting that there is a 'global work-space' system underlying conscious experience. The global workspace is the publicity organ of the nervous system; its contents, which correspond roughly to conscious experience, are distributed widely throughout the system. . . . think of the brain as a vast collection of specialized automatic processors, some nested and organized within other processors. Processors can compete or cooperate to gain access to the global workspace underlying consciousness, enabling them to send global messages to any other interested systems. Any conscious experience emerges from cooperation and competition between many different input processors.[21]

The method that Baars employs is what he calls "contrastive analysis." That is, by contrasting events that we take to be conscious with events that we take to be unconscious (where the two are similar in other respects), he believes that one can ascertain what it is that distinguishes conscious from unconscious psychological events. He notes, for example, that conscious experiences are slow, serial (i.e., occur one at a time), have limited capacity, can deal with novelty, can mutually interfere with one another, need internal consistency, and so forth. Unconscious events, on the other hand, are fast, operate in parallel (i.e., many operations occur simultaneously), have great collective capacity, deal with the known, involve little mutual interference, may be mutually inconsistent, and so forth. However, the most distinctive character of conscious events, he claims, is that they are widely available to other systems in the brain, whereas unconscious events are not.

Notice that this is in sharp contrast to Higher-Order theories, which require that a state can be conscious only if it is the object of some other *unconscious* state. For Baars, in contrast, "consciousness involves the *internal distribution of information*. Apparently both conscious and unconscious stimuli are analyzed quite completely by automatic systems. But once unattended inputs are analyzed, they are not broadcast throughout the nervous system. Conscious stimuli, on the other hand, are made available throughout . . ." (p. 35).

21. Bernard Baars, A *Cognitive Theory of Consciousness* (New York: Cambridge University Press, 1988), p. xx.

Strengths and Weaknesses of the Global Workspace Approach

Baars offers two conditions under which we can consider a person conscious of an event: (1) the person can report immediately afterwards that she or he was conscious of the event, and (2) it is possible to independently verify the accuracy of that report (p. 15). Notice the similarity with Dennett's early insistence on the importance of reportability. But notice, too, that this sort of criterion leaves the split-brain patient with only one conscious hemisphere (the left one) under experimental conditions, in spite of the fact that that patient can pick out or draw what he or she has seen with the other (right) hemisphere. Again, such criteria raise problems for the conscious experience of infants and non-human animals. One wonders, too, how one would get independent verification of people's pains or feelings.

One of the questions that arises in connection with this Global Workspace view of consciousness asks if this wide availability of information is simply a fact about conscious stimuli, or is it the case that the *distribution* of the information is what *makes* it conscious. If the latter is the case, what is it about the mere distribution of information that constitutes that information as conscious?

One aspect of Baars's theory that it shares not only with Dennett's but also with the Higher-Order theories is that it is a Physicalist theory of consciousness. For Baars, the global workspace is very likely to be found in the Extended Reticular Thalamic Activating System in the brain.

Other Approaches to Consciousness

As I noted early in this chapter, there is currently a great deal of research and theorizing about consciousness. In addition to the theories that I have discussed at some length, I should briefly mention several others that have also garnered some attention.

Biological Naturalism

Philosopher John Searle argues that consciousness is "a causally emergent property" of interactions among systems of neurons in the brain. He does not specify which kinds of interactions would cause consciousness. Searle calls his view "biological naturalism,"[22] but he also argues

22. See John Searle, *The Rediscovery of the Mind* (Cambridge, MA: MIT/Bradford, 1992).

that consciousness is not *reducible* to brain states because the subjective experience that is essential to it cannot be eliminated (as he says it would be in a scientific reduction). Subjectivity, he believes, is an *ontological* category (therefore having its own unique type of *being*). Nonetheless, Searle denies that he is either a Substance or Property Dualist. Still, his claims about the irreducibility of consciousness and the ontological status of subjectivity have motivated some commentators to see his view as some version of Dualism.

Synchronous Neural Oscillations

Physicist and biochemist Francis Crick has argued for the possibility that visual consciousness (at least) might be explained in terms of the synchronous oscillation of neural networks in the brain, firing at approximately 40 Hertz. ("Hertz" indicates the unit of frequency equal to one cycle per second.) To make this a bit clearer, Crick notes that one of the problems that must be dealt with in explaining consciousness is what is called the "binding problem." He describes it in the following way:

> Because any object will have different characteristics (form, color, motions, etc.) that are processed in several different visual areas, it is reasonable to assume that seeing any one object often involves neurons in many different visual areas. The problem of how these neurons temporarily become active as a unit is often described as "the binding problem." As an object seen is often also heard, smelled, or felt, this binding must also occur across different sensory modalities.[23]

Some German theorists suggested that the binding problem might be solved if the various neurons symbolizing the different aspects of the object were firing in synchrony. Crick (together with Christof Koch) suggested that this synchronous firing of neurons might be the neural correlate of visual awareness if the neurons were all firing (oscillating) in the range of 35 to 75 Hertz. But Crick also suggests the possibility that there may be "several forms of visual awareness, and, by extension, even more forms of consciousness in general" (p. 246). What still remains unclear, however, is how it is that oscillating neurons at some particular frequency can be the cause of conscious experience. As yet, we lack a complete answer to fill the "explanatory gap" between neurons and conscious experience.

23. *The Astonishing Hypothesis* (New York: Simon & Schuster, 1994), p. 208.

Crick's method of approach is, of course, by way of neuroscientific experiments. This approach is often referred to as a "bottom-up" approach, whereas the philosophers who begin with the experienced aspects of consciousness when they theorize are using a "top-down" approach. Crick's proposed theory of visual awareness is also clearly Physicalist.

Two other views of consciousness bear mention. Each calls into question virtually everything that the previous theories have proposed.

The "Mysteria"

Philosopher Colin McGinn, dubbed by Owen Flanagan as one of the "mysteria," argues that our minds are so constituted that it is impossible for us to ever understand consciousness. McGinn claims that our minds are simply not able to form the concepts we would need in order to understand consciousness. He calls this fact "cognitive closure" with respect to consciousness, analogous to the cognitive closure that a mouse might have in relation to subatomic physics. McGinn's argument, in its simplest form, is that consciousness surely arises from properties of the brain, but because the brain is physical our concepts of brain properties are essentially *spatial*, while our concepts of consciousness are not. He argues that we are, and will always remain, unable to form a concept that would encompass the two. Thus, the nature of consciousness will remain an insoluble *mystery* for us. For many other philosophers, however, philosophy does not come to a halt when it faces an apparent mystery. On the contrary, that is where philosophy often begins.

Eliminativism

Perhaps most radical of all, philosopher Georges Rey has argued that there really is no such thing as consciousness. Rey's strategy is to list a series of phenomena that have often been associated with or identified with consciousness. He includes such items as reportability, higher-order states, sensations, and attention. He argues that a machine could be programmed to exhibit each of the phenomena ordinarily linked to consciousness, and that in no case would one be inclined to characterize that machine as conscious. He concludes, "the *mere possibility* of a machine of the sort I have described not being conscious entails that there is no such thing as consciousness."[24] Rey's view is a version of Eliminativism, in this case involving the elimination of the notion of consciousness.

24. "A Question about Consciousness," in *The Nature of Mind*, p. 473.

One puzzle remains, however. If there is no such thing as consciousness, what would motivate anyone to deny its presence in computers? What is it that they lack? If the answer is that they can behave in many of the ways that have been associated with consciousness, and therefore those behaviors need have no connection with consciousness, then a defender of consciousness might respond that the essential aspect of consciousness is not its connection with behavior but its phenomenal "feel." (Needless to say, Daniel Dennett would make no such response.)

What Is the Function of Consciousness?

Although we all have a pretty clear *practical* sense of what consciousness is, at least in our own case, formulating a satisfactory *theoretical* account of its *nature* has proved difficult. No one of the theories that I have discussed has received unanimous acceptance. Each has its strengths; all have their problems. In spite of our lack of a completely satisfactory *theory* of consciousness, can anything helpful be said about its *function*?

Earlier, when describing the thought experiment concerning the logical possibility of zombies, I noted that some philosophers have suggested the idea that consciousness might have no function. Such an epiphenomenalist view seems counterintuitive to most of us. But what exactly is the function of consciousness? What does it do for us? A number of different proposals have been made.

Perhaps the most frequent response is that consciousness gives us *flexibility* in our dealings with our environment. This claim about flexibility comes in a couple of slightly different varieties. On one account, provided by William James, conscious states allow us to deal with information for which we have not been "hard-wired" by evolution. As he put it,

> Taking a purely naturalistic view of the matter, it seems reasonable to suppose that, unless consciousness served some useful purpose, it would not have been superadded to life. Assuming hypothetically that this is so, there results an important problem for psychophysicists to find out, namely, *how* consciousness helps an animal, how much complication of machinery may be saved in the nervous centres, for instance, if consciousness accompany their action. Might, for example, an animal which regulated its acts by [conscious] notions and feelings get along with fewer preformed reflex connections and distinct channels for acquired habits in its

nervous system than an animal whose varied behavior under varying circumstances was purely and simply the result of the change
of course through the nervous reticulations which a minute alteration of stimulus had caused the nervous action to take? In a word,
is consciousness an economical *substitute* for mechanism?[25]

For James the addition of consciousness to an organism minimizes
the need for extensive inborn mechanisms that would automatically
regulate all its behavior. Consciousness can replace rigid reflex mechanisms with a flexible guidance system that can respond to a wide variety
of stimuli.

One way of thinking about this is that the environment with which a
plant must deal is fairly limited. It needs light, water, and nutrients, but
it cannot move around in its surroundings. So its behaviors are limited
to things like being able to turn toward light, and absorb water and
nutrients. If those things are present, the plant is "hard-wired" to
respond to them. If they are absent for long, the plant will likely die. In
our case, by contrast, we have a wide variety of bodily, psychological,
and social needs. And we are able to move around in a rich and variable
environment in order to satisfy those needs. However, it would have
been extravagant of natural selection to hard-wire every possible behavior that could be useful to us in the myriad of possible circumstances in
which we can find ourselves. We are hard-wired for some; for the rest,
consciousness allows us to take in information, evaluate its relevance
for us at the time, and consider possible behaviors that might be desirable in light of that information.

Another, and somewhat related, version of the flexibility that consciousness provides suggests that consciousness allows us to consider and
evaluate possible courses of action in imagination, where we can try to
anticipate various outcomes without committing ourselves to actually
carrying out one of the behaviors until we decide which of them is most
likely to succeed. Using conscious imagination to decide whether or not
it would be wise to wrestle with a seven-foot grizzly bear can be far less
dangerous than having to actually try it to see if it will work well. This
view has its roots in the work of Kenneth Craik. He says,

> If the organism carries a "small-scale model" of external reality
> and of its own possible actions within its head, it is able to try out

25. William James's review of *Grundzuge der physiologischen Psychologie* by
Wilhelm Wundt (1875), in *The Works of William James: Essays, Comments, and
Reviews*, Frederick Burkhardt and Fredson Bowers, eds. (Cambridge, MA: Har-
vard University Press, 1987), pp. 302–3.

various alternatives, conclude which is the best of them, react to future situations before they arise, utilise the knowledge of past events in dealing with the future, and in every way to react in a much fuller, safer and more competent manner to the emergencies which face it.[26]

Yet another theory about the function of consciousness claims that it allows us to formulate for ourselves and others a coherent account of our behavior, given the fact that many of the processes that guide our behavior are unconscious.[27] So on this view, consciousness allows us to weave the disparate portions of our experience, many of which have their roots in processes of which we are unconscious, into one whole consistent story. That is, it allows us to make sense of ourselves to ourselves and to others. Such a view suggests that consciousness may play a critical role in the constitution of a Self—a topic for Chapter 5.

One final view claims that the function of consciousness is to provide us with a theory of mind that allows us to understand and predict the behavior of others. Responding to Kenneth Craik's view of the importance of constructing models of reality, Nicholas Humphrey points out that the most important reality for human beings is social reality. As social animals, humans must understand, and to some extent predict, the behaviors of their fellow humans. He puts it this way:

> Before human beings could even begin to calculate where their own and others' behaviour would take them, it was essential that they should acquire a much deeper understanding of the character of the strange creature who stood at the centre of their calculations—Man himself. They had to have a way of finding out what men as such are like, how they react, what makes them tick. They had to become sensitive to other people's moods and passions, appreciative of their waywardness or stubbornness, capable of reading the signs in their faces and equally the lack of signs, capable of guessing what each person's past experience holds hidden in the present for the future. They had above all to make sense of the enigma of the ghost in the machine. In short they had to become 'natural psychologists.' . . . Nature's solution to the problem of doing psychology has been to give to every member of the human species both the power and inclination *to use a privileged*

26. Kenneth Craik, *The Nature of Explanation* (Cambridge: Cambridge University Press, 1943), p. 61.

27. See Joseph LeDoux, *The Emotional Brain* (New York: Simon & Schuster, 1996).

picture of his own self as a model for what it is like to be another person.

And a bit later in the book,

Without introspection to guide me, the task of deciphering the behaviour of my fellow men would be quite beyond my powers. I should be like a poor cryptographer attempting to decipher a text which was written in a totally unfamiliar language. . . . In so far as we are conscious human beings we all guess in advance the 'language' of other men's behaviour.[28]

What consciousness does for us on this account is to enhance our chances of surviving and thriving in a *social* context by allowing us to attribute to others the same sort of motivations, expectations, interests, and so forth, that we find in ourselves by introspection. This in turn makes it possible for us to understand and anticipate a significant amount of their behavior. In Chapter 7 we shall return to this issue of whether or not we have a "theory of mind," and what role introspection might play.

These proposals about the function of consciousness surely imply that it is an enormously important phenomenon to study and understand. They suggest that it plays a critical role in a living organism. The various proposals are not mutually exclusive. It might be that consciousness can do all these things for us. Can you add other functions that it might have?

Issues for Discussion

1. Do you think that one should say that the right hemisphere of split-brain patients is also conscious under experimental conditions, or do you think that consciousness requires that one be able to articulate in language what one has experienced? Give reasons for your answer.

2. What do you think the function of consciousness is—or do you think that it is epiphenomenal?

3. Do you think that zombies are *logically* possible? Explain your answer. Do you think that they are a useful fiction that

28. Nicholas Humphrey, *Consciousness Regained* (Oxford: Oxford University Press, 1983), pp. 4–6, 33–4.

can help us understand something about the possible relation between consciousness and the physical or functional makeup of a system?

4. Do you think that dreaming should count as an instance of consciousness (as Descartes must)? What about sleepwalking? A person under hypnosis? What criteria are you using in making your decision?

5. How would you decide if an extraterrestrial being is conscious? What criteria would you use—behavior? Language use? Flexibility of responses? Physiological similarity to yourself? Something else? Would you apply the same criteria to nonhuman animals? To insects? To a robot?

6. Do you think that 'consciousness' is one unified phenomenon definable by a set of necessary and sufficient conditions, or do you think that the word names a number of different but related phenomena (like 'games' or perhaps 'bird')? Or do you think it names nothing? Give reasons for your answer.

7. Briefly explain what each of the theories of mind discussed in Chapter 1 would say about consciousness.

8. Which of those theories of mind seems to you to be in the best position to be able eventually to provide an adequate account of consciousness? Give reasons for your answer.

9. Why might it be the case that some (perhaps many) of our mental states are unconscious?

10. Could a system be capable of mental functions but have no consciousness at all?

11. Could it be the case that consciousness can emerge from any type of system, living or nonliving, so long as the system is capable of certain high-level mental functions? If so, what might those high-level mental functions be?

12. Which of the theories of consciousness discussed in this chapter seems to you to be the most satisfactory? Give reasons for your answer.

13. Some theorists have drawn a close connection between consciousness and language use. Do you think that instances of aphasia affect that view? Explain your answer.

Suggested Research Projects

a. In Chapter 8 of his book, *In the Theater of Consciousness*, Bernard Baars offers a series of additional possible functions that consciousness carries out. What are these? Do you agree with Baars's claims that all of them are true functions of consciousness, or do you think that some of the functions he mentions could also be carried out by unconscious mechanisms? Give careful reasons for your answer.

*b. Read Patricia Churchland's paper, "Consciousness: The Transmutation of a Concept," in *Pacific Philosophical Quarterly*, 64 (1983). She criticizes many of our common beliefs about consciousness. What are some of her criticisms? Do you agree with her? Do you think that her arguments lead to Eliminativism?

c. How does anesthesia work? Do you think it tells us something about the physical basis of consciousness? Explain your answer.

d. Read John Kihlstrom's article, "The Cognitive Unconscious," *Science*, vol. 237 (Sept. 18, 1987). What does he mean by "unconscious cognitive states"? What are some examples he gives?

e. Read Kathleen Wilkes's article, "____, yishi, duh, um, and consciousness," in *Consciousness in Contemporary Science*, A. J. Marcel and E. Bisiach, eds. (Oxford: Clarendon, 1988). What is her *central* claim in the article? What type of evidence does she offer in support of her claim? Do you agree with her? Give reasons for your answer.

*f. In his book, *The Origins of Consciousness in the Breakdown of the Bicameral Mind*, Julian Jaynes offers a unique theory about the origin of consciousness. What is it?

g. Read Section 23 in Chapter 6 of Karl Popper's book, *Objective Knowledge* (Oxford: Clarendon, 1972). What did he see as the function of consciousness? Compare his view with those discussed in the text.

h. Read pp. 94–106 in Antonio Damasio's book, *The Feeling of What Happens*. Briefly describe his accounts of *absence automatisms* and *akinetic mutism*. In what ways are these phenomena relevant to a study of consciousness?

3

Where Do Emotions Fit?

So far, we have discussed theories about what sort of "thing" the mind might be, and theories about consciousness, but little mention has been made of emotions. Do they belong to a theory of mind, or are they something quite separate? The answer to that question depends, not surprisingly, on what one takes emotions to be. Some theories of emotion claim that they are largely physiological events, and therefore not genuinely a part of the mental. Some theories see emotions as having at least some cognitive aspects, and therefore as belonging to any complete account of the mental. We shall consider several types of theories about emotions, look at some of the strengths and weaknesses of each, and see in what ways emotions ought to be included in any adequate theory of mind.

The Rational Animal

Over two thousand years ago, Aristotle defined human beings as "rational animals." In one sense, of course, the definition was entirely appropriate. Given our evolutionary history, we do indeed belong to the animal kingdom, but we appear to be distinguished from other animal species by the degree to which we are capable of rationality, or reasoning ability. On the other hand, this definition has perhaps been misleading. It is probably a mistake to suppose that rationality surfaced out of the blue with the appearance of the first human being. More likely it developed gradually in our early ancestors over a very long period of time. As we shall see in Chapter 4, studies of nonhuman animal species suggest that many of them possess some degree of rationality—some ability to categorize things, to see things in terms of means and ends, to plan certain of their behaviors with a view to their goals, and so on. So while we may possess a higher degree of rationality than other animals, we may not be the sole possessors of this quality.

But more to the point for our present purposes, defining humans as "rational animals" has led some theorists to emphasize the "rational" aspect and minimize other aspects of our psychology. In fact, one aspect of Aristotle's definition has had a particularly long and unfortunate influence on some of our thinking. His characterization depicts *man* as the rational animal, suggesting to some that *woman* is not. Aristotle himself seems to have believed that women are not fully rational. We are at a point in human history, I believe, where that particular misconception can be fully set to rest. If one is to consider the "rational animal" characterization at all, it clearly applies to *human beings*. Both men and women are sometimes rational and sometimes not-so-rational. What, then, does it mean when we say that we are rational animals? Obviously, it calls attention to the fact that we are living organisms—animals—but in addition, it signals the fact that we are capable of cognitive states like beliefs, and that these cognitive states can function for us as *reasons* that guide and motivate our behavior and our formulation of further cognitive states—for example, in making inferences from one piece of information to another.

Rationality is generally the sort of thing we recognize when we see, but it proves a bit more difficult to formulate a clean definition for it that everyone would agree to. A number of different theories about it have been proposed over the years. One thing that seems to be a matter of wide agreement is the fact that both our *actions* and our *beliefs* can be either rational or irrational. In the case of actions, they are generally considered rational when they achieve the goals that they set out to achieve. Of course the goals themselves may not always be rational. Their degree of rationality might be judged in relation to how well they fit with other, longer-term goals that one has. This appropriate relation of means to ends, or actions to goals, is often referred to as 'practical' rationality.

On the other hand, beliefs are generally considered to be rational when they are based on good evidence and when they are consistent with one's other beliefs. Notice that practical rationality is not entirely independent of the rationality of one's beliefs. Choosing to act in certain ways in order to achieve some goal surely relies on some beliefs. Notice, too, that a belief could be false and it could still be rational to hold it. One might, for example, have fairly strong evidence for it, and it might be consistent with one's other beliefs—and still turn out to be false. The long-held belief that the earth was flat was supported by people's visual experience of its apparently flat surface, and that belief fit with everything else that they believed about the earth. But it turned out to be false. So while rationality is not the same thing as having the truth about things, it does seem to involve the effort to come as close to the truth about things as one can, given one's situation.

However, just a bit of reflection on our own experiences indicates that we are not always rational. We sometimes act in ways that frustrate our goals, and we sometimes hold on to beliefs in spite of the fact that we have significant evidence that counts against them or in spite of the fact that we have no plausible evidence that supports them. So we are sometimes rational and sometimes irrational animals.

Given the fact of our sometime rationality, and given the fact that rationality does not tell the whole story of who we are, what more needs to be said about our mental lives? In addition to our capacity for cognitive states like beliefs, what else guides our behavior, what else motivates us? One essential element that must be added to our characterization as rational animals is that we are also *affective* animals. We have emotions and moods that can guide our behavior and motivate us. Notice that the terms 'emotion' and 'motivation' share a common Latin root: *moveo, movere, motus*; to move. Thus, we are living organisms capable of rational, irrational, and affective states. How do these affective states differ from simple rational or irrational states? Or do they? This is the source of this chapter's title question: Where do emotions fit? As a first step toward answering that question, let's try to get clear about what we mean by an emotion.

Methods of Approach to Emotions

There is something of a catch-22 involved in initial attempts to answer a question about the nature of emotions. To begin with, there are wide disparities in theorists' views about which states should be included in the category of emotions. As a consequence of the very different lists of emotions that have been proposed, definitions of emotion can vary significantly.

Can you name the emotions? The task is not quite so easy as you might imagine. You would likely include phenomena like fear, anger, joy, grief, hatred, or love. What would you say about curiosity? Disgust? Amusement (as in being amused)? Interest? Embarrassment? Sexual attraction? The distinction between emotions and other, possibly related, states is not as clear as one might hope it to be. That can complicate efforts to formulate a clean definition specified in terms of necessary and sufficient conditions. To get an idea of how great the differences can be when theorists provide their list of emotions, consider the following examples.

For Descartes the "primitive and simple" emotions include wonder, love, hatred, desire, joy, and sadness; all others, he claims, are derived from these six.[1] Spinoza, on the other hand, lists pleasure, pain, and desire as the primitive emotions, with all others being derived from these three.[2] They might deal with the questionable cases (like embarrassment or amusement) by saying that they are derived from some combination of the primitive emotions.

David Hume divides things a bit differently. He says that the "calm" emotions include a sense of beauty and deformity in various things, while the "violent passions" include love, hatred, grief, joy, pride, and humility. But he then further subdivides the violent passions into the "direct" (desire, aversion, grief, joy, hope, fear, despair, and security) and the "indirect" (pride, humility, ambition, vanity, love, hatred, envy, pity, malice, and generosity, "and their dependents").[3] J. B. Watson, one of the founders of Behaviorism, lists fear, rage, and sexual love as the "fundamental" emotions.[4] William James, by contrast, simply gives up any attempt to make a definitive list of emotions and says, "the varieties of emotion are innumerable."[5] These few examples should give you a good idea of how little agreement there has been among theorists about exactly which states need to be included in a theory of emotions. When there is little agreement about what counts as an emotion, there will be little agreement on how they are best defined. We might refer to this as the *extensional* problem for emotions (see box on page 100).

One conclusion that we can draw from the wide differences in specifying lists of emotions is that it is likely to be useless to approach questions about the nature of emotions by looking for a definitive list of what states count as emotions. On the other hand, it is difficult to simply construct a definition and then look to see what it applies to. It seems that such a definition would be arbitrary. Therein lies the "catch."

1. *The Passions of the Soul*, Art. 69, Stephen H. Voss, trans. (Indianapolis: Hackett, 1989), p. 56.

2. *Ethics*, Part III, Prop. XI, Proof; R. H. M. Elwes, trans. (New York: Dover, 1955), p. 138.

3. David Hume, *A Treatise of Human Nature*, L. A. Selby-Bigge, ed. (Oxford: Oxford University Press, 1739/1973), Book II, Part I, Section 1.

4. J. B. Watson, *Psychology from the Standpoint of a Behaviorist* (Philadelphia: Lippincott, 1919), p. 199.

5. *Psychology: The Briefer Course* (New York: Harper & Row, 1892/1961), p. 241.

> **Note on Terminology:** The *extension* of a term is the list of items that are properly designated by that term. So, for example, the extension of the term 'emotion' includes all those states that are emotions. The extension of the term 'dog' includes all the animals that are dogs. In contrast, the *intension* of a term generally indicates its *meaning*, or the set of properties that a thing must have in order to be properly designated by that term.

What other methods are available to us? Introspection is one possibility. It appears to give us some degree of access to our own mental states. But we have already learned that introspection is not a very reliable source of information. Like perception, it is fallible. Furthermore, if you and I both introspect our emotion states and we come to different conclusions about what they are and how they feel, there is no court of appeals to which we can look for arbitration. Introspection is also unavailable as a method of investigating nonhuman animals' emotions. And lastly, it is possible for some emotions to occur without our conscious awareness. In such cases, introspection will tell us nothing about them. Although introspection may provide us with at least some clues about emotions, it needs to be supplemented with something else (as William James pointed out).

Conceptual analysis is another approach that has been used by some theorists. It consists in looking carefully at emotion words in our language and trying to provide a detailed analysis of their meaning. For a good many years philosophers thought that conceptual analysis was the best tool for philosophical investigations. But it, too, has some serious limitations. First of all, most of our concepts—especially the most interesting ones—are not sharply bounded. They have fuzzy edges and they can change over time. Secondly, we don't have any guarantees that our concepts (or words) capture the way things really are. Words do not necessarily "cut nature at her joints."

Another avenue of approach might be by way of observing behaviors commonly associated with emotions. This has the virtue of being a matter of publicly verifiable data. Further, it can make use of the behavior of nonhuman animals as well as humans. One difficulty is that it ignores any internal states of the organism experiencing the emotion. Another difficulty is that it tacitly assumes a set of emotions that are expressed in behaviors.

A final method that has been used involves investigation of physiological changes that take place in an organism that behaves as if it is

Brain Scans: Recent developments in technology have provided us with means to view brain activity from a third-person perspective. It has long been believed that changes in blood flow in the brain correlate with brain activity, in both normal adult humans who are awake, and in unanesthetized animals. In PET scans (*Positron Emission Tomography*) the subject is injected with a radioactive substance that can be traced in the movement of blood through the system. She is then given a series of tasks (e.g., looking at words, reading words aloud, listening to words, etc.). With each task, the level of activity in different portions of the brain can be recorded as a function of changes in the flow of blood to that particular area. An even more recent procedure, fMRI (*Functional Magnetic Resonance Imaging*) takes advantage of the fact that increased activity in a particular area of the brain involves increased use of oxygen there. fMRI is able to record those areas that are using the greatest amount of oxygen during various mental tasks.

These imaging techniques do not prove that mental functions are *identical* with brain functions; rather, they appear to provide some significant *correlations* between brain function, mental function, and introspective reports.[6]

experiencing an emotion. This approach has several virtues. Like the Behavioral approach that it also uses, it involves publicly observable and verifiable data, and is able to investigate the physiological changes in nonhumans as well as humans. It may also be able to account for some unconscious emotion states. What remains unclear is precisely how to link the physiology with the *experienced* psychological states. But that is where introspection (at least in humans) might provide some assistance. (See box on page 102.)

It is likely that the most fruitful method for approaching emotions and trying to get clear about their nature and function may have to involve some combination of all the above methods—making use of behavior, physiology, introspection, and linguistic practices. Where each of them has some limitation or drawback, one or more of the other methods may be able to compensate for that. Keeping this in mind, let us turn to some of the characterizations of emotions that have been proposed.

6. See the entries in the *MIT Encyclopedia of the Cognitive Sciences*: "Positron Emission Tomography," "Magnetic Resonance Imaging" (Cambridge, MA: MIT Press, 1999); and Rita Carter, *Mapping the Mind* (Berkeley, CA: University of California Press, 1998), pp. 26–28.

La Belle Indifférence: This is a term that physician and psychologist Pierre Janet attributed to a deficit caused by damage to the right hemisphere of the brain. It generally causes a loss of emotion or an inclination to deny that there is any problem. By contrast, damage to a particular portion of the left hemisphere can cause what has been termed a 'catastrophic reaction' that includes an excess of emotional outbursts. Michael Corballis, after describing this deficit, concludes that "some of the evidence suggests that positive emotions are housed in the left hemisphere and the negative ones in the right."[7]

Theories of Emotion

Theories of emotion can be conveniently grouped into families (although even here, there are very different views about the number and character of these families). Such groupings make it easier to deal with the very large number of distinct theories that have been proposed. For convenience' sake—and some simplification—we shall consider three significant families: the Physiological/Feeling theories, Behavioral theories, and Cognitive theories.

Physiological/Feeling Theories

One of the simplest sets of theories has been called the *Physiological*, or sometimes the *Feeling* theory of emotions. The common thread that runs through this family of theories is the claim that emotions involve an awareness of some particular type of bodily events.

Descartes

Descartes provides an early example of the view. Recall that Descartes defended a Substance Dualism view of mind and body. His theory of emotions is framed within that version of Dualism. He believed that the body operates on completely mechanistic principles—like a very elaborate machine. The soul/mind, by contrast, he saw as the seat of all mental states. For Descartes, these states of the soul/mind could be either active (like volitions, which proceed from the will) or passive. The passive functions of the soul include perceptions of the external world, perceptions of our own bodies, and our passions or emotions. He defines emotions as "the perceptions or sensations or excitations of the soul

---

7. *The Lopsided Ape*, p. 264.

which are referred to it in particular and which are caused, maintained, and strengthened by some movement of the [animal] spirits."[8] So for Descartes, passions or emotions are mental events that are caused by the body, but which the mind/soul refers to *itself*. (Note that in ordinary perception, also caused by the body, the mind refers the perceptions to the external world.) Consistent with his Dualism, Descartes includes both body and mind in his account of emotions. The body is their cause, they are *felt in the heart*,[9] but they draw the attention of the mind or soul to itself.

Notice a couple of things about this way of characterizing emotions. First, emotions are *passions*, that is, they *happen* to the soul, they are states that the mind/soul *undergoes*; they are not states in which the mind/soul is active. The belief that emotions are simply undergone raises important considerations about what degree of control over them, and therefore what degree of responsibility for them, an individual can have. That is to say, if our emotions or passions just happen to us, it looks as if our experience of them cannot have any significant ethical dimension—except, perhaps, the degree to which we encourage them, "feed" them, or minimize them. However, it is significant to notice how many emotion terms in our language carry the connotation of being either virtues (love, hope, courage, etc.) or vices (hatred, pride, envy, etc.).

A second thing to notice about Descartes's theory is that, although emotions are caused by the body, the emotion itself occurs in the mind/soul. In spite of the fact that his theory is classified as belonging to the Physiological/Feeling family of theories, the claim here is that emotions are *mental* events. They are caused by physiological events in the body but they are felt by the soul. Such a view surely suggests that a theory of mind ought to have something to say about emotions.

Finally, for Descartes there is no possibility that a passion is unconscious. Recall that for him, every mental event is a *conscious* event. So presumably for Descartes the proper method for studying the emotions is introspection. By simply looking in on our mental states, including our passions, we can see that they are occurring and we can see precisely what their nature is. As he says, "one cannot be deceived . . . in connection with the passions, insomuch as they are so close and internal to our soul that it is impossible it should feel them without their

---

8. *The Passions of the Soul*, Art. 27.

9. "As for the opinion . . . [that] the soul receives its passions in the heart . . . it is founded only on the fact that the passions make [us] feel some alteration there." *The Passions of the Soul*, Art. 33.

truly being such as it feels them."[10] Unfortunately, it turns out that
things are not that easy. The simple fact that so many other theorists
have provided quite different lists of emotions and theories of emotions
indicates that simply introspecting one's emotions cannot ultimately be
a reliable source of information. If it were, there should be wide agreement on the subject, and there clearly isn't.

William James

A more recent version of the Physiological/Feeling theory comes to us
from William James. Unlike Descartes, James places his theory of psychological states squarely within the framework of Darwin's theory of
evolution. James disputes the commonsense view that emotions are
mental events that then cause certain bodily behaviors and expressions.
On the contrary, he says that emotions are the awareness of the physiological and behavioral changes that take place in us when we perceive a
particular sort of object or event. On his view, the perception does not
first cause an emotion that then causes physiological and behavioral
changes in the organism. Instead of the traditional view that one first
sees a bear, then is afraid, and then runs—James argues that the order is
reversed: I see a bear, I run, and feel fear. That is to say, the perception
itself causes the physiological and behavioral changes (e.g., increased
heart rate, running away, etc.), and the emotion is simply the awareness
of these changes. Hence, James's view is perhaps the strongest version
of the Feeling theory of emotions. According to James, my fear upon
perceiving a bear is simply my awareness of the changes in my body
and behavior that followed the perception of the bear. In fact, James
claimed that the boundary between certain instincts and certain emotions, like fear, was quite unclear. He saw some instincts as shading
imperceptibly into emotions.

One of the advantages of James's account is that it takes seriously the
importance for survival in having very speedy physical responses to
incoming information. He sees the subsequent awareness of these
responses as allowing us to continue or halt those responses. His view
also makes room for emotions in nonhuman animals who can react
immediately to what they perceive without needing to form beliefs
about things. The physical and bodily reactions are quick and *automatic*. One consequence of this seems to be that, as in the case of Descartes's theory, emotions are states we *undergo*. They happen to us and
are not a matter of choice.

10. *The Passions of the Soul*, Art. 26.

Strengths and Weaknesses of Physiological/Feeling Theories

There are important insights in the Physiological/Feeling theories of emotions. To begin with, they take very seriously the close connection between emotions or passions and the *body* of the organism. This emphasis on the important role played by the body has several dimensions. First, the body is the cause or source of the emotion. Second, most obviously on James's view, but also on Descartes's, the emotion is generated on behalf of the well-being of the body. Related to that, the experience of the emotion involves some awareness of physiological changes in the body. These changes include more than blushing or sweaty hands. Many of the physiological alterations can assist an individual in responding to the situation. The case of fear is particularly instructive. Changes in heart rate and respiration, rerouting of blood supplies, increases in adrenaline—all can assist the individual in a fight-or-flight response. Obviously, they are not guaranteed to do so. But the point is that physiological changes that occur with many emotions are not negligible. They appear to be important elements in an adequate account of at least some of our emotions.

On the other hand, the theories also have some weaknesses. First, on these accounts it is difficult to be clear about how the experience of emotions differs from the awareness of other physiological and behavioral changes that occur in the body. What is it, for example, that distinguishes the experience of lightheadedness at the sight of blood, or a case of nausea after smelling something disagreeable, from the experience of fear or anger? On the Physiological/Feeling theories it is difficult to tell. There are many changes in our bodily states, and we are aware of many of them. But only a subset of these counts as emotions. So it seems that mere awareness of bodily changes can't be the whole story.

Furthermore, most emotions are about something or someone—they have *intentionality*. (Recall our discussion of intentionality in Chapter 1.) For example, when I am angry, I am angry at you or at the IRS, or at my car that won't start. That is to say, the emotion is directed at some object other than my own body and the changes it is undergoing. Neither Descartes nor James denied the intentionality of emotions. It is just that their theories make no place for it, and in fact they make it sound as if the object of the emotion might be one's own body (or perhaps one's own mind for Descartes)—a view that clearly cannot be right in all cases.

Hence, in spite of the fact that the body and its physiology and behavior play an important role in many emotions, it seems that this cannot be the whole story.

Behavioral Theories

A second group of theories about emotions developed with *Behaviorism*. Recall that a primary motivation for the development of Behaviorism was the effort to provide a theory of mental states based solely on publicly observable data. It was an effort to bring psychology and philosophy into closer conformity with the standards of scientific investigation. The theories of emotion that emerged from Behavioral theorists were part of this same project.

J. B. Watson

One of the earliest Behaviorist accounts was proposed by psychologist J. B. Watson. His account provides an interesting transition from the sort of Physiological theory that James proposed to the fully Behavioral account that we will find later in B. F. Skinner. Watson thought that emotions are hereditary but that they are quickly overlaid with societal influences. He believed that "hard and fast" definitions of emotions are not possible, but he defined some of them as "an hereditary 'pattern-reaction' involving profound changes of the bodily mechanism as a whole, but particularly of the visceral and glandular systems."[11] You can see the emphasis on physiology in his definition. However, Watson comments in a footnote:

> . . . we have introduced physiological concepts into the behavior study of emotions. It is possible that we have given the impression that we are writing a physiology of the emotions. Such is not the case. It is perfectly possible for a student of behavior entirely ignorant of the sympathetic nervous system and of the glands and smooth muscles, or even of the central nervous system as a whole, to write a thoroughly comprehensive and accurate study of the emotions—the types, their interrelations with habits, their role, etc. We have tried to connect emotional activity with physiological processes because it seems that such formulations are now practical and no longer purely speculative (p. 195).

As Watson tries to clarify his view of emotions, it turns out that one rarely if ever finds a clear example of them in anyone older than an infant. On his account, the three hereditary emotions (fear, rage, and sexual love) are so quickly mixed with instincts and socially influenced habits that they seem to disappear into a complex set of related behaviors. One is left with very little of a theory about the emotions

11. *Psychology from the Standpoint of a Behaviorist*, p. 195.

themselves. The combination of emotion, instinct, and habit forms what Watson calls "attitudes," and he includes among these attitudes a number of things that other theorists have counted among the emotions—shyness, shame, embarrassment, jealousy, envy, hate, pride, suspicion, resentment, anguish, and anxiety. On first glance Watson's view can appear to be more confusing than helpful. But it is possible that our search for a clean theory of emotions is misguided. Perhaps they could turn out to be hybrid sorts of things—part biology, part social influence, part behavior. As we shall see a bit later, there are some more current theories that claim something very much like that.

But Watson's primary concern with emotions may not have been with formulating a precise theory or definition of them. Rather, his concern as a Behaviorist is broader than that. As he says, psychology has two goals: (1) prediction of human behavior, and (2) "formulation of laws and principles whereby man's actions can be controlled by organized society" (p. 2). With a Behaviorist account of emotions what one really wants, on this view, is understanding of what causes emotional behavior, and understanding how to control that behavior: that is, prediction and control. The precise nature of the emotion and its accompanying physiology are secondary.

As for his method of approach, Watson is quite clear. "Psychology as the behaviorist views it is a purely objective experimental branch of natural science. . . . Introspection forms no essential part of its methods, nor is the scientific value of its data dependent upon the readiness with which they lend themselves to interpretation in terms of consciousness."[12] His method is to be by way of publicly observable behavioral data. Introspection and physiology have little to contribute. Whatever we are to know about what causes emotional behavior and how to control it can be learned by observing human and nonhuman animals.

B. F. Skinner

A more recent version of Behaviorism comes with the work of psychologist B. F. Skinner. Skinner's views no longer provide a "bridge" back to the Physiological view of James. Skinner is quite explicit that physiology has nothing to do with it. He shared Watson's view of the goals of psychology—the prediction and control of behavior. So his account of emotions must also be seen within that framework: ". . . we do not have

12. "Psychology as the Behaviorist Views It," 1913, *Psychological Review*, 20; reprinted in *A History of Psychology*, L. T. Benjamin, ed. (New York: McGraw-Hill, 1988), p. 401.

and may never have this sort of neurological information [as the cause of behavior] at the moment it is needed in order to predict a specific instance of behavior. It is even more unlikely that we shall be able to alter the nervous system directly in order to set up the antecedent conditions of a particular instance. The causes to be sought in the nervous system are, therefore, of limited usefulness in the prediction and control of specific behavior."[13]

Skinner not only dismisses internal physiological events as irrelevant to a psychological study of emotions; in a sense he dismisses emotions themselves. "The 'emotions' are excellent examples of the fictional causes to which we commonly attribute behavior" (p. 160). He goes on to say, "The safest practice is to hold to the adjectival form. . . . by describing behavior as fearful, affectionate, timid, and so on, we are not led to look for *things* called emotions" (pp. 162–3). One is to look for patterns of behavior that can be described by emotional adjectives rather than for psychological or physiological states that might cause those behaviors. Nonetheless, Skinner offers a sort of definition of emotions: "We define an emotion—insofar as we wish to do so—as a particular strength or weakness in one or more responses induced by any one of a class of operations" (p. 166). Such a definition is not very enlightening, but Skinner's approving comments on what the "layman" understands by emotions are more helpful: "When the man in the street says that someone is afraid or angry or in love, he is generally talking about predispositions to act in certain ways" (p. 162).

Thus, for a Behaviorist like Skinner, emotions are not to be understood as internal mental states (as Descartes would have it) or even as closely tied to physiology (as James would have it). It seems that the term 'emotion' is a sort of shorthand for ways of characterizing various aspects of behavior. Any theory about emotions needs to be (as Watson would also have it) a theory about how to predict and control those behaviors. As in the case of Watson's version of Behaviorism, so with Skinner's, unless one accepts the goal of prediction and control as the only relevant goal in coming to understand emotions, it seems that some crucial elements are being left out.

Strengths and Weaknesses of Behavioral Theories

There can be little doubt that bodily expressions and behaviors often form a significant part of emotions. There can also be little doubt that they cannot be the whole story. Unexpressed emotions and feigned

13. *Science and Human Behavior* (New York: Free Press/Macmillan, 1953), pp. 28–9.

emotions provide strong counterexamples to Behavioral theories. Of course, a principal reason that they count against this view is that our goal is somewhat different from that of the Behaviorists. We are not concerned solely, as they were, with the prediction and control of emotional behavior. We want to know how emotions fit with theories of the mental. We are still looking for an account of the experience of emotions, their nature and their function. Given Behaviorist goals, perhaps their account of things was adequate; given our different goals, it seems inadequate.

Cognitive Theories

The third family of theories, *Cognitive* theories, includes some of the most promising candidates for a satisfactory theory of emotions. The cognitive approach to emotions goes back in history at least as far as Aristotle. In spite of the differences among various versions of the Cognitive account, one overriding commonality links them. In each case, a Cognitive theory of emotions insists on the important role played by some cognitive state—for example, a belief, a judgment, or an assessment of the situation that is the focus of the emotion. Most of these theories (but not all) also include the important contributions made by physiological changes in the organism and actual or possible behaviors by the organism. So in a sense these theories are the most inclusive and comprehensive of the three families.

Aristotle

Aristotle, for example, defined an emotion as "that which leads one's condition to become so transformed that his judgment is affected, and which is accompanied by pleasure and pain."[14] Notice the important role played by judgment, a *cognitive* state. He argued that in order to understand an emotion like anger one had to understand the temperament of angry people, the people with whom they most often become angry, and the sort of things they most often become angry about. Unless one understands all three of these elements, he said, one won't know how to induce anger in one's audience. Notice, too, that these comments occur in his work on rhetoric, in which he is concerned with how a speaker can motivate his audience. So, in spite of the fact that his theory is cognitive, Aristotle is not unconcerned with the connections between emotions and behavior.

In his treatise on the nature of the soul, Aristotle asks, "are they [affections of the soul] all affections of the complex of body and soul, or

14. *Rhetoric*, 1378a20, in *Basic Works of Aristotle*, Richard McKeon, ed. (New York: Random House, 1941), p. 1380.

is there any one among them peculiar to the soul by itself? . . . If we consider the majority of them, there seems to be no case in which the soul can act or be acted upon without involving the body; e.g., anger, courage, appetite and sensation generally. . . . It therefore seems that all the affections of the soul involve a body—passion, gentleness, fear, pity, courage, joy, loving, and hating."[15] So not only does he see the importance of considering behavior in relation to emotions, but he also sees the important role that the body and bodily functions play. Thus far, Aristotle's view incorporates aspects of both of the preceding families of theories. How strong is its cognitive dimension?

Consider his account of anger. In order to understand that emotion, and any others, one needs to know something about the frame of mind of the angry person, what sort of people does he become angry with, and about what does he become angry. In each case, one is looking for some account of the beliefs or reasons that cause anger. Aristotle makes this even clearer in his account of fear. "Fear may be defined as a pain or disturbance due to a mental picture of some destructive or painful evil in the future."[16] That "mental picture" of the impending evil is the belief or judgment about the situation.

One final note about Aristotle's account of emotions. As I mentioned earlier, much of what he has to say about them is found in his discussions of rhetoric and has to do with motivation, but a good deal is also found in his *Ethics* and concerns the relationship between emotion and moral virtues. He notes in connection with anger that it is important but difficult "to define how, with whom, at what, and how long one should be angry and at what point right action ceases and wrong begins."[17] He concludes that the praiseworthy way is to take the middle ground between being too quick to anger over everything and being too slow to ever be angered even when anger is justified. So it seems that for Aristotle a moderate degree of some emotions makes a person morally praiseworthy.

Schachter and Singer

A more recent version of a Cognitive theory was proposed by psychologists Stanley Schachter and Jerome Singer.[18] Their Cognitive view of

15. *De Anima*, 403a2–403a16.

16. *Rhetoric*, 1382a20.

17. *Ethics*, 1126a32–35.

18. See their paper, "Cognitive, Social, and Physiological Determinants of Emotional States," *Psychological Review* (1962), 69(5):379–99.

Note on Terminology: According to some philosophers, an emotion, like many other mental states, can be either *dispositional* or *occurrent*. An *occurrent* emotion is one that is actual now, it is occurring. Such emotions might be momentary, like a flash of anger that dissipates, or they might last for a longer period of time—usually occurring without a break. A *dispositional* emotion, in contrast, lasts over a long period of time in spite of the fact that it may not *occur* at every moment during that time. Envy, ambition, or love are common examples of dispositional emotions. They are usually long-lived, but they may be actualized only periodically. That is to say, one has the *disposition* to be envious of someone or to be ambitious in one's job or to love someone, and that disposition is activated on various occasions.

Some philosophers and psychologists distinguish between emotions and *moods*. One aspect of the distinction highlights the fact that moods are generally longer-term and are not intermittent (as dispositional emotions usually are). But another mark of difference is that moods are often *not* intentional in the same way that emotions are. They may have no particular object toward which they are directed. On the other hand, they often have some very generalized "object," like the great way that one's life seems to be going, or the mean way that other people seem to treat one, or the belief that everything that one tries seems to turn out badly.

emotions was prompted by what they saw as an inadequacy in William James's Physiological theory. Schachter and Singer argued that the physiological accompaniments of emotions are not sufficiently distinguishable to provide the essential aspect of the emotion. It seemed to them, for example, that a rush of adrenaline or a sense of visceral changes in the body are common to a number of different states, and something more than awareness of those bodily changes would be needed to distinguish fear, for example, from anger. In order to support their objections to James, they performed an experiment. Subjects were told that they were part of a study to test the effects on their vision of a certain vitamin compound, "Suproxin." Willing subjects were given an injection—some of them were in fact given a shot of adrenaline and others were given a placebo. Those who received the adrenaline soon began to feel more rapid breathing, tremors, some flushing, and so forth, while those who received the placebo had no side effects.

Subjects who received the shot of adrenaline were divided into three groups: One group was told what sort of side effects to expect; a second group was told nothing at all about side effects; and the third group was given misinformation about possible side effects. The subjects who received the placebo were told nothing at all about side effects. The assumption was that on the Jamesian theory, the first three groups would be expected to experience the same emotion since all three received the same amount of adrenaline. So their awareness of their bodily changes should be at least approximately the same. However, Schachter and Singer further manipulated the environments of members of the three groups. They placed the subjects with "stooges" who were either to behave in angry ways or to act euphoric. The hypothesis was that people evaluate their emotional state not simply by noticing changes in their bodily state (as James seems to say), but also in terms of their expectations about those bodily changes, and more importantly by reacting to elements in their environment—in this case, the behavior of the people around them. That is to say, *some* cognitive state would play a decisive role in the emotion experienced. The results of the experiment showed that the subjects who were given no account of the side effects of the adrenaline and who were placed with a stooge who acted angry, reported that they felt angry. Placed with a euphoric stooge, they reported feeling happy. Subjects who had been told precisely what side effect to expect from the shot reported neither anger nor happiness in spite of the behavior of the stooges.

Schachter and Singer acknowledge that their experiment did not prove that the physiological accompaniments of emotions do not differ from one emotion to another (as James's theory seems to require). Nonetheless, they suggest that the experiment provides some evidence that it is our *cognitive* state that differentiates emotions by labeling them, probably under the influence of social and environmental factors. If they are right, emotions do have a physiological dimension but their defining element is cognitive.

William Lyons

An even more recent and widely accepted version of Cognitivism has been proposed by William Lyons. He calls it an Evaluational theory. His point is that a cognitive state is indeed central to emotions, but he specifies that state as not simply a belief or judgment of *some* sort. It is, he argues, a belief or judgment that involves an evaluation or assessment of the situation. It is, on his view, this evaluative judgment that gives rise to the emotion. For Lyons it is not, as Singer and Schachter had argued, a simple matter of labeling the situation *after* the fact.

> Like Aristotle, Lyons sees emotions as a complex set of factors. The "core part of an emotion, the evaluative aspect of which . . . is what actually distinguishes this emotional reaction as being of such and

such an emotion, has three parts, the cognitive part which will involve factual judgments which give rise to belief or knowledge, the evaluative part which will involve objective evaluations or subjective appraisals, and the appetitive part which will involve desires stemming from the cognitive and evaluative aspects."[19]

But Lyons's point is not simply that cognitive states play *some* role in emotions. He claims that it is the cognitive state that *initiates* the emotion. "The emotions presuppose certain judgments, correct or incorrect, cursory or well-considered, irrational or rational, as to what properties something possesses" (p. 71). Emotions *presuppose* cognitive states; that is to say, there won't be an emotion unless there has been some cognitive state. For Lyons that cognitive state is not simply neutral but is part of an evaluative process in which the properties of a situation are assessed in terms of their desirability or undesirability. Lyons does not deny the role played by physiological changes in the organism or the possibility of some sort of emotional expression or behavior. Nonetheless, he wants to emphasize the essential role played by evaluative and cognitive states in initiating emotions. Lyons's method, by the way, is largely governed by an analysis of the *concept* of an emotion — an analysis of what we mean when we take a psychological state to be an emotion.

Joseph LeDoux

Both Lyons and Singer and Schachter rely heavily on the role that *conscious* cognitive states play in initiating or labeling emotions. More recently, experimental work by psychologist and neuroscientist Joseph LeDoux suggests a somewhat different approach to cognitive theories. He argues that certain types of stimuli can trigger the physiological responses associated with emotions like fear even before the organism has become fully conscious of the nature of the stimulus. He uses a telling example to illustrate his point. Imagine you are walking alone in the woods, and you see a coiled brown shape on the path ahead of you. Most standard Cognitive theories of emotion would be likely to say that you first recognize the object, probably forming a belief and perhaps an evaluative judgment about it, (a cognitive state); that then causes certain physiological changes in you, which in turn cause your ensuing behavior. LeDoux's experiments suggest that the order is somewhat different, at least in cases like fear. In fact, it is closer to William James's account.

19. *Emotion* (Cambridge: Cambridge University Press, 1980), p. 70.

LeDoux argues that there is experimental evidence that the stimulus first reaches the *thalamus* (a subcortical—that is, "below" the cortex—part of the brain). The thalamus in turn sends a very simple representation of the stimulus in two directions, to the *amygdala* (another subcortical part of the brain), and to the *cortex* (where conscious cognitive states are most likely to occur). The amygdala computes the affective significance of the simple representation, registering it either as possibly dangerous or harmless. That is, a quick and unconscious evaluation of the stimulus is carried out. If the amygdala computes the representation as indicating danger, it sends signals to other parts of the brain to start up the physiological responses that will be helpful in fight-or-flight behavior. These are likely to include increased heart rate and respiration, increased supplies of adrenaline, rerouting of blood supplies, and so forth. As LeDoux put it,

> By way of the amygdala and its input and output connections, the brain is programmed to detect dangers, both those that were routinely experienced by our ancestors and those learned about by each of us as individuals, and to produce protective responses that are most effective for our particular body type, and for the ancient environmental conditions under which the responses were selected.[20]

Meanwhile, back at the conscious cognitive level, the cortex is refining the representation it also received from the thalamus, gathering further information, and deciding whether this is a snake in the path or a broken tree limb. If it decides on the snake, a signal goes to the amygdala telling it to continue and speed up the physiological responses that it had initiated; if it opts for the tree branch, the signal to the amygdala is to slow things down.

From LeDoux's point of view, the process that gets the fear reaction going is not a *conscious* cognitive state, as theories like those of Singer and Schachter or Lyons would have it. Rather, it is an *unconscious* cognitive process that takes place in subcortical regions of the brain. This leaves a type of cognitive state playing a crucial role in emotions, but it also highlights the essential part played by the physiological components.

Notice that an important element in LeDoux's account of fear is the simple *representation* of the stimulus that the thalamus sends to both the amygdala and the cortex. There is surely reason to think that this thalamic representation of the stimulus is physical. It involves uncon-

20. *The Emotional Brain* (New York: Simon & Schuster, 1996), pp. 174–5.

scious information processing in the subcortical regions of the brain. But recall our earlier discussion of *intentionality*—that characteristic of mental states such that they are about something, they *represent something*. LeDoux's experiments surely suggest that in cases of fear, the thalamus *represents something*. The unconscious physiological responses of the organism are motivated by that physical representation of the stimulus. Further, remember that another of the characteristics of intentionality was that an intentional state can represent things that do not exist. Here, too, in the case of fear, the thalamic representation can represent the stimulus inaccurately (that is, give it properties that it does not really possess) or even send a representation that is completely illusory. To people who have them, hallucinations can be just as frightening in what they represent as actual perceptions can be. This looks very much like a simple—perhaps primitive—case of intentionality, but recall that in our discussion of intentionality in Chapter 1, I said that some philosophers believe that intentionality cannot be explained by Physicalism. If a simple physical version of intentionality is possible in cases like fear, it would seem that Physicalism may eventually be able to provide some more comprehensive account of intentionality.[21]

Robert Solomon

One of the most radical Cognitive theories has been proposed by philosopher Robert Solomon. In our discussion of Descartes I pointed out that Descartes (as well as many other theorists) considered emotions to be *passions*, states that happen to us. As I noted earlier, if that view is right then we have minimal control over our emotions and, consequently, minimal responsibility for them. Aristotle seemed to challenge such a view when he suggested that moderating an emotion like anger can make a person morally praiseworthy. Presumably, if one can moderate an emotion, then one is not purely passive in relation to it.

Solomon challenges in a more radical way the view of emotions as passive. In contrast to the claim that emotions are simply undergone, he argues that emotions are *constituted* by the evaluative judgments that we make about situations. For Solomon we not only actively make the judgments that are constitutive of emotions, but through them we shape our world and ourselves. As he puts it, "They [emotions] are not reactions but interpretations. They are not responses to what happens but evaluations of what happens. And they are not responses to those

21. See S. Cunningham, "Two Faces of Intentionality," *Philosophy of Science* (September 1997), 64:445–60.

evaluative judgments but rather they *are* those judgments."[22] And again, "What is an emotion? An emotion is a *judgment* (or a set of judgments), something we *do*. An emotion is a (set of) judgment(s) which constitute our world, . . . and its 'intentional objects.' An emotion is a basic judgment about our Selves and our place in our world, the projection of the values and ideals, structures and mythologies, according to which we live and through which we experience our lives" (pp. 125–6). He notes that not every evaluative judgment is an emotion; only those "intense" evaluative judgments that relate closely to ourselves and to matters in which we have heavily invested ourselves (p. 127).

Responding to some of the earlier theories that we have discussed, Solomon says, "Emotions are not feelings, yet feelings are typically if not almost always associated with our emotions. And yet neither are emotions *merely* their objective manifestations in neurology or behavior, although we may agree that such manifestations might always be found. But this hardly constitutes a 'theory of emotions'" (p. 111). What must be added, he says, is the intentional, *cognitive* act.

According to the Cognitive theory as formulated by Solomon, emotions are active and not passive, essentially cognitive and not merely physiological or behavioral or a matter of feeling, and they are the means by which we evaluate ourselves, our world, and our place in that world. At first glance such a view may appear to give us absolute control over and responsibility for our emotions. But Solomon places at least one limitation on our degree of control and responsibility. He says that the standards of evaluation that we use in our emotion judgments are not simply created by us but are given to us by society ("our parents and our peers, by instruction and by example" [p. 138]). However, he adds that we are given many divergent standards by our society, and in the final analysis we must choose which among them will be *our* standards. Our emotions are not simply unique individual creations; they operate within the framework of societal values and expectations. They nonetheless involve our choices and therefore our responsibility. The acknowledgment by Solomon of the role played by social influences leads nicely into the final version of the Cognitive theory that we will consider, the Social Constructionist view.

Social Constructionists

In many of the theories that we have discussed so far, there has been an assumption that at least some (and perhaps all) emotions are "basic" or simply part of human nature. The Social Constructionist view, by contrast,

22. Robert C. Solomon, *The Passions* (Indianapolis: Hackett, 1993), p. 127.

argues that many (perhaps most) of our emotions are "socioculturally constituted." Part of what this means is that emotions are not a matter of biology, not states that are simply "given" as part of our being human. As Claire Armon-Jones argues, "emotions are characterized by attitudes such as beliefs, judgments and desires, the contents of which are not natural, but are determined by the systems of cultural belief, value and moral value of particular communities. . . ."[23]

The general idea behind Social Constructionism is that we learn the values, standards, and expectations of our society as we grow up. And these values, and so forth, help to shape the beliefs and judgments that we make about situations, and also help to shape the behaviors and expressions of emotion that are deemed appropriate in those situations. Given the important role assigned to learning about the standards and values of one's society in the process of shaping one's emotions, it becomes clear why this view belongs to the *cognitive* family of theories. One's beliefs and judgments about those standards and values, absorbed from one's social framework, provide the basis for emotions and their expressions.

Perhaps the most plausible case for a Social Constructionist account of emotions can be given in connection with states like shame, pity, gratitude, and the like. There is considerable plausibility in the suggestion that emotions like these have a very heavy overlay of social custom and social expectations that we have been taught to observe. For example, we are generally taught from an early age just what behavior should generate shame. It is in the interest of social harmony that the members of a society learn when and how to be ashamed of their behavior. Similar things could be said about emotions like pity and gratitude. Such emotions and their expressions can contribute in important ways to enhanced relations among members of a society. One can still ask, of course, whether or not these emotions have some basis in biology. Given the fact that they can play constructive roles in social relationships, it would not be surprising if they emerged in social species through the process of natural selection. Their particular expressions and the specific circumstances under which they are experienced may, of course, vary from one culture to another even if they do have some basis in our biology.

In cases like fear, the situation is less clear. We surely can be taught what sorts of things we ought to fear—dark alleys at night, people carrying concealed weapons, and so on. It is less obvious that the experience

23. "The Thesis of Constructionism," in *The Social Construction of Emotions*, R. Harre, ed. (New York: Blackwell, 1986), p. 33.

of fear itself is little more than a social construct. One piece of evidence that seems to run counter to a Social Constructionist account of fear is that many nonhuman animals exhibit clear indications of fear. But Social Constructionists generally provide some leeway for a few "basic" emotions—perhaps fear among them. Their view does not necessarily entail that *every* emotion must be seen as exclusively the result of social influences. But they do argue that society with its values and expectations plays an enormously important role in giving shape to our experience and expression of emotions.

Social Constructionists have generally made use of cross-cultural studies in their approach to emotions. These cross-cultural studies are aimed primarily at showing how many variations there are in both the emotions that are experienced and the ways in which they are expressed in different societies. These differences are taken as evidence for the dependence of emotions on social structures and not on biology. One part of these studies investigates the differences in the way emotion *words* are used and the differences assigned to the meanings of these words in various cultures.

Another approach considers examples of cultural variations in emotions where there is an "inversion of a standard of valuation." For example, in our culture we value bravery and we disvalue cowardice. But in some other cultures, for example, the Ifaluk (a people of Micronesia), the society values those who are passive and submissive while those who are aggressive are condemned. The Japanese emotion of *amae* indicates a happy dependence on someone else (even an employer), whereas in our culture such a state might be considered immature or irresponsible.

For the Social Constructionist, emotions are not simply states that are undergone (as Descartes claimed); rather, they are attitudes and behaviors that indicate an individual's acceptance of certain social values and expectations, and his or her willingness to assume responsibility for supporting those values and expectations. Thus, for many Social Constructionists emotions are closely related to the development of moral values and moral responsibility. One interesting consequence of this view is that people can be praised or blamed for their emotions—for having or failing to have the emotions that are deemed appropriate to the situation as it is evaluated by the society.

Recall, too, that for Descartes one function of the emotions was to alert the soul to the needs of the body. They were seen to be mental states that could serve the interests and needs of the individual person. For the Social Constructionist, by contrast, emotions serve *social* needs and purposes, and one's individual needs only indirectly.

Finally, the Social Constructionist view is cautious about the role played by feelings and physiological changes in emotions. The reason for such caution is that the feelings (qualia) associated with some emotions, and the related physiology, do not seem to lend themselves to easy explanations as social constructs. Hence, some of these theorists argue that feelings and physiology are not essential factors in emotion.

Strengths and Weaknesses of Cognitive Theories of Emotion

I noted earlier that both the Physiological/Feeling theories and the Behaviorist theories of emotions point to important aspects of emotions. But each appears to be incomplete insofar as it ignores or minimizes other important aspects. One of the strengths of Cognitive theories is that they usually take account of more of the elements that appear to function in emotions than do either of the other two families of theories.

To begin with, each Cognitive theory emphasizes the central role played by some cognitive state like a belief, judgment, or evaluation (conscious or unconscious) in connection with the situation. Why is this so important? Because emotions are almost always *about something*; they are *intentional*. You don't just *feel* angry, you are angry *about something*. You are not just *behaving* fearfully. You are afraid of something. You don't just love (or hate). You love (or hate) someone. Intentional states are not simply feelings, and they are not simply behaviors. They are mental states that include a representation of some situation. In other words, they have some cognitive dimension. Thus, the fact that emotions are about something is one good reason for including some cognitive dimension in their account.

But there is good reason, too, to think that emotions are not *simply* cognitive states. There is a critical difference between a "cool" belief that there is a bear close to you, and the fear that a bear is nearby. The cool belief need not generate any response in you—the bear is on the other side of a fence and ravine in the zoo. But the belief that the bear is near you and is a danger to you will normally start your heart pumping faster, send extra adrenaline into your system, and in various other ways prepare you physiologically to run, curl into a ball, or react in some other way. Similarly, the changes in your bodily state and behavior that accompany grief, joy, or love are normally quite different from any changes that might accompany a "cool" belief or judgment.

A Cognitive theory of emotions clearly requires that an adequate theory of mind must include a theory of emotions.

One difficulty for Cognitive theories is that they might not account adequately for some states that perhaps ought to count as emotions, such as sexual attraction, disgust, or boredom. Another problem with Cognitive theories at this point in history is that there are too many of them. We may simply have to wait for more data in order to strengthen one or two of the theories and weed out some of the others.

Can Emotions Be Defined?

Notice that most of the proposed theories assume that there is *one* characterization of emotions, generally in terms of a set of necessary and sufficient conditions, that will apply to and explain the nature of virtually all emotions. This assumption may turn out to be mistaken. Recall that in the chapter on consciousness we considered the possibility that conscious states might not lend themselves to one theory that defines them in terms of a set of necessary and sufficient conditions. Might emotions be in a similar situation? Could it be the case that one reason that we lack a definitive list of the emotions is that the states that might be included are really only related by family resemblance?

Recall that according to Wittgenstein's claims about family resemblance, some collections (e.g., games) share some overlapping similarities, but also differ from one another in significant ways. They lack a set of necessary and sufficient defining properties. Are emotions best understood on the same model as games? Some have noticeable physiological aspects (e.g., fear), some may not (e.g., pride?); some usually issue in behavior (e.g., anger), some may not (e.g., hope?); some usually originate with a cognitive state (e.g., anger), some may not (e.g., sexual attraction); some probably have a basis in biology (e.g., fear, sexual attraction), some may be social constructs (e.g., guilt, gratitude); some can be instantaneous (e.g., anger, fear), some appear to need a longer duration (e.g., ambition, love).

Or would Prototype theory offer a better model? Might the prototypical cases include states like fear and anger; moving out a bit from the "center," one might list pride or ambition; moving further again one might have curiosity and boredom; and further still, states like patriotism. Might the differences in some of the theories of emotions be attributable to each theorist focusing on a somewhat different set of emotions as constituting the prototypical set?

William James suggested that there is a close connection between emotions and *instinct*. Robert Solomon saw emotions as closely connected to *judgments*. Social Constructionists relate them to *societal norms*. Is it possible that emotions actually form a series of links between biologically based instinctive reactions and highly cognitive states that are shaped, to one degree or another, by our social context? Might they be a loosely connected set of phenomena with some overlapping similarities but no one set of *defining* properties? Or might our concept of emotions depend on some best examples (maybe fear, anger, joy, grief, and the like) and some less central examples (maybe interest, boredom, disgust, embarrassment, and the like)?

What Is the Function of Emotions?

Over the centuries theorists have proposed a number of different views about the role that emotions play in our lives. Some of these roles are thought to be negative, some quite positive.

Aristotle, for example, thought that emotions can be used to motivate and persuade others. Politicians and public speakers of various sorts are usually quite good at using emotions in this way. This incitement of emotions is generally used as a means to persuade the audience to do something—fear or anger might motivate people to support the war effort, or pity might get them to contribute food to the hungry or money for victims of disaster.

Descartes thought that the passions can powerfully disturb and agitate people. You surely have experienced this. "Aversive" emotions in particular, like fear and anger, have a tendency to disturb people, particularly when the emotions are strong. In such situations, of course, these emotions are not always constructive (a view that Aristotle would also endorse). They can sometimes lead us to behave in foolish ways or to say and do things that are not helpful in the situation. An anger that leads to complete loss of self-control or a fear that paralyzes a person is rarely of any help in dealing constructively with the situation. But Descartes also saw a more positive role for emotions. He believed that they "incite and dispose their soul to will the things for which they prepare their body, so that the sensation of fear incites it to will to flee, that of boldness to will to do battle . . ."[24]

This notion that at least some of the emotions function to move the body to do what is in the interest of its survival and well-being was more fully articulated in 1872 by Charles Darwin in his book *The Expression of Emotions in Man and Animals*. In spite of the fact that Descartes lived about two hundred years before Darwin, his view of the function of the emotions was quite consistent with the one Darwin proposed in that book. For both men, the emotions can activate a living

24. *The Passions of the Soul*, Art. 40.

organism to behave in ways that can contribute to its survival and well-being. Obviously the emotions don't always do that, but the point is that they can often serve that function. (The same is true, of course, of the immune system; its normal function is to aid the body in fighting disease, but in some situations it can also attack the body.) For Descartes, this function of emotions indicates one of the very close and important connections between mind and body. For Darwin, too, with his Physicalist view of the mind, emotions can play a critical role in assisting an organism to adjust to its current environment. From both points of view emotions are not frivolous or trivial states that we would be better off without. Many of them serve a crucial function in connection with our well-being.

One feature to notice in this function of emotions on behalf of the survival and well-being of the organism is that the information that activates the organism is not merely about its environment. It must also be about the organism itself, about its current situation in the environment, its current needs and interests, its current abilities. Unless the organism can register the information about its environmental situation as it relates to itself, it would not be motivated to respond to that situation in ways that might serve its own needs and interests. This view that emotion states include an evaluation of the situation in relation to the organism itself was articulated quite explicitly by Robert Solomon, although he did not locate his view within an evolutionary framework.

In a recent contribution to the evolutionary significance of emotions, Joseph LeDoux argues in his book *The Emotional Brain* that emotions like fear can activate the physiology of living organisms (human and nonhuman) before they become fully aware of the danger. Recall from the earlier discussion of LeDoux's view, that a stimulus can activate us through unconscious processes initiated in subcortical portions of the brain. The major evolutionary advantage of this is its speed. We can begin to react to danger, for example, even before we are fully conscious of it. If LeDoux is right, emotions like fear don't even have to become conscious—they don't first have to reach what Descartes calls the mind/soul—in order to begin to function on behalf of the well-being of the organism.

One other aspect of the Darwinian view of emotions is worth mentioning. It concerns the fact that emotions can also be important sources of communication. We can tell a good deal about the attitudes and intentions of another person by looking at his or her face. Facial expressions can communicate friendliness or hostility, interest or boredom, embarrassment or intimidation, and so forth. In addition, other bodily behaviors can have a similar communicative function. Clenched fists, stamping feet, rapid movement toward or away from oneself, can all signal the feelings or attitudes of another. It is not difficult to extend the examples to the behaviors of nonhuman animals, behaviors that we associate with their emotions. Notice that the communication is not always unambiguous nor do we always interpret it correctly. Nonetheless, the communicative possibilities are clear.

Social Constructionists propose a related function for emotions. They argue that emotions, as social constructions, serve sociocultural purposes. Unlike Descartes and Darwin, the Social Constructionist does not see most emotions as originating in the body or as serving the needs of the individual. Rather, they see them as serving the needs of the social community by inculcating attitudes toward certain values and habits of response to certain situations that are deemed to be useful to the social group. For example, an individual who is taught when and how to be remorseful or ashamed or sympathetic is an individual who is likely to contribute to more harmonious relations among the members of a social community. As I mentioned earlier, this way of seeing emotions links them closely to the development of moral values and a sense of moral responsibility.

In the end, of course, it is not necessary to choose just one of these proposed functions as *the* function of emotions. It is entirely possible that they have multiple functions, some on behalf of the individual organism, some in the service of communication and persuasion, some as motivating factors on our behavior, some on behalf of social cohesion. Can you think of other functions that emotions might have?

How Do Emotions Relate to Other Aspects of the Mental?

At the outset of the chapter we considered the characterization of humans as rational animals. I noted that cognitive states like beliefs are rational when they are based on plausible evidence and when they are consistent with our other beliefs. But I noted, too, that these cognitive states can also be irrational—that is, not supported by plausible evidence and not consistent with the other things we believe.

I further claimed that we need to be understood as "rational *and affective* animals." Now a question arises concerning the relationship between rationality and affectivity. A number of answers have been suggested.

One very broad answer is that our affective states, just like our ordinary cognitive states, can be either rational or irrational. However, more can be said about the possible connections between emotions, rational cognitions, and irrationality.

As we have seen, for the Cognitive theorists of emotions, some cognitive state like a belief forms some part of the emotion—at least as its cause. This would establish one clear link between cognition and emotion, but would it settle the issue of how emotions relate to our rationality? In one sense it would. If the belief or judgment that causes our emotion is a well-founded belief, the onset of the emotion could then be said to be rational. That is to say, the emotion is based on a reasonable belief. For example, if I see someone carelessly smash into my car in a parking lot, my belief that this person has done me harm may be well founded and may cause a reasonable anger on my part. On the other hand, if I do not know who hit my car but decide to blame the nearest person regardless of the fact that I have no good reason to believe that she did it, my ensuing anger at her is not reasonable. But even in cases where my belief is well founded and therefore reasonable, more seems to be required. If I see someone carelessly smash into my car, and I then pick up a rock and begin to smash the windows on the offending car—or worse, begin to beat the driver—the reasonableness of my anger is being overwhelmed by irrational behavior. It serves no purpose other than utterly destructive revenge. Taking the driver's name, license number, and name of insurance company looks like a far more reasonable way to mend the harm that has been done. Of course, when irrational behavior follows on an emotion caused by an unreasonable belief, the whole emotion becomes quite irrational. One can construct similar examples for many other emotions like fear, jealousy, grief, and the like.

It seems, then, that emotions can be quite rational, partially rational, or quite irrational. And the degree of their rationality is a function not only of the rationality of my cognitive state but also of my behavior. One important conclusion from such examples is that if Cognitive theories of emotion are correct, it would be a mistake to simply place emotions on the irrational side of mental states. They can be as rational as their constituent cognitive states. Can the same thing be said in relation to the other theories of emotion? Not in all cases.

Consider the Physiological/Feeling theories. On this view, emotions are states that happen to us and we simply become aware of them. If this is right, the onset of the emotion does not depend on first having some belief or making some judgment. The emotional reaction to a stimulus is rapid and automatic. Here there can be no consideration of the rationality or irrationality of an automatic reaction. It simply happens and then we recognize it. The reasonableness of my emotion might then depend on whether or not it is possible for one to "feed" the emotion, "dampen" it, or simply let it run its course. It will also depend on the sort of behavior that one engages in as a result of the emotion. However, notice that if the emotion itself is nothing more than the physiological feeling, it makes little sense to characterize it as either rational or irrational.

On Behavioral theories, emotions can be rational or irrational insofar as they do or do not help the organism to achieve its own goals or to behave in socially appropriate ways. Then, of course, one needs to assess the rationality of the individual and social goals that are at stake. But emotions on this view can clearly exhibit practical rationality, just as any other behavior can.

So one possible connection between emotions and rationality is that the cognitive states involved in emotions can contribute to the rational or irrational dimension of the emotion. However, there are a number of other significant connections between emotions and rationality. One relationship that has been emphasized by philosophers for centuries is that emotions can *interfere* with rational thought or behavior. You are undoubtedly familiar with cases in which this happens. When you are grieving over a loss, it can be very difficult to work out a solution to a difficult problem. When you are profoundly angered by someone, it can be difficult to consider reasons that would minimize your anger or show the other person to be a very good and thoughtful individual. When you are jealous of a rival, it can be hard to argue for her good points. Examples like these have long given emotions a reputation for being undesirable, destructive of rationality, and the least valuable aspects of human psychology. Such a view is, however, far too narrow. While it is true that emotions can indeed disrupt rational functions on occasion, they can also, as we have seen, play highly constructive roles. Here are a couple of additional examples.

Emotions can function to focus one's attention on the matter at hand. If, for example, one is walking along a dark street alone at night, fear can heighten one's awareness of relevant sounds and movements. Footsteps behind one, or the sight of a lighted store ahead, take on special significance. This heightened and selective attention to incoming information can, on occasion, be a lifesaver. Again, feelings of sympathy can focus one's attention on what might be done to alleviate the difficulties of the suffering person. Needless to say, when an emotion serves to focus our attention on something, the results won't always be positive. But the point is that emotions can indeed serve to aid us in picking up information that can be useful, constructive, and even a matter of survival.

Related to the issue of focusing attention, if interest and curiosity do count as emotions (as they do on some accounts), they surely play an important role in guiding the learning process. When I am curious about something, I actively search and examine it. When I am interested in something, I give it my attention, often for long periods of time, in order to learn about it.

There are other significant ways in which our emotions relate to our other mental states. Emotions can alter the weight that we give to some of our beliefs. When I love someone, my beliefs about that person generally have a higher priority than do my beliefs about neighbors down the street. When I am happy about something, my beliefs about good things will generally take priority over my beliefs about unfortunate situations around me.

Our memories of events are frequently (maybe always) shot through with emotion. Recalling a first date, a Christmas morning as a child, a Thanksgiving dinner, or numerous other events from one's past usually brings with the memory feelings of all sorts. One loved the event or hated it, was happy or disappointed, had regrets about it or was thrilled by it.

Again, my emotional state can alter the way I perceive things. If I am feeling intimidated as I approach a new experience, it may contribute to my seeing you as hostile or unsympathetic. If I am in love, I am likely to see the person I love as pleasant and intelligent and witty. If I am angry with you, I may see everything you do as mean-spirited and self-serving.[25]

There are, then, a number of ways in which emotions, rational cognitions, and irrationality are related to one another, affect one another. One consequence of that fact is that for "rational and affective animals" like us, an adequate theory of mind cannot isolate affective states like emotions from other mental states. They are profoundly interdependent. This, of course, presents a difficulty for some of the theories of mind that we discussed in Chapter 1.

Emotions and Theories of Mind

At the end of Chapter 1 I suggested a series of steps that one can take when trying to evaluate the various theories of mind we had looked at. One of those steps encouraged you to consider whether or not a given

25. For further discussion of the relation between cognitive states and emotions, see S. Cunningham, "Perception, Meaning, and Mind," *Synthèse* (1989), 80:223–41.

theory is able to account for all the elements that you think that an adequate theory of mind should be able to account for—that is, how good is its explanatory power. In this case, emotions are one of the elements that a good theory of mind should be able to account for. Let's take a brief look at some of the theories of mind and see how well they explain how emotion fits into a theory of the mental.

Descartes's version of Substance Dualism has explicitly proposed a theory of emotions and has noted at least one connection between emotions and the mind. Emotions, he says, are caused by the body and are perceived by the mind/soul. One strength of Descartes's theory is that it places due importance on the role of the body while at the same time accounting for the fact that emotions are experienced by the mind—so, presumably, a theory of mind ought to have something to say about them. The difficulty, of course, is that his theory of emotions highlights the more general problem with his theory of mind: How is it possible for changes in the physical body to be perceived by the nonphysical mind?

A Physicalist theory of mind ought to be able to offer an account of emotions. It should have no difficulty in including the bodily physiology, cognitive states in the brain, and the causal links to possible behavior. The Physicalist is likely to find some problem areas in connection with the conscious qualitative feel (qualia) of the emotions. As I have noted, Physicalist theories have not yet produced a satisfactory and widely accepted account of how physical processes can generate consciousness or qualia.

Behaviorists have offered theories of emotions. But those theories face the same difficulties that their theories of other mental states have faced: It does not seem to be possible to provide a complete account of any of these states, including emotions, by attending exclusively to their associated behaviors.

Strong versions of Property Dualism, in which mental properties are not physical, seem to have the same difficulties that Substance Dualism has, the puzzling interaction between physical and nonphysical things. For emotions, the theory would probably have to say that there are changes in body physiology, leading to possible behavior (both physical), and generally accompanied by beliefs, conscious awareness, and qualia (which are nonphysical). But given the difficulties explaining the interaction between nonphysical properties and physical events, the beliefs, consciousness, and qualia would presumably be epiphenomenal. That would suggest that on a Property Dualist view, emotions would be passively undergone and would not be under any control by one's mental states.

Machine Functionalism is perhaps the least likely theory to provide a satisfactory theory of emotions. Recall that its theory of mind is meant to apply to both living and nonliving systems like computers or robots. Thus, the theory abstracts from all considerations of the composition of the system, including its physiology. It is difficult to see how a theory of emotions that makes no mention of physiology will be adequate. It might account for some analog of emotions, machine-states that might allow the computer to use emotion language, but that would be quite a different theory from the one that will explain human and animal emotions.

Teleological Functionalism, on the other hand, with its emphasis on the biological notion of 'function', should have no particular difficulty with providing a plausible theory of emotions. Teleological Functionalists have not yet, so far as I know, proposed such a theory.

Issues for Discussion

1. If there is a physiological component in emotions, what connection might emotions have with some cases of illness?

2. Some theorists claim that emotions are evolutionary adaptations with a biological basis; others claim that they are social constructions. Which view do you find more plausible? Or do you find the two views to be consistent with one another? Explain.

3. Do you think that emotions are *passions*, or do you think that we activate them? Explain.

4. What relation, if any, do you see between emotions and morality? Explain your answer.

5. One theorist has suggested that emotions should be thought of on analogy with terms like 'weather'—that is, as not having any general definition, but as fairly predictable patterns formed from *varying* combinations of elements. Do you agree? Explain your answer.

6. Which of the theories of emotions that we have considered seems to you to be the most plausible? Give careful reasons for your answer.

7. Do you think that our best strategy for understanding emotions is to continue to look for a set of necessary and sufficient

conditions that will provide us with a definition of emotions that distinguishes them clearly from all other phenomena? Or do you favor the Family Resemblance approach? Or the Prototype approach? Give reasons for your answer.

8. If the Prototype model is plausible for emotions, would you say that all the cases, best examples and less central examples, belong to the category of emotion? Or would you say that some of the less good examples shade off toward instincts or cognitive states or something else? Give reasons for your answer.

Suggested Research Projects

a. Read the final chapter in *What Is an Emotion?* edited by Robert Solomon and Cheshire Calhoun (New York: Oxford University Press, 1984). It is Cheshire Calhoun's response to Solomon's Cognitive theory of emotions. What objections does she offer to Solomon's view? Do you think that she is right? Explain your answer.

b. In *Emotions, Cognition, and Behavior*, edited by Carroll Izard, Jerome Kagan, and Robert Zajonc (Cambridge University Press, 1984), read Chapter 1, "Emotion-Cognition Relationships and Human Development," by Carroll Izard. Summarize his view and the reasons he gives in support of it. Do you agree with him? Explain.

c. In *What Emotions Really Are*, by Paul Griffiths (Chicago, 1997), read Chapter 6, "The Social Construction of Emotions." What is Griffiths's view of this approach to emotions? What reasons does he give in support of that view? Do you agree with him?

d. Read Jerome Shaffer's article, "An Assessment of Emotions," in *American Philosophical Quarterly*, 20 (2), April 1983. What is his assessment of emotions? What reasons does he give for his assessment? What theory of emotions does he hold? Do you agree with his assessment?

e. Read "Feeling and Thinking: Preferences Need No Inferences," by R. B. Zajonc, in *American Psychologist*, 35 (2),

February 1980. What is Zajonc's main thesis? What arguments does he offer in support of it? Evaluate his view.

f. Read Joseph LeDoux's article, "Emotion, Memory and the Brain," in *Scientific American*, June 1994. Describe his experiments with fear in rats. What relevance does he think that those experiments have for understanding human emotions like fear? What reasons does he give for that view? Do you agree with him?

g. Psychologist Paul Ekman, following the lead of Charles Darwin, has focused much of his research on the *expression* of emotions. One of Ekman's primary concerns was to do cross-cultural studies to see if at least some emotions are expressed in virtually the same way in all cultures. Read his article, "Are There Basic Emotions?" in *Psychological Review*, 99 (3), 1992. What answer does he give to the title question? Do his findings have any relevance for the Social Constructionist view of emotions?

4

Did the Mind Evolve?

Near the end of the first chapter I suggested that in the process of evaluating the theories of mind we had discussed, one thing to consider is whether or not each theory is consistent with other theories you take to be true. To illustrate how that might be done, let us take one of the well-confirmed theories in science, the theory of evolution, and see which, if any, of the theories of mind are consistent with it. Of course, if the mind did not evolve, then theories of mind need not have any particular relationship to the theory of evolution. So the first question that we need to address is the title question of this chapter: Did the mind evolve?

Notice that the way the title question is framed may make an assumption about *the mind*—perhaps about its being one unified, all-or-nothing sort of thing that only belongs to the normal, fully developed, human adult. As I said earlier, the assumptions that are built into a question can constrain the types of answers that will be found acceptable. If the question does indeed refer to one unified all-or-nothing adult human mind, it might seem unlikely that such a thing could spring, fully formed, from evolutionary forces. If, on the other hand, instead of asking about *the mind*, the question were to ask about the possibility that *mental states, mental functions, mental capabilities,* have evolved, an affirmative answer might seem much more plausible. As we proceed, it will be important for you to think carefully about which sense of the question seems more reasonable.

Let us begin to examine the plausibility of mental evolution by clarifying what we mean when we talk about something "evolving."

Evolution by Natural Selection

Although the most general meaning of the term 'evolution' is simply "a process of change or development; an unfolding," the sense that concerns us here is its meaning within the context of science—specifically biology. There, 'evolution' means the process by which species of plants and animals have changed and developed from earlier forms over very long periods of time. It involves the view that the types into which we currently divide all living things have developed by a natural, historical process. Its account of the origins of living things is very different from the account offered in the Bible's Book of Genesis. According to the Genesis story, all living plants and animals were created at the very beginning of the universe and have remained essentially unchanged since that time. The theory of evolution, by contrast, claims that there has been a gradual development of species over exceedingly long periods of time.

Evolution theory is actually very old. Like Dualist and Physicalist theories of the mind, it can be traced back at least as far as ancient Greece. Versions of the view can be found in the writings of Thales, Empedocles, and Anaximander, but they offer very little by way of detailed explanation of the processes supposed to be responsible for evolution.

Providing an explanation of the mechanism of evolution was the major contribution of the 19th century British naturalist, Charles Darwin. He did not invent the theory of evolution; he simply proposed a plausible account of how it occurred. Darwin called the mechanism of evolution "natural selection," and he first publicly proposed it in his book, *On the Origin of Species*, in 1859. The theory can be explained in a variety of ways, but one fairly simple, classical version is as follows.

1. One can observe numerous small variations among the individuals in any species.

2. Many of these variations can be inherited by offspring.

3. Some of these variations are helpful to the organisms in their environment; some are harmful.

4. Given the fact of limited resources, there is a struggle for life.

5. In that struggle, individuals with helpful variations are likely to survive longer, produce more offspring, and pass on some of their helpful variations.

6. Individuals with harmful variations are likely to survive for a shorter period, have fewer offspring, and to pass on some of the harmful variations to them.

7. Groups of individuals with significant harmful variations are likely to become extinct.

8. The characteristics of a group will gradually change when there is an increasing accumulation, through heredity, of variations that are generally useful in the environment of the group. (Darwin referred to such a changing group as a "variety" or an "incipient species.")

9. Over extremely long periods of time, and probably with geographic isolation, a variety can evolve into a new species that can no longer interbreed with its original group.

10. The process by which groups with favorable variations survive and those with unfavorable variations do not survive is called "natural selection." (That is, the natural environment "selects" *for* and *against* the groups that have characteristics that fit or fail to fit with the demands of that particular environment.)

11. This process of natural selection explains how variations within a group can eventually lead to the evolution of a new species.

From Darwin's point of view, one can explain the great variety of types of living forms in the world by completely natural processes of variation and selection. In this connection it is important to note that Darwin said nothing at all about *creation*. His concern is to explain how diversity among species arose, not how the world came into being.

In *On the Origin of Species* he did not say anything specific about the evolution of human beings, merely hinting at it near the end of the book. But in 1871 he published *The Descent of Man*, in which he argued explicitly for the evolution of humans by the same process of natural selection. In *The Descent of Man* he also argued that natural selection could explain not only the development of the human body from earlier forms of life, but it could also explain the development of human *mental* powers.

Darwin's theory that the human body has evolved by natural selection is widely accepted not only in the biological sciences but in many other areas as well. Most philosophers accept the view, and many religious groups do as well. In 1997 the Roman Catholic Pope urged that it be accepted as a very well founded view. However, Darwin's claims about the evolution of human mental powers are a bit more controversial. It is these claims that concern us here. Let's look first at some of the reasons for thinking that Darwin was right, that human mental capacities are indeed a product of natural selection.

Arguments Supporting Mental Evolution

Darwin's arguments for evolution rely on the gradual variation in the *properties* of systems, variations that could eventually lead to the development of new species. The sort of evidence that Darwin amassed in support of his claims about the evolution of living organisms came from the fossil record, embryology, artificial or domestic selection, the existence of rudimentary organs, similarities in morphology, and so forth. Clearly, evidence for the evolution of mental properties will be somewhat different. Mental properties, for example, don't leave fossils of themselves. Nonetheless, in the case of mental properties there are analogs to the types of evidence that Darwin used in his arguments for the evolution of species. For example, fossils of skulls can point to certain characteristics of brains—their probable changes in size and structure—that are suggestive of developing mental capabilities. Similarities in brain structures across some living species, coupled with similarities in relevant behaviors, are suggestive of similarities in their functions. We shall look more carefully at each of these, but let us begin with a more general consideration.

Perhaps one of the most obvious reasons for thinking that our mental powers are the product of evolution is the fact that everything else about us appears to be. There is strong evidence from paleontology that the human body is the most recent development from a very long series of hominid species. An enormous amount of literature supports this, but it is not our purpose here to go into the details that provide compelling evidence for the evolution of the human body. The point is that if it is the case that the human body and its brain are the product of evolution, that gives us *prima facie* (that is, on the face of it) reason for thinking that our mental powers, dependent as they are on the brain and central nervous system, have a similar origin.

There are at least four areas in which one might look for evidence of mental evolution. One approach is to ask if there is any evidence for the evolution of the physical structures on which mental capacities depend. The most important and relevant of these is clearly the brain. Second, one looks for evidence of mental capacities among early hominids, the progenitors of modern humans. Third, one looks for evidence of mental functions in a variety of nonhuman species. In the case of both hominids and nonhuman animals one looks for evidence of mental functions that might plausibly be early and perhaps simpler versions of some of the mental functions currently present in human beings. So one might look for evidence of memory, learning, problem solving, emotions, and so forth. And finally, one can ask if the processes involved in natural selection could account for the appearance and development of mental powers. That is, could variations in brain structure and/or function, coupled with the demands of the environment, have produced the complex variety of mental powers that are characteristic of human beings? Could natural selection provide a satisfactory explanation of mental evolution?

Consider first the evolution of the physical structures on which mental functions depend.

Evolution of the Brain

In their studies of the fossil remains of early hominid species, paleontologists and paleoanthropologists have uncovered evidence of the gradual enlargement of the brain. One of the earliest hominid species, *Homo habilis*, had a brain size of 500–800 cc., larger than its australopithecine predecessors, whose brains averaged 400–500 cc. After *Homo habilis*, our next most recent ancestor, *Homo erectus*, averaged a brain size of 750–1250 cc. The earliest of the modern humans had brains of 1200–1700 cc. In addition to overall increase in size, the brain of modern humans contains a larger cortex (generally associated with higher cognitive function) than did its predecessors. According to current theorists, not only did brain *size* increase from early primate ancestors to modern humans, but the brain also underwent a series of *reorganizations* during the three to four million years of evolutionary developments.[1] Once again, given the acknowledged close relationship between our brains and our mental functions, it is not unreasonable to conclude that as the brain increased in size and probably in its organization, its capacity to support increasingly complex mental functions would also have evolved.

Behavior of Early Hominids

This brings us to a second area in which to look for evidence of mental evolution—the developing capacities among early hominids. Although mental states don't leave fossils of the sort that bodies leave, they can leave fossilized evidence of their activities. For example, our early hominid ancestors have left some evidence of their ability to use tools, to create art works, to bury their dead. The earliest hand axes are generally dated to over one million years ago. (Modern humans, *Homo sapiens*,

---

1. See Ralph Holloway, "Toward a Synthetic Theory of Human Brain Evolution," in *Origins of the Human Brain*, J.-P. Changeux and J. Chavaillon, eds. (Oxford: Clarendon, 1996).

did not appear until sometime between 100,000 and 200,000 years ago.) There is, in addition, some evidence that the Neanderthals, who emerged about 125,000 years ago, occasionally buried their dead.[2]

Activities of this sort suggest that our early hominid ancestors were capable of mental states of some sort. For example, notice that construction of a tool requires some understanding of the spatial characteristics of the stone or bone or wood in order to shape it in a specific way. It also requires a sense of the temporal steps that are needed in order to complete the tool. In addition, toolmaking suggests some sense of causal relationships, in this instance between the tool and its use. Burial of the dead, on the other hand, could be seen as indicating some degree of respect for other members of their species ("conspecifics"), or perhaps some desire to protect their bodies from scavenging animals. Taken together, these activities point rather strongly to the development of mental capacities. Early hominids did not write any epic poetry that we know of, nor did they invent computers. Nonetheless, they appear to have had rudimentary concepts, beliefs, and desires that could develop more fully in later ages.

Although mental capacities don't leave fossils of themselves in the same way that bodies do, they nevertheless do leave some evidence of their presence in the form of artifacts and remnants of purposive behaviors. What these suggest is that some of our current mental capacities had forerunners in the early hominids who preceded us. Our ability to understand spatial and temporal properties, causal relationships, and some of the consequences of death, belong to a long lineage of abilities that appear to antedate the evolution of fully modern human beings.

Animal Minds

Turn now to the third area of evidence, in which one looks for some relevant similarities between humans and certain living nonhuman species. This is currently a very active area of research, and it is an avenue that Darwin himself explored in some detail. While paleontology provides us with some evidence from past history, studies of living nonhuman animals provide us with current evidence that is available for controlled experimentation. Keep in mind that there is a great deal of evidence that the human body shares its evolutionary history with other

---

2. References to these items and accounts of many other evolutionary developments can be found in Steven Mithen's book, *The Prehistory of the Mind: The Cognitive Origins of Art, Religion and Science* (London: Thames & Hudson, 1996).

species and that we and the other primates (chimps, gorillas, and orang-utans) share a common ancestor. We also share 96 to 98 percent of our DNA with those primates, and our sensory systems as well as our brain structures are remarkably like theirs. As one theorist put it,

> Our brain, like our other organs, is essentially similar to its coun-
> terpart in all higher mammals. Its principal structures have the
> same functions, approximate locations, and names as they do in a
> variety of other species. . . . Our brain contains most of the same
> chemical neurotransmitters, is subject to many of the same dis-
> eases, and has the same types of neurons as those of other primates.
> Moreover, most higher mammals, including humans, have sub-
> stantially similar cerebral organizations on a microscopic level;
> there is a typical topographic, laminar, and columnar organization
> according to which the sources of inputs and outputs, and the vari-
> ous interconnections between areas of the mammalian brain are
> laid out. On the available evidence, the brains of apes and humans
> are so similar that one is left at a loss to explain the remarkable,
> and apparently discontinuous, nature of the mental capacities of
> humans in comparison with those of our primate cousins.[3]

Given our acknowledged close bodily relationship with these ani-mals, it is quite reasonable to investigate how much of our mental func-tion we might also share with them. The idea is that if we can find evidence that at least some nonhuman animals have some mental capacities, then it would be clear that such mental capacities are not unique to human beings. Mental functions in nonhuman animals would point to the likelihood that both they and we have inherited such capacities from an earlier ancestor. That is, it would provide addi-tional evidence that our mental capacities are indeed one of the prod-ucts of evolution.

In looking for evidence of possible mental capacities in nonhuman species, investigators have used a number of different approaches. We shall look briefly at four of them: anecdotal evidence, laboratory experi-ments, ecological studies, and theoretical considerations.

Anecdotal Evidence

Anecdotal evidence involves everyday descriptions of situations or events, in this case animal behavior that appears to indicate some

---

3. Merlin Donald, *Origins of the Modern Mind* (Cambridge, MA: Harvard University Press, 1991), pp. 20–1.

degree of intelligence or mental function. Such evidence does not arise from carefully controlled experiments but simply from informal observations. Darwin made extensive use of stories about intriguing animal behavior. He was, in fact, somewhat uncritical of the stories that people sent him to support the view that animals are capable of certain mental states. A recent example may illustrate what is meant by anecdotal evidence. In a small town where I was spending some time in the summer, a man accidentally fell into twelve feet of water in a pond on his property. He had never learned to swim, and no other people were nearby to see what had happened. After he had gone under the water twice and came up for the third time, his dog saw him, jumped into the water, swam to him and let the man hold onto him while the dog swam back to shore. The interpretation that one very much wants to give to the incident is that the dog saw that his master was in trouble, cared for his master, and swam out to save him. If that is a correct interpretation, then it would certainly seem that the dog has some mental states—recognizing a problem, caring about someone, solving the problem. But for opponents of this sort of evidence, there may be other explanations of the dog's behavior that have little to do with these sorts of mental states. They might say, for example, that the dog was perhaps just acting out a game of "fetch" that he had played many times with his master, having little or no understanding of what was really happening. Obviously, dog lovers will not be satisfied with such an account. But from the point of view of rigorous scientific investigation, anecdotal evidence is generally taken to be the weakest kind. Science looks for more carefully controlled accounts—explanations that have effectively eliminated all or most other possible explanations.

Lab Experiments

A more rigorous approach, favored by some comparative psychologists, makes use of laboratory experiments. In these situations, the investigators try to control for the many variables that may provide alternative explanations of the animals' behavior. If, for example, they were working with the dog in the previous story they would try to construct experiments that would test the dog's recognition of problems, its ability to solve problems, and so on, in ways that could eliminate "fetching" as an explanation. Here is a description of an actual and relevant experiment:

> One study examined the ability of rats to respond differentially according to their own behavior. Rats are trained to press one among four levers when a buzzer sounds. This buzzer signals the availability of a food reinforcement. The correct response depends

on the behavior the rat is engaging in at the time of the buzzer
onset. Four frequent and spontaneous behaviors are considered:
immobility, face washing, walking, and rearing. Each lever press
is associated with the occurrence of one of the four behaviors.
The results indicate that the rats can discriminate the four behaviors. Moreover, detail[ed] behavioral analysis discounts the possibility that rats are using cues from their locations in the
experimental room or from fields of visual stimuli.[4]

Notice that the fact that the rats can distinguish various of their own
behaviors and can press the appropriate lever, based on that discrimina-
tion, is suggestive of some ability to categorize and to use the categori-
zations in guiding their behavior. The experimenters make no claims
about whether or not the rats were *conscious* of what they were doing.
As I noted in the chapter on consciousness, a function need not be conscious in order to count as mental. So, in saying that the rat exhibits evidence of some mental function, one can leave open the question of its
conscious awareness.

Perhaps some of the best-known examples of lab studies of animal
behavior are the efforts to teach some of the primates, particularly
chimpanzees, to use language. You may remember that Descartes had
argued that animals do not have minds, that they are simply mechanistic systems. One of his reasons was that only human beings have language. One way to prove Descartes wrong would be to teach some
animals to use and to understand language. Some primates have been
taught American Sign Language, others were taught to use a system of
colored plastic shapes that represent different objects, properties, and
actions. The chimps were able to learn the language that they were
taught, and that fact has seemed to many to undo Descartes's claim.

More recent investigations suggest some limits to the success that
was achieved. The chimps' use of the language so far has been somewhat circumscribed. They have used it primarily to ask for things and
rarely, if ever, to make spontaneous statements about things. They
seem to have no significant ability to generate new words in the language, as humans do. Nonetheless, their apparent ability to understand
and remember what the symbols mean and their ability to use them to
communicate their needs and wants, is in itself an indication of some

---

4. Recounted in Jacques Vauclair, *Animal Cognition* (Cambridge, MA: Harvard University Press, 1994), p. 145. The original research is reported in R. J.
Beninger, S. B. Kendall, and C. H. Vanderwolf, "The Ability of Rats to Discriminate Their Own Behaviors," *Canadian Journal of Psychology* (1974), 28:79–91.

mental capabilities. They are not as complex or as flexible as the mental capabilities of humans, but they do appear to be present. This, of course, is what one might expect on an evolutionary account of mental abilities—their gradual development rather than the sudden appearance of the full-blown and most sophisticated version of the abilities.

Ecological Approach

A third approach to the issue of animal mentality, the ecological approach, is in a sense something of a compromise between anecdotal evidence and laboratory experiment. It studies animals in their natural habitat, describing their normal behavior with minimal interference from the investigators. Part of the rationale for this approach is that lab experiments may influence the animals to behave in ways that are not really normal for them. The laboratory environment is, of course, controlled and therefore to some extent artificial. The ecological approach claims that it studies animals in their normal environment and can, therefore, provide more accurate descriptions of their natural behavior and possible mental capacities. One well-known example concerns vervet monkeys. They have at least three distinct calls that they make in the presence of three different predators—leopards, eagles, or snakes. When one of the monkeys makes the "eagle" call, the other monkeys that are present generally look up or run for cover in deep brush. On the other hand, in response to the "leopard" call the monkeys will run to a tree and begin climbing. These reports are not merely anecdotal. Investigators played recordings of the different calls in the absence of the indicated predator and got the same response from the monkeys. That suggested that the monkeys had some sense of what the different calls mean and what kind of behavior was appropriate to each call. What the investigators had done was to eliminate some other possible explanations of the behavior—for example, that the monkeys simply saw or smelled the predator.

Whatever the merits of anecdotal evidence, it seems clear that the evidence gathered by both investigators in the lab and ethologists in the field suggests that at least some nonhuman animals behave in ways that strongly indicate some degree of mental function. Add that to the fact that we share with a number of species a good deal of similarity in our physiology and anatomy, particularly in the brain and nervous system— areas that are critical to mental function. Of course, none of the evidence to date indicates that any of these animals possess *all* of the same mental functions that the normal adult human being does.

Evidence from these various approaches to the study of animal mental capacities provides fairly clear evidence that they perceive aspects of their environment and can guide their behavior on the basis of the information received. Furthermore, many of them show evidence of certain types of memory—remembering where food sources are, the location of a nest, or what certain linguistic signs mean. The famous dance of honeybees tells other bees at the hive about the direction in which the nectar has been found and its distance from the hive. This, of course, involves more than just memory. It includes a rather remarkable capacity to communicate variable information. The dance is not equivalent to what most theorists consider to be a full-blown language—it has a limited set of meanings and doesn't appear to grow or change. Nonetheless, it is a system of communication that appears to make use of both perception and memory. The calls of the vervet monkeys, mentioned earlier, are also part of a limited, but significant, system of communication. Furthermore, in addition to the efforts to teach chimps and gorillas various languages, theorists are beginning to do careful studies of the communication systems used by dolphins and whales. It should be noted, too, that not all communication systems are vocal. Some animals communicate by gestures, some by electrical signals, some by chemical transfer.

The ability to communicate information relies on the ability to categorize some things, to recognize similarities among certain *types* of things. The vervet monkeys recognize different types of predators. The rats described earlier appear to recognize different types of behaviors in themselves. Many species (perhaps most) recognize conspecifics, and many primates at least also appear to distinguish animate from inanimate things.

Various species of animals also give evidence of an ability to solve problems. For one anecdotal example close to home, watch the local squirrels deal with your efforts to prevent them from getting to your bird feeder. Squirrels are prodigious problem solvers, especially where food is concerned. Also, certain species of birds will pick up a shellfish, fly fairly high with it, and then drop it on a hard surface to crack it open. In 1953 an 18-month-old Japanese macaque monkey was seen washing sand off a piece of sweet potato she had been given. Gradually, other members of her troop learned to do the same thing. (If, as some have claimed, culture involves the ability to teach and to learn, this example may be indicative of very simple cultural transmission.) Some time later, the same monkey took some wheat mixed with sand and threw it in the water; the sand sank and the wheat stayed on the surface.[5] Rhesus

5. See Michael Tomasello and Josep Call, *Primate Cognition* (New York: Oxford University Press, 1997), pp. 276–8.

macaques and bonobo chimps have also shown ability in solving mazes on a computer. Using a joystick, they appear to solve the maze, not by brute trial and error, but by apparently anticipating and avoiding obstacles.[6] As the authors of the study point out, it is highly unlikely that such a skill could be the result of hard-wiring in these primates.

Evidence of this sort strongly suggests the presence of certain, albeit limited, mental capacities in various species of nonhuman animals. This in turn would indicate that these capacities are not uniquely human. Furthermore, the fact that they generally appear to occur in a simpler or less developed form in many animals points to the plausibility of their evolutionary history.

Theoretical Approach

We have considered three approaches to animal studies: anecdotal, lab studies, and ecological studies. There is one other approach to consider. It is what we might call "theoretical." That is to say, the view is not primarily the outcome of detailed experimental work. Instead, it considers what sorts of competences would be required for animals to cope with the environments in which they live. An interesting and important example comes from the work of Nicholas Humphrey. (Recall his account, in Chapter 2, of one of the functions of consciousness.) He has argued that social animals *require* some degree of intelligence just to be able to live in a socially structured group. Humphrey argues, in fact, that intelligence has developed precisely because of the demands of social living. What he has in mind is that an animal (human or nonhuman) who lives as part of a group must have the capacity to recognize other members of the group, must be able to keep track of at least some of the relationships among members of the group (e.g., dominance relations, perhaps kinship relations, etc.), and must be able to learn how to deal with other members of the group (perhaps avoiding them, or competing with them, or manipulating them). All of these skills, he argues, require some degree of intelligence—some memory, some recognition of one's place in the group, some recognition of relationships among other members of the group, some knowledge of how to get others to do what one wants them to do, and so forth.

According to one version of this view, what social animals require is a "theory of mind." The general view is the same in the case of nonhuman animals as it was for conscious human beings: in order to relate successfully to other members of the group, each individual needs to

6. Tomasello and Call, pp. 51–2.

have some sense of the fact that the behavior of those members is guided by beliefs and desires, much as its own behavior is. Otherwise, no individual would be able to anticipate the behavior of another or be able to manipulate that behavior. There is strong evidence that many social animals, especially the primates, have some ability to both anticipate and to manipulate the behavior of others. (In Chapter 7 we shall explore in greater detail this proposal that some organisms have such a theory of mind.)

I should mention one other important piece of evidence for the existence of some mental states in certain animals. There is considerable evidence, both from field studies and from laboratory experiments, that various types of mammals have emotions not unlike ours—in particular they exhibit fear, anger, affection, and the like. The behavior, the physiological accompaniments, and the precipitating causes connected with these emotions are quite similar to those found in humans. If, as I argued in the chapter on emotions, emotions count as genuine mental states and should be included in any adequate theory of mind, then this counts as one additional piece of evidence for the mental capacities of some nonhuman animals.

Objections of Anthropomorphism

There are, however, some theorists who object to this whole line of argument about the mental capacities of nonhuman animals. According to this objection, claims about the mental capacities of animals are based ultimately on *anthropomorphism*. To speak of animals as having desires or beliefs or even emotions is, on this view, anthropomorphic, just as speaking of computers as being stubborn, or God as angry, are also examples of anthropomorphism. It amounts to interpreting things exclusively from a human point of view, and to projecting on nonhuman systems the characteristics that we have.

Note on Terminology: An *anthropomorphic* view is one that attributes human properties or abilities to nonhumans. The notion originated in theological contexts, with concerns about attributing human characteristics to God.

A recent book criticizing claims about animal minds cites Descartes's view as being the more accurate one. "Descartes thus sowed the seed of a materialist conception of animal behavior. The seed fell on rather stony ground and took 200 years to germinate, but by the 1960s the majority of professional students of animal behaviour had rejected traditional anthropomorphism in favour of Descartes on this point." (Recall that Descartes believed that nonhuman animals have no mental states at all; they are simply mechanisms.) The author's reason for rejecting the attribution of mental states to animals is that "our penchant for anthropomorphic interpretations of animal behaviour is a drag on the scientific study of the causal mechanism of it."[7]

His reasoning raises two questions. If it implies that *mental states* cannot be studied in relation to their causal mechanisms, that introduces a serious difficulty for both neuroscience and psychology. A standard assumption of both sciences is that mental states do indeed have causal histories, and that these causal histories can be studied. If, on the other hand, it implies that human mental states can be studied scientifically in terms of their causal mechanisms, but animal mental states (if there are any) cannot be so studied, that raises troubling questions about how one could know that animals' mental states are of a radically different sort from those that belong to humans.

There is, however, a different sort of reason for objecting to anthropomorphism. This has to do with the issue of *evidence*. The complaint is generally put in terms of our inability to really *know* what is going on within nonhuman animals. How can we be sure that we are not just imposing on them the categories of our own experiences when they don't really apply to them at all? This is not necessarily a denial that animals could have mental states. Rather, it is an *epistemological* worry, a concern about what can be *known*. And it draws a cautious conclusion: Since we cannot be certain about the mental states of nonhumans, we should not make any claims at all about them.

One possible response to this worry is that in our dealings with other human beings, we also do not *know* for certain what is going on inside them. In fact, we are never sure of what someone else is thinking or feeling. We attribute those internal states to other humans on the basis of their behavior. It won't quite do to respond that other people, unlike nonhuman animals, can *tell* us what they are thinking or feeling. First, certain chimps who have been taught American Sign Language, seem able to "say" what they want. And when the dog picks up his leash and goes to the door, whining, why is that behavior a less clear indicator of what he wants than if he could say, "I want to go out"? Second, we users of language are sometimes unclear or simply mistaken when we speak about our internal state. So language use, by itself, is no sure guide to

7. J. S. Kennedy, *The New Anthropomorphism* (Cambridge: Cambridge University Press, 1992), pp. 1, 5.

the mental states of individuals. And finally, there are human beings who are unable to tell us what they think or want or feel, and yet we are often capable of inferring it from their behavior. Consider the case of very young children before they learn language, or a deaf mute who has not yet learned a sign language. Most of us have few doubts about the existence of some mental states in these individuals. So the epistemological worry covers our interactions with other living organisms of all sorts. Actually, concern about a *simple-minded* anthropomorphism (perhaps based exclusively on anecdotal evidence) has motivated scientists to construct careful tests for animal mental function in such a way as to eliminate most or all of the competing explanations of their behavior.

Notice that the anthropomorphic objection presupposes that there is some unbridgeable gulf between us and nonhuman animals. In fact, it simply assumes without argument that there is no evolutionary continuity between human mentality and that of nonhuman animals. The claim that attributing some mental capacities to nonhumans is necessarily an error requires some careful supporting argument of a sort that has not yet been given. Much of the appeal of anthropomorphic objections seems to lie with some intuitive preference for Descartes's account of things—an account in which humans are absolutely unique. This may sometimes include either an inplicit adherence to Dualism or a refusal to consider even the possibility of mental evolution.[8]

As I noted, objections to attributing mental states to nonhuman animals because we don't know what *really* goes on inside them, appear to overlook the fact that our attribution of mental states to other humans faces that same ignorance. Such attributions in all cases (except perhaps our own) are based on observable behaviors and their causal antecedents, the flexibility and appropriateness of responses to environmental factors, habitual patterns of behavior, and so on. The case for nonhuman should rest on similar considerations.[9]

An Instrumental Reply?

Perhaps this is the place to mention one other way of thinking about mental states that has not yet been discussed. It is, in a sense, a way of avoiding the epistemological worry posed by anthropomorphic concerns.

8. For an insightful discussion of this issue, see John Andrew Fisher, "The Myth of Anthropomorphism," in *Readings in Animal Cognition*, Marc Bekoff and Dale Jamieson, eds. (Cambridge, MA: Bradford/MIT, 1996).

9. See John Dupre, "The Mental Lives of Nonhuman Animals," in Bekoff and Jamieson.

The view has been proposed by Daniel Dennett, and he refers to it as taking the "intentional stance." In its simplest form, the view argues that there are three different ways in which one can look upon a system: One can consider its *physical composition*; one can consider its *design*; or one can consider it as an *intentional* system. When one takes the "physical stance," one simply looks at the system in terms of what it is made of, or perhaps in terms of physical science. When one takes the "design stance," one is concerned not with what the system is made of but how it is structured, how it is organized. Each of these stances allows one to deal with the system according to the needs of the moment. If one needs to deal with its weight or color, for example, the physical stance will do. If one needs to fix the system after it has broken down, one probably needs to turn to the design stance and look at how the parts works together. Simple physics won't be enough; one needs to work at the level of the system's organization. But finally, if one wants to predict the behavior of the system, one way to do that is to attribute intentional states to it—states like beliefs, desires, and the like. This involves taking the "intentional stance." Dennett argues that the considerations that lead one to take one stance rather than another are pragmatic. That is to say, one takes the stance that is most likely to get the results one wants. And from Dennett's point of view, one can take the intentional stance with *any system at all*. If it is convenient or useful to talk about your computer as *wanting* to mess up the paper you are writing, then do so without any qualms. If it is convenient and useful to predict your dog's behavior by talking about him as *thinking* that his dinner is coming soon, that's also fine. And if it is convenient and useful in predicting how your neighbor will react to your new car to speak of her as *feeling envious*, feel free to do so. In *all* cases, according to Dennett's view, the talk is merely *instrumental*—that is, it is a useful device for achieving some goal (for example, predicting behavior), but it makes no necessary commitment to the existence of any actual intentional mental states in any of these systems.

If Dennett's view is right, then perhaps one can stop worrying about anthropomorphism because our attributions of mental states to people as well as to animals are just a convenient manner of speaking that allows us to make some sense of their behavior. Not everyone is equally enthusiastic about using an *instrumentalism* of this sort in order to avoid the problems associated with animal studies. Nonetheless, Dennett's view emphasizes an important insight I mentioned earlier: We do go by the behavior (linguistic or otherwise) of various systems, people or animals, in deciding what internal states they may be in.

So far, I have reviewed some of the reasons and evidence that have been offered for the view that at least some nonhuman animals are capable of some mental functions. This evidence, taken together with the evidence gathered from paleontology and paleoanthropology, suggests that mental functions are not unique to modern humans. It seems that versions of them have been shared by earlier hominids as well as by a number of other species. All of this in turn seems to support the view that mental functions, mental capabilities, mental states are a product of evolution.

Natural Selection of the Mental

One final consideration deserves mention. Could the processes involved in natural selection account for the evolution of mental functions? Could such mental functions be explained by a process of small variations, gradually accumulating over long periods of time? Furthermore, would favorable variations, particularly in the structures and functions of the brain that relate to mental function, enhance an organism's ability to survive and to reproduce more successfully than competitors who lack such variations? Might such small variations include things like an improved ability to perceive one's environment, increased memory capacity, increased ability to learn from conspecifics, more refined awareness of spatial and temporal relations, recognition of causal relationships, and so on? And might such variations be further enhanced by increasing awareness of them and increasing flexibility in their use? If the answer to these questions is affirmative, as it clearly seems to be, then we have good reason to believe that human mental functions are indeed a product of evolution by natural selection.

One note of caution is important here. Talk of "increasing capacities" may suggest that evolution is a *progressive* process. And part of our inclination to see it as progressive arises from our tendency to see ourselves as the pinnacle of evolutionary development. We think of ourselves as "the brightest and the best." And our improvements in medicine, in technology, and other areas, encourage that view of our species. But keep in mind that the processes involved in natural selection are *random*. They involve the selection of *accidental* variations that happen to be advantageous in some particular environment, and that happen to be more adaptive than the other variations that are available. But the process has no goal, no particular direction. It leads to extinctions as well as to improvements.

Arguments against Mental Evolution

Consider some of the reasons that have been offered for thinking that mental capabilities have *not* evolved, that they are indeed unique to the human species.

Religious Argument

Some of those who argue against the idea that mental capacities are a product of evolution believe that the mind is a direct creation of a Divine Being. In some cases, this belief may be related to the belief in immortality. If we are immortal, the argument says, then there must be something about us that is nonphysical, something outside the scope of the natural forces that cause death. That "something" is the nonphysical mind or soul; this was Descartes's view. If the mind is nonphysical, then it would presumably be beyond the generating power of natural selection, since natural selection is a process that involves only the physical world.

Alfred Russel Wallace

Not all those who deny the evolution of the mental do so by arguing for immortality. In fact, the man who formulated the theory of evolution by natural selection at about the same time that Darwin did, Alfred Russel Wallace, offered several arguments against *mental* evolution. We'll look at three of them.

Natural Selection and the Future

Wallace's first argument begins with the claim that natural selection cannot possibly select for some property that is not yet needed and used by the organism. That is, natural selection does not provide for *future* possibilities; it merely selects what is currently available and currently useful. Darwin would have agreed with him on this. Wallace then assumed that the size of the brain is one of the most important factors in determining mental capacity. However, he said, since the size of the human brain has not changed over very long periods of time, the mental powers of our primitive ancestors must have been equal to the powers of 19th-century Britains. However, those primitive individuals did not make use of the enormous mental capacities that their brains possessed. He concluded that the mental capacities of our primitive ancestors could not possibly have been the product of natural selection — those capacities far exceeded anything that they needed or used at the time. In short, he argued that the mind is too complex and has too much unfulfilled promise to be explainable by a process of natural selection. Wallace concluded that the mind must have been created by God. In fact, he eventually concluded that the human being, mental and physical, is outside the scope of natural selection.[10]

In spite of its initial plausibility, there are a couple of problems with Wallace's argument. First of all, his assumption that the size of the brain is one of the most important factors that determines mental capacities appears to be false. Apart from the fact that whales, elephants, and dolphins have larger brains than humans, a more relevant factor is the ratio of brain size to body size. Even when one takes that into account, Wallace's general assumption appears to be unfounded. Some highly intelligent people, like Anatole France, had brains that were considerably smaller than the average human brain.[11] Even more to the point, there is considerable evidence that it is not the *size* of the brain that is critical; it is the quality and quantity of neural connections in the brain that correlates with mental capacity. Experiments with animals placed in cages that were rich with stimuli revealed that their brains had far more neural connections than conspecifics living in sterile cages. This would suggest that the quality of an organism's interaction with its environment is critical to establishing the kind of complex neural organization that could support more complex mental activities. In the case of humans, an environment in which the attention of primitive humans was focused largely on food sources, sexual mates, and climate, is likely to generate simpler neural connections than an environment that has rich social relations, increasingly complex political relations, and an advancing technology. Among other problems, Wallace's argument seems to overlook the importance of environmental influences in developing nascent mental capacities.

Biology versus Culture

A second argument offered by Wallace capitalizes on a somewhat paradoxical relationship between human beings and natural selection. It appears that most other species are effectively at the mercy of nature. If they do not possess variations that assist them in their environments, nature will select against them. Human beings, on the other hand, have the ability, in virtue of their mental capacities, to alter their environments

10. Alfred Russel Wallace, *Contributions to the Theory of Natural Selection* (London: Macmillan, 1870).

11. See Michael Corballis, *The Lopsided Ape*, p. 66.

in such a way that they can control some of the forces of nature rather than being completely controlled by them. Wallace used this argument to conclude that natural selection could not have produced the mental capacities that are able to disarm it.[12]

Of course, our mental capacities don't *disarm* natural selection. On the contrary, they provide us with one more *adaptive* capacity that can enhance our efforts to cope with our environments. Given their function, there is every reason to believe that they have emerged by a process of natural selection.

Nevertheless, the dichotomy that Wallace proposed—between nature and our mental capacities with their cultural products—has raised questions for some theorists about the precise relationship between nature or biology, on the one hand, and mind and culture, on the other hand.

Biologist John Bonner distinguishes between biological and cultural evolution on the basis of differences in their respective means of transmitting information. Biological or genetic information is transmitted slowly and is fairly rigid. Culturally based transmission of information, in contrast, is fast and flexible, and can be conveyed from one individual or artifact to innumerable others in a very short time. He notes that both can be "guided by selection."[13]

Some theorists have further argued that cultural factors have a profound influence on biology. As Merlin Donald put it, "Cultures restructure the mind, not only in terms of its specific contents, which are obviously culture-bound, but also in terms of its fundamental neurological organization. . . . Culture can literally reconfigure the use patterns of the brain . . ."[14] He suggests, for example, that someone learning a new skill, like reading Braille, literally restructures the portion of the sensory cortex that relates to the fingers.

On the most radical view of the relationship between biology and culture—a view that appears in the writings of some Sociobiologists—culture and the behaviors associated with it are simply reducible to biology, to a matter of genetic endowment (see box). But perhaps the most balanced view is that biology and culture are mutually interdependent and profoundly influence one another. Merlin Donald's view, as well as that of some Sociobiologists, belongs in this group.

12. Alfred Russel Wallace, *Social Environment and Moral Progress*, Chapter 14, 1913.
13. John Bonner, *The Evolution of Culture in Animals* (Princeton, NJ: Princeton University Press, 1980), pp. 17–18.
14. *Origins of the Modern Mind*, p. 14.

Note on Terminology: *Sociobiology* is the theory that social behavior has its roots in biology. The view comes in several varieties. In its most radical form, it argues that cultural factors—and the disciplines that study them, like the humanities and social sciences—are reducible to biology. In its more moderate form, some Sociobiologists have argued that human evolution must be understood as an *interplay* between the biological and the cultural. They refer to this as "gene-culture coevolution," where the biological/genetic component affects the development of the mental, and the mental/cultural in turn affects the genetic by supporting behaviors and institutions that contribute to the survival of individuals having certain types of genetic makeup. E. O. Wilson, the founder of Sociobiology, has argued at different times for both views.[15]

In the end, Wallace's position appears to be untenable. Our mental capacities have enabled us to establish cultures with their science and technologies. These in turn have enabled us to protect ourselves against some of the harsher forces of nature. This is clearly an adaptive variation very much within the scope of natural selection. One is tempted to suspect that Wallace's objection implicitly assumed that natural selection has some goal—at least its own preservation—such that it would select for nothing that opposed it. Not only does such a view appear mistakenly to personify natural selection, but there is no reason to think that the theory entails, or even allows, for such a goal-oriented interpretation.

Consciousness and the Physical

The final argument from Wallace also has its 20th-century counterparts. Wallace argues that physical facts could not possibly account for consciousness. As he puts it, "If a material element, or a combination of a thousand material elements in a molecule, are alike unconscious, it is impossible for us to believe, that the mere addition of one, two, or a thousand other material elements to form a more complex molecule, could in any way tend to produce a self-conscious existence. The things are radically distinct."[16] But recall Marvin Minsky's little story in the

15. See Charles Lumsden and E. O. Wilson, *Promethean Fire* (Cambridge, MA: Harvard University Press, 1983); E. O. Wilson, *Consilience* (New York: Knopf, 1998).

16. Wallace, 1870, p. 365.

chapter on consciousness, about how a box could not hold a mouse because each individual side of the box lacks 'containment'. His story disarms objections like this one and highlights the importance of recognizing the possibility of emerging properties.

Several current philosophers of mind, however, agree with Wallace. Although most of them do not couch their arguments within the context of evolution, they argue that there is nothing in physical nature—including brains and their neural activity—that could conceivably explain the emergence of consciousness. Most of these philosophers are Property Dualists of the strong variety. They hold that at least some mental properties, particularly consciousness, are nonphysical properties. (Recall the view of David Chalmers.) As such, they could not be the result of the physical processes involved in natural selection.

One contemporary argument against mental evolution has been expressed by philosopher Thomas Nagel.[17] It was also voiced by philosopher Bertrand Russell, and it echoes one of A. R. Wallace's concerns. In its most generic form it goes like this: If mental capacities are a product of natural selection, they must contribute to the survival of the organisms that have them. But a substantial portion of human mental capacities are exercised in ways that have nothing to do with survival. The development of higher mathematics, much of philosophy, and physics, all seem to indicate that human mental powers are not properties that have been picked out by natural selection because they contribute to our survival. They are far removed from such mundane considerations.

One of the difficulties with such a view (as well as with Wallace's first argument) is that it appears to collapse the distinction between mental *capacities* and the *contents* to which those capacities can be applied. Surely curiosity, the ability to recognize and manipulate spatial and temporal and causal relations, the ability to make inferences and to generalize, all contribute to our ability to survive. Without them humans would have quickly succumbed to the competition in our environments. The things to which we have directed these capacities have gradually developed over the millennia. While food and mates and climate might have absorbed all the attention of our early ancestors, an increasingly rich environment would have invited the extension of our mental capacities to deal with new and more complex objects. Every new tool, idea, or organization would offer new contents on which to exercise our mental abilities, until we now find ourselves

17. Thomas Nagel, *The View from Nowhere* (New York: Oxford, 1986), pp. 78–82.

with an enormously rich and complex set of things that engage our mental powers. Thus, our mental *capacities* are clearly connected with our survival. And just as our bipedal capacity could be extended into dance, which may or may not have survival value, and our visual perception could be extended into the visual arts or the use of makeup, which also may or may not relate directly to survival, so our curiosity, our powers of inference, our recognition of relations could be extended into exploring other subject matters that may have no obvious bearing on our survival. By itself, these extensions don't appear to bear any negative consequences for the effects of natural selection.

Language

One final reason that has been offered for rejecting the evolution of mind has its origin in Descartes. One of his principal reasons for denying that animals have minds was that they are incapable of using language. The implication is that the human mind, with its unique capacity for language, must be of a wholly different type from anything that preceded it.

The plausibility of the view depends on how one interprets the two terms "using" and "language." If one means by "language" a system of signs with a generalizable grammar, a generative system (one in which a virtually infinite number of new expressions can be formulated), and a system with a large number of lexical items—then there is no evidence yet that nonhuman animals have constructed such a system. If, on the other hand, one counts a system as a language when it has even a few signs that can refer, and when it is used among conspecifics to communicate on a standard and predictable basis, then some animals do indeed have a (minimal) language. And, of course, if language use, along with other mental capacities, does belong to the evolutionary context, it would hardly be surprising to find earlier and simpler forms of it in use among some nonhuman species.

With regard to the notion of "using" a language, it is important to keep in mind that articulating a language is just one way of using it; understanding a language is another use of it. While some animals do communicate with a minimal language, many can be taught to understand portions of even human language. It might be useful here to recall some of the minimal languages that some nonhuman animals use. I have already mentioned the three predator calls of the vervet monkeys and the dance of the honeybees, which indicates both the direction and the distance of a nectar source. A wide variety of species have communication systems that are used primarily in the service of finding mates. Cuttlefish and squid send "messages" by changing the pigment in their skin. Certain web-spinning spiders tap out "messages" to one another on the web. Birds learn the appropriate song for their species when they are exposed to adults of the species, and they then use these songs both to attract mates and to announce their territory.

In the end, the argument against mental evolution, based on the human capacity for language, depends heavily on how narrowly one wants to define "language," and whether or not one is willing to see human language as belonging to a continuum of communication systems. There can be little doubt that human language is far more complex and rich than any of the animal languages that we are aware of, but that by itself does not necessarily exclude it as a product of natural selection.

Mental Evolution and Theories of Mind

I began this chapter by reminding you that at the end of Chapter 1 I suggested that one of the factors that is useful when you are trying to evaluate a theory is to see if it is consistent with other theories that you take to be true. I also suggested that one such theory might be the theory of evolution. If, as I have tried to show, that theory can reasonably be applied to the development of human mental function, then it will be useful to see which theories of mind that we have studied are consistent with the theory of evolution.

Let's begin with Substance Dualism. It should be fairly obvious by now that this view has significant problems with the theory of evolution as it relates to mental capacity. If the mind is a simple, unified, nonphysical substance, there appears to be no plausible evolutionary explanation for how such a substance came into existence. If it is true that mental capacities have evolved, it surely seems that Substance Dualism is at least *prima facie* inconsistent with the theory of evolution.

What about Behaviorism? As I mentioned in our earlier discussion of Behaviorism, one aspect of that view is supportive of the theory of mental evolution in a very important way. For both the Methodological and Metaphysical versions of the theory, it is important to see mental capacities in the context of an organism's interactions with its environment. And while neither version of Behaviorism *requires* that mental capacities have evolved, it seems that at least one of them is fully consistent with it. The Methodological Behaviorist makes no claims about the nature of mental states and is simply concerned to operate with publicly observable behavior as the primary scientific indicator of the mental. Nothing in this view contradicts the theory that the mental has evolved over time. The case for Metaphysical Behaviorism is more problematic. Recall that this theory denies the existence of any internal mental states. The mental is to be found completely in publicly observable stimulus-response relations. On one reading of the theory, one could simply say that it obviously supports the evolution of the mental because it recognizes evolution in the behavior of organisms. But given the evidence that mental states and capacities are closely tied to brain structures and functions, it now seems implausible to claim that mental evolution is nothing more than behavioral evolution. While the two are closely related, there is little reason to suppose that one is completely reducible to the other. So while Methodological Behaviorism is consistent with the evolution of the mental, its Metaphysical relative appears to oversimplify the connection.

What about Physicalism? The most fundamental aspect of all versions of Physicalism is the claim that mental states belong to the natural physical world. To that extent, it surely seems to be consistent with the evolution of the mental. In fact, all but one of its many permutations is indeed consistent with it. The one exception is Type Physicalism. Recall that according to that theory, each type of mental state is identical with a particular type of brain state. When one considers the evolution of mental states through various animal species, each with slightly different brains, the claim that a particular mental state—for example, remembering—must be the exact same brain state in all those species becomes difficult to maintain. In fact, it was considerations such as these that led many philosophers to move away from Type Physicalism to Token Physicalism. According to the latter, every case of remembering will be *some* physical state of the brain, but a variety of such states in different species might all be cases of remembering. We considered several other variations of Physicalism—Reductive, Nonreductive, and Eliminative. Reductive Physicalism is consistent with the view that as the brain evolved so did its mental capacities; the same is true with most versions of Nonreductive Physicalism, which argue for the necessity of more general *theories*, but not for anything that is nonphysical. However, the case with Eliminative Physicalism is a bit more ambiguous. It differs from the other versions of Physicalism in that it insists on eliminating reference to the 'mental' and explains behavior completely in terms of brain structure and function. The view is clearly consistent with the evolution of the brain and its various capacities. But since it is not committed to the notion that there are *mental* states like beliefs, desires, and so forth, the issue of their evolution would be of no concern to Eliminativists.

For Functionalism the case is also a bit complicated. Recall that Functionalists argued that the composition of the system was irrelevant to its mental capacities. And part of the motivation for this claim was the desire to include nonliving systems like computers and robots in theories of the mental. When Darwin formulated the theory of natural selection, he was concerned to explain the development of species of *living* systems. And on his view the mental capacities of animals were adaptations that assist them in their dealings with their environments, assist them in their struggle to survive and to provide for their well-being. Computers and robots don't fit easily into such a framework. The simple reason is that since they are not alive, they do not struggle to survive; and since they have no interests of their own (they work *for us*), what they do is not in the service of providing for their own well-being. Does it follow that Functionalism is inconsistent with a theory of the evolution of mental capacities? Some versions of it appear to be—those that insist that any theory of the mental must apply equally to living and nonliving systems. But if one were to construe Functionalism as a theory about *living* organisms (humans, nonhuman animals, ETIs), then while continuing to deliver us from our earlier chauvinism, it would also be consistent with mental evolution. And one might then formulate a *secondary* (or "derivative") application of the theory to *nonliving* systems like computers and robots, in which the attribution of "mental" states to such systems would be understood as having a somewhat different meaning from what it has for living systems. The "evolution" of such systems might then be a product of human ingenuity rather than a product of natural selection.

The final theory we considered was Property Dualism. On its completely physicalist interpretation, where mental properties are construed simply as special complex physical properties, it is fully consistent with mental evolution. On its metaphysically stronger version, where mental properties are construed as nonphysical properties, it shares all the difficulties that Substance Dualism has with mental evolution. The theory of natural selection provides no explanation for the origin of such nonphysical properties.

Exploring the consistency relations between each theory of mind and the theory of evolution does not, of course, resolve the issue of which theory of mind is correct. But it does give one some additional reasons for preferring one or more of the theories over some of its competitors. Additional considerations have already come from your examination of the adequacy of each theory of mind to deal with emotions.

Issues for Discussion

1. Do you think that the evidence for the evolution of mental capacities is adequate? Explain your answer.

2. Why is the question of the possible evolution of mental functions so much more controversial for some people than is the question of the evolution of the body?

3. Why do anthropomorphic interpretations seem to come so naturally to us, not only in our discussion of animals but also in our thinking about a Divine Being?

4. Can you provide additional reasons for thinking that mental functions are or are not a product of evolution?

5. If it is the case that some nonhuman animals possess certain mental capacities, should that make any difference in the way that we treat them? Explain.

6. What are some consequences of the view that mental capacities, like bodily characteristics, are a product of evolution by natural selection?

7. Do you think that consciousness frees us from the influence of natural selection? Explain your answer.

8. Do you think that biology and culture are two independent domains, or do you see them as interdependent? Explain your answer and be explicit about what you include in the notion of "culture."

9. Tomasello and Call, in their book, *Primate Cognition*, say: "The Western intellectual tradition was created by people living on a continent with no other indigenous primates. It is therefore not surprising that for more than 2,000 years Western philosophers characterized human beings as utterly different from all other animals, especially with regard to their mental capacities" (p. 3). Do you agree that this was indeed a significant factor? Explain your answer.

Suggested Research Projects

a. What is the theory of *Punctuated Equilibrium*, and how does it differ from Darwin's account of evolution? (Some of Stephen Jay Gould's work is a good source.)

b. Find accounts of at least two other experiments that have been done by comparative psychologists studying animal mental function. Describe the experiments and the results that were reached by the investigators. (Cite your sources.)

c. What are some of the problems that have been cited in connection with efforts to teach languages to chimpazees? What conclusions do they suggest? (Cite your sources.)

d. Describe some of the art works that have been attributed to earlier species of hominids, and explain where they were found.

*e. Read pages 225–81 in Michael Ruse's interdisciplinary collection of essays, *But Is It Science?* (1996). Summarize the arguments for and against creationism. Which side seems to you to have the better arguments? Explain your answer.

*f. Read J. S. Kennedy's short book, *The New Anthropomorphism* (1992), and Frans de Waal's article, "Are We in Anthropodenial?" (*Discover*, July 1997). Outline the arguments of each author and evaluate them.

*g. Read Chapter 2 of Anthony O'Hear's book, *Beyond Evolution* (Oxford: Clarendon, 1997). O'Hear argues that although reason may have evolutionary roots, it also has what he calls a "transcendent dimension." What does he mean by the "transcendent dimension" of reason, and what reasons does he offer in support of his claim?

h. Read pages 260–8 in M. Tomasello and J. Call, *Primate Cognition*. What are some of the arguments they discuss for and against the claim that some primates are able to learn a language that allows them to communicate with humans? Which do you find most persuasive? Why?

i. Read Chapter 6, "The Evolution of Language," in Michael Corballis's book *The Lopsided Ape*. What evidence does he give for the claim that human language is unique? What arguments does he offer for the claim that language evolved? Are these two claims compatible? Explain.

j. Read Roger Crisp's article, "Evolution and Psychological Unity," in *Readings in Animal Cognition*, Marc Bekoff and Dale Jamieson, eds. What is Crisp's view of the mental capacities of some nonhuman animals? What arguments does he offer in support of that view? Do you agree with him?

5

What Is a Self?

By this time you may be wondering just where *you* fit into all this. What is the "Self" or "Subject" that we talk about, and how does it relate to mind or to consciousness? Is it the same thing as one's body? Is it a product of evolution? Or is 'Self' one of those words, like 'phlogiston', that doesn't really name anything—a verbal relic of an earlier and less-informed time? These are the issues that will concern us in this chapter. We will consider a number of different views about the Self, or 'Personal Identity' as it is often called, each with its advantages and its unresolved puzzles.

Actually, a number of somewhat different notions are sometimes bundled together under the term 'Self'. They include a notion of an *enduring* Self, sometimes referred to as 'Personal Identity'. In addition there is a notion of Self as the *subject of experience* and sometimes referred to as 'Subject' or 'Subjectivity'. And there is the notion of Self as *agent*, including *moral agent*, sometimes referred to as 'Person'. As you will see, some theories of Self emphasize one of these notions over the others; some theories attempt to include all of them. As you read, consider the possibility that one comprehensive theory of Self may not be plausible, and we may need a series of theories in order to provide an adequate account of each of these related notions.

Let's begin by taking a look at some of the theories that have been proposed.

Theories of Self

Self as a Nonphysical Entity

This view goes back in history at least as far as Plato, and apparently versions of the view have also been held by a number of Native American groups. But it was articulated in greatest detail by Descartes as part of his larger philosophical project. One of Descartes's primary goals was to find some indubitable foundation for knowledge, from which he could

not only prove the existence of God and immortality but could also provide a solid basis for science. Using his "method of doubt"—that is,
doubting but not denying anything that could conceivably be false—he
established the one certain truth, "*Cogito ergo sum*" (I think, therefore I
exist). One of the consequences of his view was that, although he could
conceivably be mistaken about his body—he mentioned the mistaken
experience of the phantom limb—he was certain that any time he considered the matter, he was necessarily thinking. Even trying to doubt or
deny that he was thinking was itself a form of thinking. It was on this
basis that he constructed his theory of Self. He says,

> Then, examining with attention what I was, and seeing that I
> could pretend that I had no body and that there was no world nor
> any place where I was, I could not pretend, on that account, that
> I did not exist at all; and that, on the contrary, from the very fact
> that I thought of doubting the truth of other things, it followed
> very evidently and very certainly that I existed; whereas, on the
> other hand, had I simply stopped thinking, even if all the rest of
> what I had ever imagined had been true, I would have had no
> reason to believe that I had existed. From this I knew that I was a
> substance the whole essence or nature of which is simply to
> think, and which, in order to exist, has no need of any place nor
> depends on any material thing. Thus this "I," that is to say, the
> soul through which I am what I am, is entirely distinct from the
> body and is even easier to know than the body, and even if there
> were no body at all, it would not cease to be all that it is.[1]

It should not come as a surprise that Descartes decided that he was a
substance. We have already discussed that in connection with his Substance Dualism theory of mind. What may be more surprising is that he
identified his Self, not with the combination of the physical and the
nonphysical substances, but exclusively with the nonphysical substance. He defined himself as a mind or soul, a *thinking* substance.

Descartes's account appears to address each of the three notions of
Self that I mentioned at the beginning of the chapter. As a *substance*,
this type of Self would endure and can therefore account for Personal
Identity through time. His *mental* substance also functions as the locus
of agency and is the seat of consciousness, hence it would also count as
a Person and as a Subject of experience. Furthermore, Descartes's theory of Self as a mental substance can also account for the first-person

1. René Descartes, *Discourse on Method*, in *Philosophical Essays and Correspondence*, p. 61.

point of view on the Self (that is, what *I* think of as myself), since it depends on the *cogito* that each individual must arrive at for herself. As we shall see, the third-person point of view (how *others* identify me as a Self) is a bit more complicated.

Strengths and Weaknesses of the Theory of a Nonphysical Self

Descartes's view of the Self has a couple of advantages. First, if the Self is a *substance*, then that would account for what some have thought to be its unity, its continuing identity through time, in spite of any changes in its accidental properties. This view that the Self has some continuing identity would explain its status as an agent with responsibility for its choices through time. Second, if the Self is nonphysical and entirely distinct from the body, then that would explain the possibility of immortality. When the body dies, the nonphysical Self could continue to exist in an afterlife.

This view, however, raises some questions and has some puzzling consequences. First, is it really the case that you are the same person you were in kindergarten? Are all the changes that have taken place, physically and emotionally, really irrelevant to who you are? People have conflicting intuitions here. On the one hand, there does seem to be some sense of continuity with who you were in the past; on the other hand, in some respects you seem to be quite a different person. The difficulty is highlighted when one tries to specify what it is that has remained unchanged. It certainly isn't your body, or your skills, or how you feel, or what your goals are. What, then, is it? The theoretical notion of *substance* would account for what did not change because it is by definition the thing that is supposed to remain the same while its properties change. But do we have any evidence for its existence? As we shall see, the philosopher David Hume will argue that we can find no such evidence in our experience.

A second difficulty that Descartes's view poses is that it seems to leave a severely "stripped-down" version of the Self. Is it the case that your sex, your athletic or musical skills, your emotions, and so forth, play no part in determining who you are? (Keep in mind that even for Descartes, your emotions begin in your body. Without a body it seems that you would have no emotions.) Is your Self really nothing more than your thoughts? If the only part of you that is immortal is your nonphysical mind, would that be *you* in an afterlife, or would it be just a shadow of your full Self? Again, people's intuitions differ here. It seems clear that if immortality is a genuine possibility, one's conscious awareness must survive. Otherwise, *something* might survive your death, but if it does not include your consciousness it is difficult to see that *you* have survived death. So Descartes's insistence on the importance of the mind in connection with immortality seems right. But many people take themselves to be more than conscious thoughts. And of course, if consciousness originates in the brain, Descartes's position would become even less tenable.

Finally, there is a problem of individuation. How could one distinguish one mental substance from another? We normally individuate things by their publicly observable properties—color, size, sound, location, and so forth. A mental substance has none of these properties. Each mental substance might be able to distinguish itself from everything else because of its special access to its own thoughts. But it would not be able to distinguish among other mental substances without acquiring some capability that we currently lack.

One thing to be aware of in evaluating certain theories is the effect that a philosopher's *method* may have on the conclusions he or she draws. Sometimes a particular method can skew the problem or its possible solutions. As we look at the various philosopher's views, ask yourself whether or not you think that the particular method has distorted the problem or generated unwarranted conclusions.

Descartes's "method of doubt" is one that calls into question many beliefs that seem to common sense to be true. The existence of one's body, for example, doesn't normally seem to be open to doubt. Yet it is his temporary doubting of his body that allows him to conclude that his mind is the only thing about which he can be certain, and the only thing that is required for his existence. Other philosophers have challenged Descartes's method. Some have argued that it is only because we have functioning bodies that we are even capable of thought or doubt. Still others have argued that his method of doubt presupposes the use of language, and that in turn presupposes that we are part of a physical human community from whom we learned the language. The objections have taken many forms. What is important to notice is that if they are reasonable objections, then they may call into question the conclusions that Descartes drew about the nature of the Self.

The Psychological Self

About fifty years after Descartes published his views on the Self (1637), John Locke offered his views (1690) in his *Essay Concerning Human Understanding*. Like Descartes, Locke believed that there are substances, and like Descartes he believed that *mental* events are essential to the Self. But unlike Descartes, he does not equate the Self with a mental *substance*. He says,

> *Self* is that conscious thinking thing, (whatever substance made up of whether spiritual, or material, simple, or compounded, it matters not) which is sensible, or conscious of pleasure and pain, capable of happiness or misery, and so is concerned for it*self*, as far as that consciousness extends. . . . That with which the *consciousness* of this present thinking thing can join itself, makes the same *person*, and is one *self* with it, and with nothing else; and so attributes to it*self*, and owns all the actions of that thing, as its own. . . .[2]

For Locke, the Self is identified with consciousness and whatever consciousness can join to itself. Among the things that it can join to itself, Locke mentions the body as well as past and future actions. However, insofar as a part of the body is cut off (he mentions a finger as an example), it ceases to belong to the conscious Self. Similarly, past or present actions that are completely lost to consciousness cease to be part of the Self.

> For, whatsoever any substance has thought or done, which I cannot recollect, and by my consciousness make my own thought and action, it will no more belong to me, whether a part of me thought or did it, than if it had been thought or done by any other immaterial being anywhere existing (p. 147).

Locke's notion of Self does not coincide completely with his notion of *man*. A man is "nothing but a participation of the same continued life, by constantly fleeting particles of matter, in succession vitally united to the same organized body" (p. 137). So where a man is identified with the living body, the Self is identified with consciousness and all that it joins to itself. One interesting consequence of the view is that while a *man* may be legally punished for what he did, if he is no longer conscious of having done it, he (his Self or Person) will not be morally responsible for it.

Locke's view clearly accounts for Self as the Subject of experience. But if Personal Identity requires some *enduring* reality (and it may not), then Locke's view appears to be problematic. He would account for Personal Identity by the continuing presence of consciousness and its appropriation of things to itself. But one standard objection to such a view is that it may tacitly presuppose some sort of enduring Self that *has* the consciousness without offering any explanation of that tacit Self. Furthermore, his claim that one is morally responsible for only those

---

2. *An Essay Concerning Human Understanding*, Vol. I, Book II, Chapter 27, Kenneth Winkler, ed. (Indianapolis: Hackett, 1996), pp. 143–4.

actions that consciousness retains in memory may also raise some questions about the adequacy of his account in relation to the Self as moral
agent.

Strengths and Weaknesses of the Theory of a Psychological Self

There is something initially appealing in Locke's emphasis on consciousness, just as there was in Descartes's insistence on the importance
of the mental. However, given our earlier discussion of the difficulties
we are currently having in formulating a satisfactory theory of consciousness, this emphasis may be less helpful than its intuitive appeal
suggests. Furthermore, the exclusive emphasis on consciousness raises
puzzles that Locke could not have anticipated. Cases involving split-
brain individuals have raised the possibility that two distinct centers of
consciousness may function under certain experimental conditions.
On Locke's theory, this would seem to entail that these individuals
occasionally develop two distinct Selves. Under normal circumstances,
then, when the two hemispheres are able to communicate, would we
say that the two Selves disappear and a third, unified Self reappears? It
may be that the split-brain phenomena point to the possibility that we
should not think of Self as a unified thing at all. Perhaps it would be
more useful to think of Self as a series of capacities that sometimes
function as a harmonious whole and other times become fragmented
and disjointed.

One of the classic objections to Locke's theory (and to more recent
versions of the Psychological theory that place even more stress on
memory) is that there is a great deal of our experience, both past and
present, that is lost to consciousness (or memory). That fact seems to
make a psychological notion of even the normal Self fragmented and
full of gaps, rather than a unified and enduring sort of thing.

Locke was quite aware of this possible objection, and it seems not
to have bothered him. He appears to suggest that the fact that consciousness can lose portions of one's past has a parallel in the relation
between the conscious Self and the body. If we lose a finger, it simply
ceases to be part of the Self in a relatively unproblematic way. He
apparently believed that similar losses in the psychological realm
should be equally unproblematic. Keep in mind that he did not
equate Self with one enduring *substance*. He apparently saw it as a
genuinely psychological phenomenon and explained it entirely in
terms of the first-person perspective. As such, it should not be
expected to retain *every* aspect of one's life. Perhaps anticipating this
sort of objection, Locke makes use of his distinction between the Self

(or 'Person'), on the one hand, and the *man*, on the other hand. The latter is the enduring substance and is treated from the third-person, or public, point of view.

It is difficult to be very precise about Locke's method. He is generally characterized as an *empiricist*—that is, a philosopher who limits his theories to claims that can be supported by evidence found in *experience*. But, in fact, some of Locke's views go well beyond what experience reveals—for example, his assumptions about the existence of substances. He was, in addition, concerned to give an account of the meaning of certain terms associated with Self. So one might say that his method combines some empiricism, some speculation, and an early version of language analysis. Do you think that this combination of methods has distorted the issue of the nature of Self and generated a problematic theory, or do you think that his method provides a reasonable approach to the nature of Self?

Since Locke takes consciousness to be constitutive of Self, his theory could perhaps be made consistent with any theory of mind that can provide a plausible theory of consciousness. Behaviorism might be the only theory that is not compatible with Locke's account. On some versions of Functionalism it would be possible for a system to have a mind without being conscious, so some minded systems might lack the sort of Self that Locke describes. Although Locke's view favors Dualism (he speaks of both mental and physical substances), his insistence on detaching consciousness from any necessary link to mental substance seems to make his theory especially compatible with Property Dualism.

More recently, philosopher Derek Parfit, in his book, *Reasons and Persons*, offers a revised version of Locke's theory (which he characterizes as claiming that "experience-memory provides the criterion of personal identity"[3]). On Parfit's account, the Psychological theory won't be sufficient by itself, but it should constitute at least part of an adequate theory of Self. Parfit's account of the psychological element in the Self includes memory, but this portion of Self does not require that memory recall every aspect of one's life (no reasonable theory could), but rather that there be "continuity of memory." By that Parfit means that today one can remember at least some of yesterday, and yesterday one could remember at least some of the day before, and the day before one could remember at least some of the previous day, and so on. Some content will undoubtedly be lost, but the continuity from day to day will be an important contributor to Personal Identity. In addition to memory, he notes that there needs to be a direct connection

---

3. Derek Parfit, *Reasons and Persons* (Oxford: Clarendon Press, 1984), p. 205.

between other psychological events, for example between an intention and the later act that completes it. He also emphasizes the role of enduring beliefs and desires (p. 205). What Parfit proposes for the psychological element in his theory of Self is a series of overlapping chains of connected psychological events. Gaps will not be troublesome, particularly when other elements are later added.

Amnesic syndrome (see box) raises some problems for a theory of self that would rely exclusively on memory.

Amnesic Syndrome: Amnesic syndrome can be caused by surgery to alleviate epilepsy, by chronic alcoholism (then usually referred to as "Korsakov Syndrome"), by encephalitis, and so forth. It results in an inability to form new memories. A person with amnesic syndrome can usually remember events that occurred before the onset of the disease, and often retains normal intelligence and previously learned skills, including language use and social skills. But he or she is unable to recall what happened just moments ago. The individual can even learn new skills but then has no memory of having learned them. A person with amnesic syndrome can speak with a friend or relative, and if that person leaves the room for just a few moments, the amnesic person has no memory of having just spoken with them. The fact that memory of much earlier events appears to remain intact while the ability to lay down new memories is lost, suggests that it is likely that there are *at least* two distinguishable memory systems (although they probably work in tandem under normal circumstances).[4]

Bundle Theory of Self

In the mid-18th century, philosopher David Hume approached the problem of Self using a quite distinctive method. Although like Locke he was an *empiricist*, his version of empiricism was much more rigorous than Locke's. As an empiricist, his general approach to any philosophical issue was to look to experience to see what evidence he could find to support one view or another. But his view of *experience* was very precise: It consists of two types of phenomena: *impressions* (that is, sensory perceptions or passions) and *ideas* ("faded" versions of impressions, as in imagination or memory). Everything we can know, he argued,

4. See Lawrence Weiskrantz, *Consciousness Lost and Found*, pp. 8–9, 100–26; also "Neurophysiology of Vision and Memory," in Marcel and Bisiach, eds., *Consciousness in Contemporary Science.*

should be grounded in one of these phenomena. His question about Self, then, amounted to the question of whether or not we have any impression, and thereby any idea of Self. Put more simply, do we have any *perception* of the Self? His answer:

> There are some philosophers, who imagine we are every moment intimately conscious of what we call our SELF; that we feel its existence and its continuance in existence; and are certain, beyond the evidence of a demonstration, both of its perfect identity and simplicity. . . . Unluckily all these positive assertions are contrary to that very experience, which is pleaded for them, nor have we any idea of *self*, after the manner it is here explain'd. For from what impression cou'd this idea be deriv'd? . . . It must be some one impression, that gives rise to every real idea. But self or person is not any one impression, but that to which our several impressions and ideas are suppos'd to have a reference. If any impression gives rise to the idea of self, that impression must continue invariably the same, thro' the whole course of our lives; since self is suppos'd to exist after that manner. But there is no impression constant and invariable. . . . passions and sensations succeed each other, and never all exist at the same time. It cannot, therefore, be from any of these impressions, or from any other, that the idea of self is deriv'd; and consequently there is no such idea.[5]

Notice that Hume is looking for an impression of something that is *enduring* and unified. This is what he fails to find. So he denies in effect that the sort of Self that Descartes defended can be supported by any evidence from our experience.

> . . . when I enter most intimately into what I call *myself*, I always stumble on some particular perception or other, of heat or cold, light or shade, love or hatred, pain or pleasure. I never can catch *myself* at any time without a perception, and never can observe any thing but the perception (p. 252).

Hume goes on to say that the notion of a simple, *enduring* Self (of the sort that Descartes defended) is a fiction. But then what is it that the term 'Self' refers to? Hume claims, on the basis of his reflection on his experience, that we can only be referring to collections of perceptions, since that is all that experience ever finds. He notes that we often treat

5. *Treatise of Human Nature*, Book I, Part 4, Section 6; Selby-Bigge, ed. (Oxford: Oxford University Press, 1739/1973), pp. 251–2.

things that are variable or serial as if they were one—an acorn that becomes an oak tree, or a boat that has had various of its parts replaced, are still treated as if they were the same objects. From his point of view, all that experience can show us is that the human person is a series of constantly changing perceptions. But our imaginations have a tendency to lump the series of impressions together as if they formed one thing, a Self. He suggests that memory aids in this by noting resemblances among earlier perceptions and later ideas. But memory alone will not be enough to account for an enduring Self, because we forget a great deal of what we have experienced. However, he believes that memory gives us a notion of the causal relations among our perceptions, allowing us to extend our notion of Self beyond what memory can recall. His account at this point sounds almost like the Functionalist theory of mind: "the true idea of the human mind, is to consider it as a system of different perceptions . . . which are link'd together by the relation of cause and effect, and mutually produce, destroy, influence, and modify each other. . . . memory does not so much *produce* as *discover* personal identity, by shewing us the relation of cause and effect among our different perceptions" (pp. 261–2).

But in an Appendix to the book, Hume notes that even his own theory is filled with problems and that he has no idea how to fix it. Having argued that experience gives us no evidence of an enduring, substantial Self, that all we find are distinct perceptions, he is left with the problem of explaining how those distinct perceptions are supposed to form one unified Self. His earlier suggestion—that we recognize the causal relations among them (for example, impressions cause ideas, and so on) and thereby discover their unity—is inconsistent with other claims he has made about causality.

> But having thus loosen'd all our particular perceptions [i.e., shown them to be distinct existences], when I proceed to explain the principle of connexion, which binds them together, and makes us attribute to them a real simplicity and identity; I am sensible, that my account is very defective. . . . If perceptions are distinct existences, they form a whole only by being connected together. But no connexions among distinct existences are ever discoverable by human understanding. We only *feel* a connexion or determination of the thought, to pass from one object to another (p. 635).

His central concern is undoubtedly with his earlier appeal to the causal connection supposedly discoverable among perceptions. Hume had argued elsewhere in the *Treatise* that we have no direct experience of the relation of *necessary* connection that would be essential to causal relations. The most that our impressions show us is that things can be related by spatial and temporal togetherness, by one succeeding another, or by two (or more) always being experienced together. But experience fails to give us a perception of any *necessary* connection between two things; and this alone, he believes, could guarantee a genuine causal connection between them. If that is right, and clearly Hume believes that it is, then he cannot justify his claim that the causal connections among our perceptions account for our treating them as if they are unified into a Self. Experience does not show us causal connections between them. So at best, the Self is experienced as a "bundle" of perceptions. Hume does, however, seem to allow for some version of a *Subject* of experience (as distinguished from an enduring, unified Self)—a version he does not make explicit, but it will be elaborated much later by another philosopher in the empirical tradition, William James.

Strengths and Weaknesses of the Bundle Theory of Self

One of the strengths of Hume's approach is its caution, its avoidance of speculation. It is always desirable to look for *evidence* that supports the view one is proposing. And for Hume the only reliable place to look for that evidence is in experience. Another strength of his view is that it highlights the difficulties one faces when appealing to *introspection* for one's theory of Self. The stark differences between what Descartes claimed to find when he introspected, and what Hume claimed to find, surely suggest at the very least that introspection alone is not likely to provide the theory of Self that we seek. If it could, both Descartes and Hume should have found the same data when they introspected. Obviously they did not.

On the other hand, Hume himself notes some of the problems with his view. He needs to appeal to a recognition of real causal relations among our impressions and ideas, but such an appeal is inconsistent with the rest of his empiricist philosophy. Whether or not Hume's characterization of the enduring Self as a fiction is tenable remains an open question. Whatever its merits, the view is still current among some philosophers and has not been decisively refuted.

One final point on Hume: Recall my suggestion that you pay close attention to method. Hume's conclusions are based very explicitly on his views about the nature and limits of experience, and his insistence that we cannot know anything beyond what we find in that experience.

It may surprise you to know that some two thousand years before Hume proposed his Bundle theory of self, Buddha proposed a similar view. His method, too, was like Hume's. Buddha argued that there is simply no evidence for the existence of an enduring, unified Self. He believed that human beings consist of five elements: the body, sensations and feelings, cognitions, character traits and dispositions, and consciousness. Notice that these five elements are the sorts of things that one seems to find in experience. And although there are some noticeable similarities with Hume's basic aspects of experience (perceptions, passions, ideas), Buddha's approach is not quite so radical as Hume's. The body, for example, seems to Buddha to be clearly available to experience. Unlike Hume, he was not heir to Descartes's cautions about unquestioned acceptance of the existence of the physical world. But notice, too, that Buddha does not include in the five elements anything that could be construed as a permanent soul or Self. He sees these elements of the human being as always changing—a claim that has considerable plausibility. Our sensations, feelings, consciousness, dispositions, even our body—all do change almost constantly. For Buddha, the only aspect of a human being that survives death is our "moral identity," but that is not some unified or permanent thing. It is a set of qualities that we accumulate during our lives. And he sees no problem with assuming that these qualities could be reincarnated in another body after our death. So the Bundle theory of Self is a very old view indeed.[6]

Kant's Transcendental Self

The 18th-century philosopher Immanuel Kant took issue with Hume's method, arguing that it was too narrow. On Kant's view, Hume had neglected the question of what makes experience itself *possible*. (Questions relating to the *possibility* of something—in this case the possibility of experience—are referred to as *transcendental questions*.) From Kant's point of view, the Self is simply one of the preconditions for the very possibility of experience, so he didn't find it surprising that Hume failed to find the Self as one of the contents of experience.

> This consciousness of oneself is merely empirical and always mutable; it can give us no constant or enduring self in this flow of inner appearances. . . . But what is to be presented *necessarily* as numerically identical cannot be thought as such through empirical data. A condition that is to validate such a transcendental

6. For additional information on Buddhist views, see Damien Keown, *Buddhism* (Oxford: Oxford University Press, 1996) for a brief and nontechnical discussion; for a more comprehensive account, see David E. Cooper, *World Philosophies* (Oxford: Blackwell, 1996).

presupposition must be one that precedes all experience and that makes experience itself possible.

Now there can take place in us no cognitions, and no connection and unity of cognitions among one another, without that unity of consciousness which precedes all data of intuitions, and by reference to which all presentation of objects is alone possible.[7]

Strengths and Weaknesses of Kant's Transcendental Self

This precondition for the very possibility of all experience is what some philosophers have called 'Self', the unifier of experience and the source of continuing identity through time. Given Kant's view, this Transcendental Self would be "systematically elusive." That is to say, any effort to find it in experience must necessarily *use* it, and therefore never find it. This transcendental notion of the Self lacks most of the rich content that one normally looks for in a theory of Self. Nonetheless, if Kant's methodological point is right, it would seem that such a Self would not be simply a fiction.

Self as (at Least) the Body

Few philosophers argue that the Self is nothing more than the body. However, some have argued that the body is at least a necessary, if not sufficient, condition for Selfhood. Bernard Williams, for example, argues vigorously for the importance of recognizing the role that the body plays in one's sense of oneself. He supports his claim by appealing to our intuitions by way of a thought experiment (see box on page 172).

Williams uses a thought experiment to test our intuitions about what we count as Self. A simplified version of his story goes like this: Suppose that you were told that tomorrow you were going to be tortured. But you were also told that before the torture another procedure would be performed that would wipe out all your memories and give you a different set of memories, perhaps a set belonging to a different person (enter the science fiction portion of the story). The procedure could even change aspects of your character. In other words, before your torture your *psychological* states that have sometimes been identified with Self would be erased and exchanged for someone else's. Would you then stop worrying about tomorrow's torture, deciding that it would be someone else's problem—because tomorrow's body would have someone else's psychological states and therefore belong to someone else—or would

7. *Critique of Pure Reason*, Werner S. Pluhar, trans. (Indianapolis: Hackett, 1996), A 107, p. 158.

> **Note on Terminology:** A *thought experiment* usually employs a bit of science fiction. It proposes a story that is intended to test the limits of conceivability for some situation. For example, if I were to ask you to imagine that you had discovered, in some foreign environment, a substance that was pink, tasted like strawberry ice cream, but was warm and had the texture of sand, would you say that it was ice cream? In other words, what conditions absolutely must be fulfilled in order to apply the concept *ice cream*? Must it be cold? Must it be relatively smooth? How many of its features are negotiable? Thought experiments can sound far-fetched, but their purpose is not to describe some empirical possibility but rather to see how far one can alter a familiar situation and still have the normal concept(s) apply — or how far one must alter things before the normal concept(s) no longer apply.

you still dread the torture — because it would still be *your body*, and to that extent, part of *your Self*?

He is relying, of course, on the expectation that your answer will be that you would still dread the torture, and that the change in memories and character traits would not eliminate that dread. Williams concludes from this thought experiment that our concept of Self includes the body as a necessary element. He says,

> The problem just is that through every step of his predictions I seem able to follow him successfully. And if I reflect on whether what he has said gives me grounds for fearing that I shall be tortured, I could consider that behind my fears lies some principle such as this: that my undergoing physical pain in the future is not excluded by any psychological state I may be in at the time, with the platitudinous exception of those psychological states which in themselves exclude experiencing pain, notably (if it is a psychological state) unconsciousness.[8]

For Williams the fact that we are likely to dread some future pain to our bodies, in spite of any changes in our psychological states, is evidence that a purely psychological theory of Self cannot be adequate. Our bodies are a primary center of concern to us.

One might think that theorists who focus exclusively on psychological facts in their account of the Self or Person are approaching the issue

---

8. "The Self and the Future," in *Problems of the Self* (Cambridge: Cambridge University Press, 1973), p. 53.

from the first-person point of view. That is to say, they are concerned with what *I* take to constitute *my* Self. And from that first-person point of view, there may seem to be something essential about my consciousness or other psychological states. And it may seem that theorists who approach the issue primarily from the third-person point of view are likely to place less emphasis on one's conscious experiences and more on physical continuity of the body. Williams's view seems to contradict this simple division. His defense of the important role played by one's body appeals to first-person considerations, to one's fear or dread of the expected torture.

> **Asomatognosias:** Asomatognosias is a deficit that comprises several syndromes relating to one's knowledge of one's own body. In one syndrome, *autotopagnosia*, a person is unable to name her own body parts or is unable to point to them when they are named. In another, called *anosognosia*, the person fails to recognize some bodily deficit, like blindness or paralysis. The person literally does not know that she is blind or paralyzed, and denies it when asked about the inability to move an arm or leg. In some cases, the person can even deny that the limb belongs to her.[9] Neurologist Antonio Damasio adds, "Patients with anosognosia offer us a view of a mind deprived of the possibility of sensing *current* body state, especially as it concerns background feeling. I suggest that these patients' self, unable to plot current body signals on the ground reference of the body, is no longer integral. Knowledge about personal identity is still available and retrievable in language form: anosognosics remember who they are, where they live and worked, who the people close to them are. But that wealth of information cannot be used to reason effectively on the current personal and social state."[10]

The method of using thought experiments has come under some criticism. For some theorists, imaginary cases prove nothing about real situations. Arguments of this sort have been raised particularly against thought experiments involving zombies. The main point of these arguments is that we cannot conclude much with certainty based on what we can or cannot happen to imagine. However, Williams's story may

---

9. See J. L. Bermudez, A. Marcel, and N. Eilan, eds., *The Body and the Self* (Cambridge, MA: MIT/Bradford, 1995), p. 205 *ff.*; and Weiskrantz, p. 186 *ff.*

10. Antonio Damasio, *Descartes' Error. Emotion, Reason, and the Human Brain* (New York: Putnam, 1994), pp. 154–5.

seem to be closer to what one can imagine rather readily. We do seem to feel that our bodies are indeed a special element in who we are. Still, the concern remains that thought experiments may reveal little more than our long-standing—and perhaps quite limited and mistaken— habits of thought.

Strengths and Weaknesses of the Theory of Self as Body

If Williams is right, and our bodies form some essential aspect of the Self, the view does at least confirm our habit of seeing ourselves as intimately connected with our bodies. And although our bodies do indeed change over time, we don't seem to face Hume's problem of trying to find something that will relate a series of "distinct existences" to one another. While portions of our bodies change, other portions continue on. That is to say, we don't experience the body as a series of distinct existences that must somehow be linked together by something else. We experience it as a continuing and slowly changing entity. Furthermore, if Williams is right, his view would explain why we consider our sexual identity and our physical skills to be so much a part of our Selves.

One standard sort of objection to a view like Williams's goes like this: Given the availability of organ transplants and prosthetic devices (artificial limbs), how many organs could be transplanted into a person, and how many limbs replaced, before that person stopped being the Self that he had been? In other words, if the body is essential to Self, is there any part of it that cannot be replaced without also replacing the Self? One obvious attempt at an answer to the last question is to say that the brain cannot be replaced. And this suggestion has led to another whole series of thought experiments.

Imagine that you and a person of the opposite sex are in a terrible automobile accident. Your head is crushed beyond repair; your companion's head is fine, but his or her body is destroyed. Medical emergency teams manage to save your body and the head of your companion, and by the miracles of future medicine they join the two and form a living, healthy human being. Who is that person? Is it you (it has your body with all its skills, sexual apparatus, etc.), or is it your companion (it has his or her brain, memories, cognitive skills, etc.), or is it some third, new person? What kind of answer can be given—and on what grounds? Or is the question unanswerable?

Derek Parfit has argued that some questions about identity are indeed undecidable. By way of an example, he describes a club that has met for some years. Then it ceases to meet. After a few years, some of its former members come together again, call the club by the same name and have the same rules. Is it the *same* club or is it simply one that is similar to the first? Parfit says that if there are no rules in the club's charter specifying either way, the question may simply be unanswerable.[11] Similarly, he believes, in some problematic cases of personal identity (perhaps like the one I described above), there may be no determinate answer to the question of who a person is. Do you think he is right?

Self as Multidimensional

In most of the theories we have discussed so far, the Self has been identified with *one* particular sort of thing—a nonphysical substance, a set of memories, or a bundle of impressions and ideas. But for some theorists the Self cannot be identified with any one type of thing. It is, rather, to be understood as a complex collection of several sorts of elements.

Perhaps the best example of this sort of view can be found in William James's *Principles of Psychology*. There he offers a very broad and multifaceted account of Self.

> *In its widest possible sense*, however, *a man's Self is the sum total of all that he CAN call his*, not only his body and his psychic powers, but his clothes and his house, his wife and children, his ancestors and friends, his reputation and works, his lands and horses, and yacht and bank-account.[12]

Claiming that one's wife and children, along with one's horses and bank accounts, are part of one's Self may raise interesting questions about the extent of male chauvinism in late 19th-century New England. But James goes on to explain that what unites all these things is that they give a man the same emotions. "If they wax and prosper, he feels triumphant; if they dwindle and die away, he feels cast down. . ." (p. 280). Notice the close connection he suggests here between our *feelings* about things and the part they play in relation to our Self. His is easily the richest and most far-reaching account of Self that we have so far encountered.

James divides the "constituents of the Self" into four categories: (1) the *material* Self, (2) the *social* Self, (3) the *spiritual* Self, and (4) the *pure Ego*. The first three of these he counts as elements in the "empirical" Self. It seems that these are the aspects of the Self that are easily discernible in experience.

11. *Reasons and Persons*, p. 213.

12. William James, *Principles of Psychology* (Cambridge, MA: Harvard University Press, 1981/1890), p. 279.

He describes the *material* Self as including the body (which he characterizes as the "innermost part of the material self"), the clothes, one's immediate family, one's home. In ordinary conversation we would normally refer to such things as "mine" rather than as "me." But James was especially concerned to give *relations* their full due in his philosophy. He believed that philosophers had for too long ignored the important role played by relations in constituting the nature of things. He believed that experience is a *stream* of related happenings rather than a series of isolated bits of things (as Hume seemed to suggest). So, as he looked to his experience for some insights into the nature of Self, he noted all the relations that on his view contribute to the reality of Self. Unlike Descartes, he did not look for one unified, enduring substance; unlike Locke, he did not limit his considerations to psychological events; and unlike Hume, he did not look for one *distinct* perception that could be the source of our idea of Self. Instead, he elaborated on all the relations that he took to be constitutive of his experience of Self.

His account of the *social* Self again emphasizes relatedness. He characterizes this aspect of the Self as

> the recognition which he gets from his mates. . . . *a man has as many social selves as there are individuals who recognize him* and carry an image of him in their mind. . . . we may practically say that he has as many different social selves as there are distinct *groups* of persons about whose opinion he cares. . . . From this there results what practically is a division of the man into several selves; and this may be a discordant splitting, as where one is afraid to let one set of his acquaintances know him as he is elsewhere; or it may be a perfectly harmonious division of labor. . . (pp. 281–2).

Needless to say, neither James's material Self nor his social Self coincide with the notion of an enduring Personal Identity that some other theorists have been concerned with. They will not do, either, to account for Subjectivity or for moral agency, although James describes in some detail how each can lead to morally good or morally bad attitudes and behavior. Still, something more is needed if his account of Self is going to answer to some of the traditional views of what is essential to a Self. He approaches those views in his next two categories. And both of those categories emphasize another aspect of James's philosophy. As a Pragmatist, James put a good deal of emphasis on the importance of *action*. He believed that we come to know things best not simply by looking at them, but by interacting with them.

His third category of the empirical Self, the *spiritual* Self, makes this aspect of his philosophy explicit. The *spiritual* Self is the *active* knower.

> By the Spiritual Self, . . . I mean a man's inner or subjective being, his psychic faculties or dispositions, taken concretely; . . . our considering the spiritual self . . . is the result of our abandoning the outward-looking point of view [of the material and social Self], and of our having become able to think of subjectivity as such, *to think ourselves as thinkers.* [James asks,] ". . . *what is this self of all the other selves?*" . . . the *active* element in all consciousness; . . . It is what welcomes or rejects. It presides over the perception of sensations, and by giving or withholding its assent it influences the movements they tend to arouse. It is the home of interest, . . . It is the source of effort and attention, and the place from which appear to emanate the fiats of the will (pp. 283–5).

James insists that the spiritual Self is not purely cognitive; it is not a mere bundle of perceptions or memories; it is an experienced center of active engagement with its world, a center of interest, a source of choices and preferences. Once again, the theme of relatedness appears. The spiritual Self is not a self-contained ego but is that aspect of Self that is actively related to its world.

The fourth and final category of Self that James discusses is perhaps his most famous: the Pure Ego. He says that this is the "pure principle of personal identity" (p. 314). It is, he suggests, an aspect of the Self with which we are intimately familiar, recognizing it as belonging to us in a way that no other thing does. In an apparently paradoxical claim, he says, "The passing Thought then seems to be the Thinker; . . ." (p. 324). He goes on to say that what we know with such "warmth and intimacy" is not simply the present thought, but also the past thoughts that it "appropriates" to itself. He uses the metaphor of a herdsman gathering up and branding as his own any of those past thoughts that share with the present one the same feeling of warmth and intimacy. This, he believes, gives temporal continuity to our sense of Personal Identity. While this might sound much like a version of Locke's Psychological Self, James is careful to give our awareness of the body a special place. "*Resemblance among the parts of a continuum of feelings* (especially bodily feelings) experienced along with things widely different in all other regards, *thus constitutes the real and verifiable 'personal identity' which we feel*" (p. 319).

So we string together our past experiences (including bodily sensations) not by attributing them to some substance, and not simply by memory, but also by their feeling of warmth and intimacy, familiarity.

Notice that James is here speaking from the first-person point of view. His method is largely descriptive and clearly belongs to the same empiricist tradition that Locke and Hume followed. But there are several differences between their version of empiricism and that of James. He did not begin with distinct substances or distinct impressions. As I noted earlier, on his view the experienced relations that things have are as important in defining them as are any other aspects. The other important difference, especially in contrast to Hume's empiricism, is his great emphasis on the importance of the body. This is probably a result of several things. Unlike Hume, James was trained as a medical doctor and was also a practicing psychologist. He was, as Hume could not have been, greatly influenced by Charles Darwin's theory of evolution. All of these factors may well have contributed to James's emphasis on bodily considerations in his account of Self.

James's emphasis on the Pure Ego as the present thought is clearly intended to account for our sense of Subjectivity, and he also intended it as an account of Personal Identity. But he does not see the latter as one unified enduring entity. Rather, as it was for Locke and Hume, it is a psychological reality.

Strengths and Weaknesses of the Multidimensional View of Self

One obvious advantage of James's theory is its lack of questionable metaphysical speculations. He makes no claims about substances, physical or mental, and no claim about the need for a transcendental ego that is inaccessible to experience. In addition, his view takes account of the importance of feeling as well as cognition, body as well as thought, in our understanding of ourselves.

Such a view of Self, even including the three empirical elements (material, social, and spiritual) does not provide a foundation for immortality as Descartes's theory does. His account obviously includes one's social relations of various sorts, but for some philosophers these seem to be somewhat extraneous to what is at the heart of Self. As we shall see, for other philosophers these social relations are the very core of the matter.

Self as Social Construct

Most of the earlier theories of Self that we have discussed—the Nonphysical, the Psychological, and the Bundle theories—treated it as self-contained. For Descartes, it had no need even of a body. Locke and Hume described it completely in terms of the "internal" experience of the individual. It was not until the late 19th century that James produced a more relational account of the Self. But early in the 20th century another philosopher, George Herbert Mead, pressed the relational view of the Self much further than James had.

Mead begins by insisting that the Self is not a substantive thing of any sort. Rather, he says, it is a *process*. Presumably, he means that it is a developing reality rather than a fixed and enduring one. Mead picks up on James's category of the *social* Self and elaborates it in quite a different way from the one James discussed. For Mead, the Self is literally constituted by its interactions with others. At first, as a child one takes part in the give and take of "gestures" of a certain sort. Gradually this develops into *play*, where one is again exchanging bits of behavior with others. And lastly, one learns to participate in *games* that have rules. All of this involves some degree of role-playing. It also involves learning what responses are expected in certain situations, and learning how to elicit those responses both in oneself and in others. In all of this Mead sees a gradual incorporation of a set of attitudes arising from one's interactions with others. This set of attitudes comes to constitute what Mead calls the *"me."* He says, "It is the social process itself that is responsible for the appearance of the self; it is not there as a self apart from this type of experience."[13] And later, "one has to be a member of a community to be a self" (p. 162). What is it that unifies the Self amid all these social interactions? He explains:

> What goes to make up the organized self is the organization of the attitudes which are common to the group. A person is a personality because he belongs to a community, because he takes over the institutions of that community into his own conduct. He takes its language as a medium by which he gets his personality, and then through a process of taking the different roles that all the others furnish he comes to get the attitude of the members of the community. Such, in a certain sense, is the structure of a man's personality (p. 162).

As a consequence of this process, society comes to exercise a degree of "control over conduct" of its members. This mention of "control over conduct" should remind you of what the early Behaviorists, Watson and Skinner, stated as the goals of Behaviorist psychology—prediction and control of behavior. Mead, too, is operating within a framework of Behaviorism.

13. "The Self," in *Mind, Self, and Society*, vol. 1 (Chicago: University of Chicago Press, 1934), p. 142.

In spite of his emphasis on the public aspect of the Self, Mead is careful to distinguish it from the body. Although the body is essential to a Self, he says that body and Self can still be distinguished. The Self is constructed by the body's relation to and interaction with its social environment. Furthermore, and a bit more surprising given Mead's emphasis on the social, he sees the Self as "essentially a cognitive rather than an emotional phenomenon" (p. 173). One might have expected him to give great importance to our emotional responses to one another—love, fear, anger, jealousy, sympathy. These would seem to be among our first responses to our social environment, even before language emerges. However, Mead sees things differently. The cognitive appears to him to be the formative influence in the development of the social Self.

Having said all this about the Self as a socially constructed "me," Mead then asks about the nature of the "'I' which is aware of the social 'me.' The 'I' is the response of the organism to the attitudes of the others; the 'me' is the organized set of attitudes of others which one himself assumes. . . . The 'I' is his action over against that social situation within his own conduct, . . ." (p. 175). The "I" is also the source of freedom and novelty. This response of the "I" to itself and to its social situation is capable of changing social situations and attitudes. Mead's account of "I" appears to coincide with that aspect of Self that others have termed "Subjectivity."

Putting the "I" and the "me" together, Mead broadens his characterization of the Self: "The self is essentially a social process going on with these two distinguishable phases. If it did not have these two phases there could not be conscious responsibility, and there would be nothing novel in experience" (p. 178). He sees the two phases of the self, 'I' and 'me,' as interdependent. Thus, the Self is partially constituted by its social interactions, but it is also actively reflective on itself and on its social situation—making it not only an essentially social being but also a responsible and sometimes creative agent.

Strengths and Weaknesses of the Theory of Self as Social Construct

It is difficult to characterize Mead's method with any degree of accuracy, due to at least two factors: (1) His writing style is sometimes disorganized, and (2) he rarely offers explicit evidence or argument in support of the claims that he makes.

Nonetheless, there are some important strengths in Mead's view of the Self. He gives full weight to the role of social relations in helping to shape us. We are, after all, born into a culture and language that contribute in essential ways to the development of our identity. We also learn how to behave in that culture through an extended series of interactions with some of its other members. In addition, we learn a great deal about values, motives, goals, appropriate ways to express emotions, and so on, from the people around us. So there is much of value in Mead's account.

On the other hand, Mead is intent on emphasizing the essential role of society in shaping the Self. As he says, "The self is not something that exists first and then enters into relationship with others, but it is, so to speak, an eddy in the social current and so still a part of the current" (p. 182). Nonetheless, he clearly believes that something more is needed if one is to have an account of freedom, responsibility, and creativity, so he introduces a notion of "I," with no explanation of its origin or nature. Its primary justification seems to be that its presence solves a problem for Mead's theory. However, the elements in a theory should have some greater degree of justification than the mere fact that they help to disarm objections to the theory.

A more recent version of the Social Constructivist view of the Self has been introduced by some feminist thinkers. As I noted at the outset of the discussion of Mead's view, many of the previous theories of Self treated it as an independent, atomistic sort of thing. Some feminists have argued that such a view is not only unrealistic but can be downright damaging. Given the obvious influence on us of culture and language, from our earliest years, it is unrealistic, they say, to ignore their role in shaping us. Furthermore, our relationships with other individuals—parents, siblings, children, other loved ones—surely play decisive roles in our lives. On their view, the evidence suggests that the notion of a Self that is simply given, wholly formed and unchanging, at birth, is at best unrealistic. As a consequence, some recent theorists have argued for a notion of a Reciprocal (or Relational) Self, a Self that arises out of relations of reciprocity.

It is perhaps not surprising that the emphasis on reciprocity has emerged from some feminist thinkers. Traditional roles for women have emphasized the importance of their relationships with others—parents, partner, husband, children. There can be little doubt that such relationships contribute in important ways to who we are.

Yet one finds the same tension here that I mentioned in connection with Mead's view. If I am constructed by my social relations, is there a place for my freedom, my individuality, my capacity to distance myself from my social context? This tension has led other feminist thinkers to look for a somewhat different view of Self that takes account of both social relations and influences, on the one hand, and

individuality and some degree of autonomy, on the other. The issue is
far from resolved.[14]

Narrative Self

The Narrative view of Self has dimensions of both the Psychological
and Social theories of Self, but it adds a distinctive component. This
theory sees the Self as a character in a relatively coherent *story*. The psychological aspect of the Narrative Self involves an individual's awareness of her part in the narrative, but that narrative is not simply spun
out by the lone individual. It opens as the individual begins to recognize some of the roles designated for her by the culture into which she
is born. She learns this through interactions with parents, siblings, and
so forth, and through the stories she is told about kings, queens, and
pirates and good and bad animals. He learns that he is a son, a younger
brother, she learns that she is a daughter, a sister, each expected to
behave in certain ways toward others. Gradually, the individual begins
to make his or her own contributions to the narrative that will give life
some degree of coherent meaning.

In her book, *The Constitution of Selves* (Ithaca: Cornell, 1996), philosopher Marya Schechtman notes that narratives can vary in their
degree of coherence. The less coherent the story becomes, the less we
are able to understand the behavior of the individual who is constructing it. She also notes one important aspect of the Narrative account:
We are not free to spin out any story that we would like. Our story needs
to mesh with the stories that others construct about us. That is, there
must be some reality check on the narrative that each of us weaves. Our
stories interlock with one another. When they don't, we may begin to
lose touch with the social context in which we live — and perhaps to
some extent lose touch with aspects of reality.

Philosopher Alasdair MacIntyre also describes the Narrative Self in
his book, *After Virtue*:

> What the narrative concept of selfhood requires is thus twofold.
> On the one hand, I am what I may justifiably be taken by others
> to be in the course of living out a story that runs from my birth to
> my death. I am the *subject* of history that is my own and no one
> else's, that has its own peculiar meaning. . . . To be the subject of
> a narrative that runs from one's birth to one's death is . . . to be
> accountable for the actions and experiences which compose a

14. For a fuller discussion of some of these issues, see *Feminists Rethink the
Self*, Diana Tietjens Meyers, ed. (Boulder, CO: Westview Press, 1997).

narratable life. . . . [P]ersonal identity is just that identity presupposed by the unity of the character which the unity of a narrative requires. . . . The other aspect of narrative selfhood is correlative: I am not only accountable, I am one who can always ask others for an account, . . . I am part of their story, as they are part of mine. The narrative of any one life is part of an interlocking set of narratives.[15]

The Narrative Self, as described by MacIntyre, clearly includes moral agency as well as the Subjectivity involved in experiencing one's life. This view of Personal Identity includes some degree of unity and coherence, but it does not appear to involve a commitment to an enduring, unchanging substance.

Strengths and Weaknesses of the Narrative Self Theory

The view is appealing in that it takes seriously the role that culture and social relations can play in the development of a Self. The family, country, language, and religion that we are born into are not a matter of our choosing, and they surely make important contributions to who we are. On the other hand, the theory also includes a weaver of the story, perhaps thereby relieving some of the tension that we found in Mead's theory. On the Narrative theory, social relations are given their full due, but the individual makes a unique contribution to narrating her portion of the story in which she is the leading character. It is she who weaves many of the events and experiences into a reasonably coherent whole. It is she who gives them some degree of meaning and value.

Moreover, the view has some advantages over the theory proposed by Hume. Unlike the Bundle theory, the Narrative Self has an ongoing coherence. The fact that some experiences are forgotten is not especially important; they simply may not be required for a reasonable narrative.

The theory discards any claims to be offering a metaphysical account of Self. If one looks to a theory of Self to provide the underpinnings for immortality, the Narrative theory will disappoint. If one wants a theory of an unchanging, permanent Self, one will not find it in the Narrative account. But if one looks for a view that incorporates social relations, memory, coherence, and accountability, then perhaps the Narrative Self is satisfactory.

15. *After Virtue* (South Bend, IN: Notre Dame University Press, 1981), pp. 217–8.

In a recent oral presentation, philosopher Diana Meyers suggested that the Self is perhaps best understood as having a number of different aspects. She mentions the rational Self, the social Self, the relational Self, the divided Self (including unconscious as well as conscious drives and motivations), and the embodied Self (dimensions partially reminiscent of James's view). Each of these manifests itself primarily in a variety of *skills*. And the different aspects are given some degree of unity and coherence by being woven together into one's Narrative Self.

Evolution and the Self

None of the theories of Self that we have so far considered raise the question of the possible evolutionary significance of Self. If we are indeed products of evolution, and if we do possess something of the nature of a Self or Subjectivity, it seems reasonable to ask why evolution selected such a Self.

One very general way to approach the issue can begin with William James's suggestion that the core of the Self (what he calls the "Pure Ego") is the passing momentary thought. Such a present thought would, of course, be essential to the survival of an organism. Without it, the organism would have no information about its present environment, with its possible food source or mates or predators. Without such information, the organism would be unlikely to survive for long. But momentary thoughts by themselves would hardly be enough. The organism needs to be able to remember at least some of its past experiences. Otherwise, every encounter with its environment would be brand new, and therefore would involve a lucky (or unlucky) guess, and wild risk. As James noted, each momentary thought must re-collect to itself some of the past thoughts. Thus, present awareness and some memory of past experiences are minimal requirements for survival.

But more is needed. In addition to a present thought about one's environment, plus a recognition of what is being seen or smelled or heard, an organism needs to be able to relate this information to its own current needs or interests. Without such a capacity, an organism might see food and recognize what it is, but not notice that it relates to its own hunger.

Here we begin to see the basic outlines of a Self or Subject. An organism that can relate incoming information to information about its own bodily states and needs begins to have the minimal requirements for Self or Subjectivity. One other element is needed in order to make this Self *functional*. The organism needs to be able to relate all of this information to its capacity for *action*. It must be able to actively respond to what it sees, recognizes, and relates to its own current needs. Anything less would put the organism in serious jeopardy for survival.

So there are perfectly good evolutionary reasons for the selection of these capacities in living organisms. Notice that they do not require a sophisticated level of what we think of as "self-consciousness" — reflective consciousness on one's own mental states or on oneself as a moral agent. Neither is there any requirement for some kind of unified entity that is unchanging and might be immortal. From an evolutionary point of view, the minimal requirements for any degree of Selfhood or Subjectivity include some cognitive capacities (at least some degree of perception and memory), awareness of one's own bodily needs, and the ability to direct bodily actions in light of these. These minimal requirements can plausibly be seen as providing the foundation on which any richer notions of Personal Identity, moral agency, and the like, could be constructed.[16]

Psychologist Jaak Panksepp also proposes that we consider the evolutionary origins of Self. On Panksepp's view, we should look for the development of self — perhaps a "proto-self" — in the early affective states of organisms as they actively respond to their environments. He says, "I ascribe to the evolutionary view which assumes that the primordial self arises from certain body-linked neurosymbolic brain processes that we share . . . with all other mammals and perhaps a diversity of other creatures as well. . . . I ascribe to the proposition that every moment of our conscious lives is undergirded by feelings, and that if the biological infrastructure of those intrinsic value-signaling systems were destroyed, one's sense of self would degrade."[17] Several important themes emerge from his account: the notion of a Self need not belong exclusively to human beings; the sense of Self is deeply rooted in emotional or affective states; some degree of Selfhood plays a critical role in the survival of a number of types of organisms; and Self is first and foremost an active responder to its environment, rather than a passive spectator of it. Panksepp believes that this early, core Self (or "self-representation") iterates up through higher levels of brain structure as the brain develops, playing its role in higher cognitive functions as it does so. Neuroscientist

16. See the discussion of subjectivity and evolution in S. Cunningham, *Philosophy and the Darwinian Legacy* (Rochester, NY: University of Rochester Press, 1996), pp. 201–10.

17. Jaak Panksepp, "The Periconscious Substrates of Consciousness: Affective States and the Evolutionary Origins of the Self," *Journal of Consciousness Studies*, 5, No. 5/6 (1998), p. 567.

Antonio Damasio argues for a view that is in many respects in agreement with this.[18]

Perhaps it is through the development of these higher levels of brain structure that some organisms eventually develop a sense of Personal Identity and moral agency. Such a view would be consistent with our earlier discussion of the evolution of the mental.

Issues for Discussion

1. Do you think that a theory of Self should explain or justify belief in immortality? Explain your answer.

2. Could a robot have a Self? Explain your reasons.

3. Do you think that William James's emphasis on our experience of relations provides an adequate response to Hume's concerns about his Bundle theory of Self? Explain.

4. What sort of theory of emotions do you think that Mead would be likely to offer? Explain.

5. Do you think that James's view of the "present Thought as the Thinker" is an adequate account of how the Psychological Self could be unified? Explain.

6. How would you resolve the tension between the notion of Self as a social construct and the notion of Self as an autonomous individual? Explain your view.

7. Which *method* seems to be the most reasonable one in constructing a theory of Self—introspection? Behavioral considerations? Examination of the meaning of the word "Self"? Investigation of social influences on indivduals? Some other approach?

8. Do you think that the body is an essential element in the Self? Explain your answer.

9. Does the fallibility of memory, or the possibility of amnesia, make it unlikely that memory is constitutive of Self? Explain your answer.

18. See his books, *Descartes' Error* (New York: Putnam, 1994) and *The Feeling of What Happens* (New York: Harcourt Brace, 1999).

10. To what extent do you think that social factors contribute to the constitution of Self? What implications might such a view have?

11. Which theory of mind do you see as the most promising source for a satisfactory theory of Self? Explain your view.

Suggested Research Projects

a. Read Daniel Dennett's essay, "Where Am I?" in *Brainstorms*. How do you think that Dennett means to answer the title question? Give reasons from his essay for your answer. Do you agree with him?

b. Read Jerome Shaffer's article, "Persons and their Bodies," *Philosophical Review*, 25 (1966): 59–77. What view of Self or person does he defend? What arguments does he offer? Do you think his view is plausible? Explain your answer.

c. Read "Classical Confucian and Contemporary Feminist Perspectives on the Self: Some Parallels and Their Implications," Chapter 4 in *Culture and Self: Philosophical and Religious Perspectives, East and West*, Douglas Allen, ed. (Boulder, CO: Westview Press, 1997). What is the primary parallel that the author sees between certain Confucian and certain feminist views of the Self?

d. What is the Hindu view of the Self? Does it differ from the Buddhist view? If so, how?

e. Read the thought experiment at the beginning of Chapter 10 in Derek Parfit's book, *Reasons and Persons*. How is it connected to issues of Personal Identity?

f. Read the entry on "Dissociation of the Personality," in *The Oxford Companion to the Mind*. Briefly describe the phenomenon—often referred to as "Multiple Personality Disorder." What are some of the main points that the article makes about the phenomenon? What implications might it have for a theory of Self?

g. Read Chapter 5, "The Narrative Self-Constitution View," in Marya Schechtman's book, *The Constitution of Selves* (Ithaca,

NY: Cornell, 1996). What does she mean by the "narrative form"? What are some of its characteristics?

h. Read Chapter 13, "The Reality of Selves," in Daniel Dennett's book, *Consciousness Explained*. What theory of Self do you think he supports? Explain.

i. Read Chapter 2, "The Lost Mariner," in Oliver Sacks's book, *The Man Who Mistook His Wife for a Hat*. What implications does it have for the Narrative theory of Self? For the Bundle theory? For the Psychological theory of Self?

6

Could a Machine Have a Mind?

Recall my earlier comment about the importance of clarifying a question before attempting to answer it. Unless one has a clear understanding of what the question means, proposed answers may turn out to be quite irrelevant to the real issue. So what does the question, "Could a machine have a mind?" really ask?

First, notice that the question is framed in terms of possibilities: *Could* a machine . . . ? The question isn't about your present-day computer, but rather it concerns the possibility in principle that *some* machine might turn out to "have a mind." Second, recall my earlier suggestion that it may be a mistake to think of "mind" as some unified, all-or-nothing sort of thing. Given the evidence of mental dissociations and mental deficits—the possible loss of some mental functions without the loss of all of them—it appears more promising to think of collections of *mental capacities*, *mental processes*, or *mental functions* rather than simply "mind."

Machines and Mechanisms

So far, then, the reformulated question reads, Is it possible in principle for a machine to have mental capacities (functions, processes, etc.)? One more thing needs to be clarified. What exactly counts as a "machine"? It might surprise you to know that some theorists count the human body or the brain as a machine. Descartes, for example, considered the body to be a machine, that is (roughly), a system whose behavior can be explained in terms of the movements of bits of matter. And the 18th-century thinker, Julien de La Mettrie, pushed Descartes's view to the limit and argued that the soul as well as the body must be understood on material, mechanistic principles—that is, as a machine. His book, published in 1748, was titled *Man a Machine*. If either Descartes or La Mettrie is right, then the quick answer to our opening question is clearly yes. For Descartes, the human body is a machine that has a mind—but that mind, of course, is not itself physical. For La Mettrie, on the other hand, the human person, mind and all, is a machine. More recently, Marvin Minsky put it this way: "There is not the slightest reason to doubt that brains are anything other than machines with enormous numbers of parts that work in perfect accord with physical laws."[1] Again, if Minsky is right, then the answer to our original question seems obvious, at least for the Physicalist: Of course brains are machines that are capable of mental functions.

What is it that constitutes something as a "machine"? One common answer is that machines are systems that are controlled completely by physical forces, sometimes described in terms of "matter in motion." The view that everything, including living organisms, is a machine came to be known as a *mechanistic* view. It was generally opposed to the view, sometimes called *vitalism*, that living organisms are radically different from nonliving things in that they are controlled by some internal "vital" force and not simply by the ordinary external physical forces in nature. The philosopher Henri Bergson called this internal force the "*élan vital.*" Such a view is not widely accepted today for at least two reasons: (1) Science has found no evidence of such a vital force, and (2) it has found evidence for the view that the movements of living bodies are caused by chemical-electrical events in the nervous system. This current scientific view doesn't *prove* that living things are best understood as machines, but it does provide a serious challenge to vitalism.

Even if one believes that the body of living organisms is best explained mechanistically, that the brain is a machine, the question with which we began is obviously not asking if human beings are capable of mental function. The puzzle behind the question concerns things like computers and robots. So the reformulated question really asks: *Is it possible in principle for a nonliving system like a computer or robot to be capable of any mental functions (processes, capacities, etc.)?*

Before we consider some possible answers to that question, a couple of preliminary cautions are in order. First, keep in mind that mental functions are not necessarily *conscious* functions. As I noted in the chapter on consciousness, theorists now have evidence that a good deal of our mental functioning goes on at the unconscious level. Second, the theory of mind that one accepts will have some consequences for the type of answer that one will be likely to give. While a Physicalist could accept an affirmative answer to the question (although she need not), some Dualists appear to be committed to a negative answer unless they believe that computers and robots can be united with a nonphysical

1. *The Society of Mind,* p. 288.

substance or have nonphysical properties. The weak form of Property Dualism, which merely argues for nonreducible theories of the mental, and not for a nonphysical type of reality, could give an affirmative answer. A third caution—at the start we shall limit the discussion to *digital, serial* computers. We shall turn to the issue of parallel systems later in the chapter. And finally, keep in mind that it is possible for a system to carry out a mental function without doing so in exactly the same way that a human being would do it. If there is any extraterrestrial intelligence (ETI), it is possible that it functions in a somewhat different way from the way that we do. We would not for that reason deny the very possibility that it could carry out any mental functions.

The question of whether or not computers and the like are capable of mental function is studied by an interdisciplinary field called Artificial Intelligence (AI). The title is not as helpful as it might be. "Artificial" sometimes connotes "not real," as it does when one talks about artificial fur or an artificial fireplace. A more accurate term might be "artifactual," that is, "human-made." Bridges and automobiles are artifacts, but they carry no connotation of being unreal. And as for "intelligence," the term is very broad and probably too vague to lend itself to careful testing. On the other hand, a science of "Artifactual Mental Processing" (AMP) may be a more accurate name, but it is probably also too cumbersome. So I suspect we shall need to stay with "AI," keeping in mind what the terms really intend. I offer one final word of caution: AI comes in at least two varieties, depending on the strength of the claims that it makes. "Weak" AI involves efforts to *mimic* or *simulate* certain mental functions like problem solving, decision making, and so forth, without making any claims about the actual mental competence of the computer. "Strong" AI, by contrast, has as its aim the production of genuine mental functions in the computer.

Symbol-System Theories

The first group of AI theorists we shall consider is committed to the view that if machines have mental functions, they are carried out in a symbol system, generally a language of some sort. The view is sometimes referred to as the "Representations and Rules" theory, sometimes as "Good Old-Fashioned AI" ("GOFAI" for short), sometimes simply as "Classical AI," and more generally as "Symbol-System AI." For simplicity's sake I'll stick with the "Symbol-System" tag most of the time. But it might be helpful first to explain how it came to be called a "Representations and Rules" theory. That title is apt because these AI theories generally require that the system have at least two components: representations or symbols, and rules that govern them.

First, consider the *representations* or *symbols*. They are usually coded in *binary* form, that is in strings of 0s and 1s (or ON and OFF switches). These representations have no intrinsic meaning; they are given an interpretation by programmers. They can be used to represent almost anything—numbers, letters of the alphabet (e.g., in one system, the letter A is coded by the binary string 1000001), ordinary objects, people, and so forth. The codes represent things in a discrete and unambiguous way. Each binary string normally represents just one clearly specified item, with no ambiguity, no fuzziness. Representations are stored at an "address" in the computer's memory. From there they can be retrieved, combined, and manipulated in a variety of ways.

The *rules* of the system dictate the ways in which representations can be combined, manipulated. One common rule takes the form of a conditional: "If such-and-such occurs, then do so-and-so." Rules in these systems are normally rigid, allowing no exceptions unless another rule explicitly notes how that type of exception is to be handled.

This combination of unambiguous, discrete representations governed by rigid rules explains the inflexibility of most Symbol Systems. They are normally unable to handle ambiguous or incomplete input or situations that are not governed by the programmed rules. You have likely encountered some inflexibility in your dealings with computers. One reason is that, in all probability, the computer that you use operates as a Symbol System.

Linguistic Model

Given their inflexibility, why have some AI theorists insisted on using Symbol Systems? One very important reason is that they are *linguistically* structured systems. But that raises at least two questions: (1) In what way are they linguistically structured? (2) Why is it important for an AI system to be linguistically structured? An answer to the first question, at a basic and intuitive level, is that a Symbol System has a series of individual symbols that have been given some meaning—much like words in a language. And the proper relationships among these symbols are dictated by a set of rules—somewhat like the grammar of a language. One cannot simply combine the representations in any random way. The representations in the system are supposed to have an internal structure that is logical and meaningful—like grammatical combinations of words in a language.

But the second question is fundamental: Why must an AI system be *linguistically* structured? For Symbol-System AI theorists, a language-based system provides for certain characteristics that they believe are apparent in our mental processes. Philosopher Jerry Fodor argues for a close connection between thought and language (as Descartes did before him), and he believes that some of the properties that character-ize language also reflect the properties of our thoughts, our mental pro-cesses. Both language and thought have what he calls a "combinatorial" character—a structural capacity to have their elements combined in certain rule-governed ways. As he puts it, "belief states have combinato-rial structure; . . . they are somehow built up out of elements and . . . the intentional object and causal role of each such state depends on what elements it contains and how they are put together."[2]

More particularly, Fodor argues that language and thought share characteristics like *productivity, systematicity,* and *inferential coherence. Productivity* involves the capacity to produce a virtually unlimited num-ber of syntactically structured (i.e., grammatically structured) thoughts or sentences. By *systematicity* Fodor means the characteristic of lan-guage such that if one understands a sentence like "John loves Mary," then one must also understand the sentence, "Mary loves John." That is, there are certain systematic relations among various syntactically structured pieces of language such that the relations among their mean-ings are not random.

One final argument that Fodor offers for insisting on a linguistic model of mental states is that it takes account of the *inferential coher-ence* of those mental states, that is, it accounts for their *logical* relations. For example, if one believes that sugar is sweet and that rain is wet, one can also reasonably infer from that conjunction of truths that one part of the conjunction—that sugar is sweet—is true. (In slightly more for-mal notation, If *p and q* is true, then *p* must also be true—where *p* and *q* stand for any proposition you might substitute.) His point is that our thoughts (like our language) are normally related by certain rules of logic; they are not entirely random and unconnected. These inferential relations need to appear, he says, in any adequate theory of mental function. And these logical relations, along with productivity and syste-maticity, are characteristics of a *linguistically structured* system. Thus, any attempt to mimic mental function, or to produce it, in an artificial system, would on this account require a Symbol System—a system of representations and rules.

2. Jerry Fodor, *Psychosemantics* (Cambridge, MA: MIT/Bradford, 1987), p. 147.

A Symbol-based system is neat—there is no room for ambiguity since the meaning of each representation is explicitly specified. It is ordered and predictable—the relations among the binary representations are specified by programmed rules. Furthermore, such a system is able to duplicate many of the features of language that appear to be central to *logically structured* mental processes. Finally, it is widely agreed that representations do indeed form an essential aspect of mental states. Recall the description of intentionality—the characteristic of mental states in virtue of which they are *about* something. They achieve this "aboutness" by means of representations. The role of explicit *rules* is, as we shall see, more controversial.

Supporters of a linguistic model for the mental, like Jerry Fodor, argue that we operate with a neurally instantiated language system that he calls a "Language of Thought" (LOT). It is not a language to which we have conscious access, but it provides the linguistic structure that allows us to learn natural human languages like English or Arabic. It is also the system in which our unconscious computational processes are carried out.

Hemispherectomy: Hemispherectomy is a surgical procedure in which one hemisphere of the brain is removed, usually because of serious disease. If the surgery is performed on the left hemisphere (generally the center for language) before the patient is two years old, the right hemisphere usually takes over the language capability. However, in an older individual, a hemispherectomy impairs language to some degree, and by the age of twelve or thirteen the surgery often results in permanent aphasia.[3] It seems, then, that the brain comes programmed in some way to learn language. And while that "program" is normally in the left hemisphere, if the surgical procedure is done early enough in the individual's development, the other hemisphere is usually able to replace that language-learning capacity. Subjects who undergo hemispherectomy do, however, sometimes have other deficits, for example, in motor control on the side opposite the missing hemisphere.

On Fodor's view, and the view of many Symbol-System AI theorists, since our thoughts and our mental processes appear to share these features of language, they therefore need to be modeled in a linguistically structured system. This, of course, is consistent with the view that the

3. See Michael Corballis, *The Lopsided Ape*, p. 288.

computer provides a good model for the mind. Fodor has been quite explicit on this point: "The claim that the mind has the architecture of a Classical computer is not a metaphor but a literal empirical hypothesis."[4]

This view is also consistent with a Functionalist theory of mind. Recall that the Functionalist (in particular, the Machine Functionalist) argues that the physical makeup of a system is not relevant to the question of whether or not it can have mental capacities. The issue is not what the system is made of, but what the system can do. If it can carry out certain types of *functions*, then it can count as having mental capacities. The decisive issue, of course, revolves around what sort of functions the system must be able to carry out. For Fodor and many supporters of Symbol-System AI, the relevant functions are essentially linguistically structured logical functions—what philosophers for many years have referred to as "reasoning."

Philosopher William Bechtel and psychologist Adele Abrahamsen note that "[t]he idea that intelligent cognitive processes are essentially processes of logical reasoning has a long history, captured in the long-held view that the rules of logic constitute rules of thought."[5] They go on to point to various figures in the history of modern philosophy— Thomas Hobbes, Gottfried Leibniz, and others—who have advocated a view of thinking as a kind of logical manipulation of ideas. If these philosophers were right, and logical reasoning is the essence of mental function, then perhaps Symbol-System AI is on the right track. But as we shall see, some theorists, including Bechtel and Abrahamsen, suggest that this emphasis on logical inference may not provide the most plausible way to model our mental processes.

Computer Capabilities

Clearly the computer is capable of performing certain logical and mathematical operations. In fact, it is commonly thought to be quite superior to most of us in its problem-solving capacities in limited domains like logic and math. Philosopher Jack Copeland reports that a computer was able to prove thirty-eight of the first fifty-two logic theorems in *Principia Mathematica*, a scholarly book about logic published by Bertrand Russell and Alfred North Whitehead in 1910.[6] Copeland

---

4. Jerry Fodor and Zenon Pylyshyn, "Connectionism and Cognitive Architecture: A Critical Analysis," *Cognition*, 28 (1988), footnote 35, p. 62.

5. W. Bechtel and A. Abrahamsen, *Connectionism and the Mind* (Cambridge: Blackwell, 1991), p. 10.

6. Copeland, *Artificial Intelligence* (Cambridge: Blackwell, 1993), p. 7.

also notes, contrary to what you might think, that in certain circumstances a computer can "exhibit more intelligence than the person who programs it" (p. 22). He gives the example of a program for playing checkers; it learned through practice to improve its performance and eventually beat the man who created it, Arthur Samuel. One might object that playing a good game of checkers is not exactly the same thing as being intelligent. But the program at least seemed to learn from its mistakes, and that should count for something. In fact, as you undoubtedly know, some computers (e.g., IBM's "Deep Blue") play a very respectable game of chess—a feat that has traditionally been associated with a fairly high degree of intelligence. Furthermore, some computers exhibit considerable competence in other limited domains like diagnosing certain illnesses, analyzing chemical compounds, or landing airplanes. These capacities all bear some resemblance to the use of information in what we usually consider *reasoning*.

Note that we also speak of computers, even PCs, as having *memory*. They can take in data, store it, and retrieve it on command. Computer memory is, in fact, considerably more powerful and reliable than the memory of most humans. However, as we shall see later, it also lacks some desirable features that human memory has.

In spite of all this, some critics ask if these capabilities—problem solving in logic or math, game playing, memory, and so on—are enough to justify the claim that such computers are intelligent systems. In answering this question, one needs to keep in mind the fact that philosophers are really interested in two quite different sorts of questions in connection with the intelligence of AI systems. On the one hand, they ask if a particular type of system—for example, a Symbol-based system—is capable of performing certain functions that have traditionally been seen as intelligent—solving logic problems or playing chess. The answer to this question clearly appears to be affirmative; some computers can indeed perform some of these functions exceedingly well. On the other hand, philosophers also ask if these systems provide plausible models for *human* mental functions. It is here that opinions diverge sharply. One of the problematic areas concerns the limited domains within which AI systems work. They can be quite good at performing apparently intelligent functions in one very limited area (chess, or checkers, or math) but show little capacity to transfer their skills into any other area. Programs that are very good at chess are not as a rule capable of diagnosing illnesses. Humans, in contrast, regularly transfer their mental capabilities in one domain to numerous other domains.

In the early years of AI (the 1950s and 1960s) researchers tried to duplicate this ability to operate across diverse domains. There were significant efforts to create a computer that had general intelligence. It was assumed at the time that the term 'intelligence' means *the ability to solve problems*. The best-known example of such a program was called the "General Problem Solver," and it was created in the late 1950s. Early optimistic theorists believed that it would be possible to construct a computer program that could solve virtually any problem given to it. It gradually became clear that such a goal was far more difficult to achieve than anyone had realized, so projects were gradually scaled back, and programs were limited to dealing with one very specific and circumscribed domain—playing chess, *or* analyzing chemical compounds, *or* solving math problems. *General* intelligence, of the sort that could handle any problem, proved elusive. The pressing question now is whether or not it will be possible to "scale up" from these limited areas of expertise and create programs that exhibit an ability to perform intelligently across a broad spectrum of domains. So far, the prospects have not been promising.

However, the defender of AI might ask whether or not genuine mental function *requires* the ability to exercise a capacity across domains. We seem willing to credit young children and certain animals with mental capacities even where they are applied very narrowly. Ought we to be willing to do the same in the case of computers or robots?

In spite of the fact that some of these Symbol-based systems can carry out limited functions that have traditionally been seen as intelligent, some philosophers have asked if a system must *understand* what it is doing in order to qualify as genuinely intelligent even in some limited domain. The debate over this issue has focused on what is called the "Turing Test."

The Turing Test

In spite of the difficulties involved in defining intelligence, and programming general intelligence, the idea that a computer might one day be intelligent led to the formulation of a test that was supposed to decide the issue. It has come to be known as the Turing Test, named after its creator, the mathematician Alan Turing. One of its simplest versions goes like this: Place a person in one room at a computer terminal; in a second room, not visible to the first, place a second person at one computer terminal along with another computer that has a program for receiving and answering questions. The person in the first room is to ask questions of the two in the other room in an effort to find out which one of the two is a computer. The computer program is allowed to mislead and even to lie; the person is supposed to answer all questions truthfully. There is no limit to the kind of questions that can be asked, and the interrogator is generally given a half hour to decide. If the interrogator cannot identify the computer program within that time, presumably because its responses to questions are indistinguishable from those of its human companion, that fact is supposed to indicate that the computer is intelligent, is indeed thinking.

"Chinese Room" Response

The Turing Test has generated considerable discussion over the years. Perhaps the best-known criticism of it comes from philosopher John Searle. Searle's objection comes in the form of a thought experiment generally referred to as the "Chinese Room." Searle asks us to imagine a room with two slots in it—one for incoming questions written in Chinese, and one for outgoing answers, also in Chinese. There is a person inside the room, receiving the questions and sending out the answers, but he understands absolutely no Chinese. What he does is to follow a rule book that shows the shape of the marks to make when responding to incoming marks that have a certain other shape. Notice that the person in the room is manipulating *representations* by means of a set of *rules*. The person is functioning as a sort of central processing unit (CPU) in a Symbol-based system. Searle's point is that even if the responses are perfect Chinese responses to the Chinese questions being asked, the person inside the room still does not understand a word of Chinese. He is simply following rules that are based solely on the *shape* of the incoming material, and he has no idea what any of the shapes— incoming or outgoing—*means*. Searle concludes that the case is exactly analogous to the case of a symbol-based computer. When it receives data, it simply follows rules that allow it to respond based purely on the order of a string of 0s and 1s (or some comparable system), and it has absolutely no understanding of what any of the symbols mean. In other words, even if a computer passes the Turing Test, that is no indication that it is thinking or is intelligent, since it *understands* nothing. All it is doing is manipulating symbols that are meaningless for it, according to a set of programmed rules that are equally meaningless for it.

Many objections to Searle's Chinese Room argument have been posed. One of the more common ones says that the man in the room may not understand Chinese, but the system taken as a whole does. Part of what is at stake here may come down to a dispute between two quite different sets of criteria for deciding if a system is intelligent or has any understanding. Searle's critics seem to rely primarily (perhaps exclusively) on *behavioral* criteria; if the system behaves in ways that we normally use to attribute intelligence or understanding, then we should count it as being intelligent or understanding what it is doing. Searle, on the other hand, seems to appeal to an internal or *experiential* sense of what it means to understand something. Any agreement on the validity of the Chinese Room argument is likely to depend on agreement on the criteria to be used in deciding when one has cases of intelligence or understanding—and such agreement is not expected to come soon.

There is, however, another objection to the Turing Test. It is willing to grant the behavioral criterion for understanding or intelligence, but it argues that the test assumes that *linguistic* behavior by itself is a sufficient indicator of their presence. The objection argues that intelligence requires a good deal more than the ability to use language in plausible but limited ways. This sort of objection goes to the heart of the dispute between those who argue that mental functions essentially involve the manipulation of linguistic symbols, and those who argue that there is more to it than that (perhaps the ability to use mental images, perhaps bodily interaction with the environment, perhaps emotions, perhaps evidence of some degree of internal awareness, etc., in addition to language use).

Skepticism about Symbol-System AI

The critics of Symbol-System AI generally fall into two camps, those who are skeptical of AI itself, and those who argue that AI is a worthy research program, but the Representations and Rules approach is a failure and needs to be replaced with a more promising model. First, the skeptics.

One of the earliest critics of AI was philosopher Hubert Dreyfus. In his book, *What Computers Can't Do* (1972)—later revised and issued as *What Computers Still Can't Do* (1992)—Dreyfus offered an extended analysis of the ways in which he believed that Symbol-System AI failed to provide a plausible model for understanding human mental processes. I shall mention just three areas of concern to him: (1) the reliance on representations, (2) the focus on "knowing *that*" to the exclusion of "knowing *how*," and (3) the inability to establish relevance.

Role of Representations

As I noted earlier, it is widely agreed that representations play an important role in knowledge. Fodor, in fact, says that it is the presence of representations that establishes a state as cognitive. But the agreement is not universal. Dreyfus, for one, disagrees. He says, following the lead of philosophers like Martin Heidegger, "there is usually no need for a representation of the world in our mind since the best way to find out the current state of affairs is to look to the world as we experience it."[7] At least part of what Dreyfus means here is that our knowledge of the world is grounded in our *activities*, our interactions with it, and not primarily by means of mental representations of it. This is a view argued as well by the philosopher John Dewey. For these philosophers we are not simply spectators of our world; we build things in it, we dance in it, we eat portions of it—and all these activities contribute to our knowledge of the world. Mental representations, if they play any role at all, cannot tell the whole story of our acquaintance with the world.

Knowing *That* versus Knowing *How*

The concern about representations relates to a second point that Dreyfus makes: Symbol-System AI reduces mental processes to *propositional* knowledge, that is, to knowing *that* various things are the case. He argues that our mental processes involve much more than knowledge of facts about the world (e.g., knowing *that* roses are flowers). Perhaps our most basic type of knowledge, he argues, is knowing-*how*. Examples include some obvious cases, like knowing how to walk or to ski or to dance, but he also means knowing how to deal with various types of situations in which we find ourselves. When we arrive at a party, we don't have to go through a list of facts about parties in order to know what to do. We have developed a level of know-how that guides our behavior without any need to review a set of factual propositions about parties. More generally, we know *how* to get along in the world without having to consult mental representations with programmed rules for combining them. "In general, human beings who have had vast experience in the natural and social world have a direct sense of how things are done and what to expect. Our global familiarity thus enables us to respond to what is relevant and ignore what is irrelevant without planning based on purpose-free representations of context-free facts" (p. xxix).

Relevance

A third area of concern for Dreyfus involves one of the most problematic issues for Symbol-System AI: determining the *relevance* of one thing to another. "My first take on the inherent difficulties of the symbolic information-processing model of the mind was that our sense of

---

7. Hubert Dreyfus, *What Computers* Still *Can't Do* (Cambridge, MA: MIT/ Bradford, 1992), p. xxxi.

relevance was holistic and required involvement in ongoing activity, whereas symbol representations were atomistic and totally detached from such activity" (p. xi). More broadly, we experience things in a context, not in isolation. And that context includes not only other objects and events, but also our own active engagement with things in ways that reflect the fact that we are living bodies with needs and interests. We see things as relevant to situations and to us because we use them, need them, are interested in them. Symbol-based systems manipulate symbols that are abstracted from any normal human activities, and from any context that would provide relevance relations.

What makes the problem of determining relevance so difficult is that anything is potentially relevant to anything else, depending on the circumstances. At present, we don't have any clear idea about how to structure a system of rules and representations in such a way that the system can recognize what is relevant to what, in a given situation. The system needs to be told everything, and telling it everything would require an *immense* amount of programming. But perhaps worse, we don't as yet know precisely how to *organize* the programmed information so that the system would be able to recognize what is relevant to what and under what circumstances. Human beings are very good at recognizing relevance in a vast number of situations, and the suspicion of critics of Symbol-System AI is that we don't do it by following a set of rules that manipulate the appropriate representations.

I should mention, however, that there is a project underway that is attempting to program a computer with all the commonsense knowledge that it would need. Doug Lenat is the director of the project (called "Cyc," as in "encyclopedia"), which began in 1984. His prediction is that by the year 2015 it will be common for computers to have the type of knowledge that we refer to as "common sense." He believes that such knowledge will require about 100 million items of information.[8]

Dreyfus is skeptical that the mere massing of information will allow the computer to recognize relevance relations. "In order to retrieve relevant facts in a specific situation, a computer would have to categorize the situation, then search through all its facts following rules for finding those that could possibly be relevant . . ." (p. xxi). The problem is that in a classical computer, when you increase the number of facts, you increase the search time, so you add more rules in an effort to shorten the search, but soon you have what is called a "combinatorial explosion"—that is, the number of facts to be searched and the number of

---

8. See Jack Copeland's book, *Artificial Intelligence*, for a more detailed account of the project. Dreyfus also discusses the project in some detail.

rules to be used becomes unmanageably large. Add to that the fact that
we don't yet know what sort of rules would enable a computer to discover what is relevent to what in a given situation. The possibilties for
relevant information are virtually limitless. Daniel Dennett illustrates
the point in his characteristically entertaining way:

Once upon a time there was a robot, named R1 by its creators. Its
only task was to fend for itself. One day its designers arranged for
it to learn that its spare battery, its precious energy supply, was
locked in a room with a time bomb set to go off soon. R1 located
the room, and the key to the door, and formulated a plan to res-
cue its battery. There was a wagon in the room, and the battery
was on the wagon, and R1 hypothesized that a certain action
which it called PULLOUT (WAGON, ROOM) would result in
the battery being removed from the room. Straightaway it acted,
and did succeed in getting the battery out of the room before the
bomb went off. Unfortunately, however, the bomb was also on
the wagon. R1 *knew* that the bomb was on the wagon in the
room, but didn't realize that pulling the wagon would bring the
bomb out along with the battery. Poor R1 had missed that obvious
implication of its planned act. Back to the drawing board. "The
solution is obvious," said the designers. "Our next robot must be
made to recognize not just the intended implications of its acts,
but also the implications about their side effects, by deducing
these implications from the descriptions it uses in formulating its
plans." They called their next model, the robot-deducer, R1D1.
They placed R1D1 in much the same predicament that R1 had
succumbed to, and as it too hit upon the idea of PULLOUT
(WAGON, ROOM) it began, as designed, to consider the implications of such a course of action. It had just finished deducing
that pulling the wagon out of the room would not change the
colour of the room's walls, and was embarking on a proof of the
further implication that pulling the wagon out would cause its
wheels to turn more revolutions than there were wheels on the
wagon—when the bomb exploded.

Back to the drawing board. "We must teach it the difference
between relevant implications and irrelevant implications," said
the designers, "and teach it to ignore the irrelevant ones." So they
developed a method of tagging implications as either relevant or
irrelevant to the project at hand, and installed the method in
their next model, the robot-relevant-deducer, or R2D1 for short.
When they subjected R2D1 to the test that had so unequivocally

selected its ancestors for extinction, they were surprised to see it sitting, Hamlet-like, outside the room containing the ticking bomb . . . "Do something!" they yelled at it. "I am," it retorted. "I'm busily ignoring some thousands of implications I have determined to be irrelevant. Just as soon as I find an irrelevant implication, I put it on the list of those I must ignore, and . . ." the bomb went off.[9]

As Dreyfus suggested, solving the relevance problem will be no easy task. Defenders of AI, of course, will respond by saying that since human beings have solved it, it must be solvable.

These three considerations—the role of representations, knowing how, and relevance—lead Dreyfus to the general conclusion that Symbol-System AI is not a likely candidate for modeling the way mental processes work, at least not the way they work in human beings.

Computers versus Humans

It is, of course, clear that there are some significant differences between computers and human beings. While there are some obvious differences that don't appear to affect the issue of mental function (computers don't get measles or eat hot dogs), some are clearly relevant to it. To mention just a few:

- Since computers are not alive, they have no body chemistry and hence appear to be incapable of experiencing those emotions that involve body chemistry (like fear and anger).

- They give no indication of being conscious (although that alone would not prevent unconscious mental processes).

- They appear to have no sensations like pain or hunger.

- They appear to have no interests of their own that would provide them with a framework for evaluating things in relation to those interests (although they could perhaps be programmed to behave as if they have some).

I shall have more to say about further differences shortly, but these examples are sufficient to give some sense of a few of the reasons for hesitation that some theorists have felt in connection with using serial

9. Daniel Dennett, "Cognitive Wheels: The Frame Problem of AI," reprinted in *The Philosophy of Artificial Intelligence*, Margaret Boden, ed. (Oxford: Oxford University Press, 1990), pp. 147–8.

computers as the model for understanding human mental function. None of these factors, taken individually, entails that the computer must necessarily be incapable of any mental function at all. But they do suggest that if the computer has any such functions, it will nonetheless provide an incomplete model for understanding the mental functions of normal adult human beings.

Some theorists have suggested another difference between us and computers, one that poses a direct challenge to Symbol-System AI. While there is considerable agreement among theorists that cognitive processes must involve *representations* of some sort, one area of dispute among AI researchers is whether or not mental processes are essentially *linguistic* in nature. One objection, for example, suggests that an exclusively linguistic theory omits all consideration of the role of *images* or *models* in mental processes. These images are sometimes characterized as *analog* rather than *digital* representations. The difference between the two has been a matter of some controversy, but one common distinction parallels that between digital and analog watches. A digital watch registers a precise set of numbers, with no room for ambiguity, no range of interpretations—for example, 3:47:15 (forty-seven minutes and fifteen seconds after three). An analog watch, by contrast, indicates time on a *continuous* scale. So the same time on an analog watch would show the minute hand somewhere between forty-five and fifty minutes after three. A further distinction is that analog representations often bear some resemblance to what they represent. Images and models are usually similar in some respect—perhaps in the spatial relations among elements—to the objects or situations that they represent. Digital representations need not have any similarity to their referents. The relevance of these distinctions here is that linguistic representations are often characterized as digital, while images (like other types of pictures) have been seen as analog. The conclusion is that if, as some theorists have argued, at least some mental processes involve images as well as language, then a digital system, using exclusively linguistic representations, will provide an inadequate model of mental processes.

Nevertheless, digital computers might still be seen as instantiating at least certain mental processes. Furthermore, there does not seem to be any reason to *require* that every mental system be capable of having images. In fact, some *people* claim that they don't have them. Research scientist Philip Johnson-Laird has argued that it is possible for a system to have linguistic (or "propositional") representations at one level, and imagistic representations at a higher level. Digital computers, then, might simply lack the "upper," imagistic, level but be capable of the sort of mental functions that rely exclusively on linguistic representation.

Balint's Syndrome: Balint's Syndrome is a deficit sometimes caused by damage to the parieto-occipital regions of both hemispheres of the brain. It results in an inability to locate objects in space in spite of the fact that the subject can recognize them. They appear unable to reach for them, to direct their gaze toward them, or to estimate their distance. Psychologist Stephen Kosslyn notes that this deficit is generally quite distinct from **Kluver-Bucy Syndrome** in which subjects can locate objects in space, but they are unable to identify them. This deficit usually follows damage to the temporal lobe in both hemispheres. Kosslyn argues that these two syndromes provide evidence that we store two distinct representations of objects: one for *what* the object is and one for *where* the object is.[10] As a consequence, he sees the process by which we generate mental images to be a *constructive* process, involving the retrieval and composition of the different aspects of the object. Kosslyn has also done considerable experimental work on the role of images in certain types of mental processes.[11]

Connectionism (or Parallel Distributed Processing)

In an effort to understand how Connectionism developed as an alternative to Symbol-System AI, consider some of the criticisms that Connectionists have leveled at Symbol Systems.

Connectionist Critique of Symbol-System AI

A good deal of the Symbol System approach to AI relies on the assumption that the mind or mental functions are best understood on analogy with *computer function*. Within this framework, computer systems became the dominant metaphor for theorizing about the mind. Connectionism, in contrast, uses *brain function* as the model for understanding mental function. As you will see, the two approaches involve some very important differences in both starting points and conclusions.

10. See Stephen Kosslyn, "Seeing and Imagining in the Cerebral Hemispheres: A Computational Approach," *Psychological Review*, 1987, 94(2); see also "Aspects of Cognitive Neuroscience of Mental Imagery," *Science*, June 17, 1988.

11. See *Image and Brain: The Resolution of the Imagery Debate* (Cambridge, MA: MIT Press, 1994); and see his article on Imagery in *The MIT Encyclopedia of the Cognitive Sciences*, R. A. Wilson and F. C. Keil, eds. (Cambridge, MA: MIT/Bradford, 1999).

In addition to the issues cited in our discussion so far, a number of other problems with Symbol-System AI have been noted by Connectionist theorists who are, nonetheless, optimistic about the prospects for AI. All of these problems, they say, can be solved by approaching AI by way of *Connectionist* systems rather than by way of Symbol-based systems. Before looking more carefully at these Connectionist systems, consider some of the problems that they see in Symbol-System AI. This will give you some sense of why Connectionist systems developed in the way that they did. These problems include: (1) Symbol-based AI systems are inflexible; (2) they do not degrade gracefully when damaged; (3) they are not good at tasks like pattern recognition; (4) they do not make generalizations easily; (5) they are not very good at learning from experience; (6) they have difficulty dealing with "soft" constraints; and (7) their version of memory is deficient in important respects.[12] The fact that they generally operate serially is a further drawback. Connectionists argue that each of these problems points to a fundamental difference between the way in which the *brain* carries out mental functions and the way in which Symbol-System AI does. A brief look at each of these criticisms should help to illuminate some of the reasons that motivated Connectionist systems to use the brain rather than the digital computer as the model for AI. Each criticism points to a sharp contrast between Symbol-based systems on digital computers, on the one hand, and the human brain, on the other.

Flexibility

The inflexibility of Symbol-based systems is a result of the rigid rules that govern its computations over its discrete and unambiguous representations. The system normally cannot work with ambiguity or indeterminateness (as your own experience with computers undoubtedly demonstrates). In order to deal with these to any degree, it has to be given additional explicit rules. And while these may give the impression of some flexibility, the latter is rigidly circumscribed by the very rules that make even a small amount of flexibility possible. Human beings, in contrast, are quite good at dealing with ambiguity, with metaphor, with indeterminateness. We can respond to information flexibly, depending on the circumstances—both external and internal to ourselves. That is, we can usually disambiguate things by considering what else we know about the situation. "I went to the bank this morning," can mean one

---

12. For a fuller discussion of some of these issues, see Bechtel and Abrahamsen, *Connectionism and the Mind*, pp. 56–66.

thing in the city and quite a different thing at a camp on the edge of a river. Our knowledge about the world we live in and interact with provides the background against which we can usually untangle ambiguities. Symbol-based computers lack most of this background knowledge. That lack is commonly referred to as the "frame problem." What we know is "framed" by a great deal of other, related, knowledge. Our understanding of things involves an extensive web of related beliefs that impact one another. And the bet is that their mutual impact is not simply a matter of rule-governed logical inferences. It is probably also a function of an individual's past experiences, current interests and needs, and even emotional associations. The computer, in contrast, has limited and often isolated bits of information at its disposal; they have purely logical relations and have little or nothing to do with experience of the world.

System Damage

When a significant portion of a computer is damaged, it "crashes." Damage to the hard drive, or a "virus," can bring the system to a complete halt. The human brain and nervous system, by contrast, can suffer a fair amount of damage without bringing the person to total collapse. Human cognitive function can degrade gradually in the face of damage. A stroke may leave a person partially blind or with a language deficit, while at the same time leaving other cognitive functions, like memory or hearing, intact. Again, this difference points to some discrepancy beween the Symbol-System AI model and the human version of mental function. (See box on page 208.)

Pattern Recognition

One of the cognitive abilities that humans are particularly good at is pattern recognition. We do it quickly and with little effort in most cases. We recognize faces and voices and similarities in patterns of all sorts, often after very brief exposure. But it has been extraordinarily difficult to program Symbol-based systems to do likewise. I shall return later to consider how important this ability may be to our cognitive function.

Generalization

Related to our ability to recognize patterns is our ability to generalize, to categorize, to classify things into groups. Again, this is something that we do with little or no effort and do on a regular basis, over a wide range of items. Symbol-based systems must have their generalizations

Neurogenesis: Neurogenesis is the process by which new brain cells are produced. Scientists have known for a long time that various parts of the human body can be repaired by manufacturing new cells where they are needed. However, it was long believed that the one exception to this process of regeneration was the adult human brain. Although it was known that brain cells, *neurons*, die as we grow older, scientists believed that it was not possible for them to be replaced. New evidence now suggests that the adult brain is capable of producing new neurons under certain conditions. The process of cell production begins with *stem cells* which are *totipotent*—that is, they are able to give rise to any type of cell in the body. It is these stem cells that are responsible for the development of the many different types of cells in an embryo. Evidence now points to the fact that stem cells are also able to produce new brain cells in adult human beings. As we learn more about the precise conditions under which neurogenesis occurs, it may be possible to enhance the process in ways that will lead to improved treatments for brain diseases and the mental deficits that result from them.[13]

programmed for them. They don't normally generate spontaneous generalizations on their own. They are more likely to use concepts that are specified in terms of necessary and sufficient conditions, whereas we are able to generate prototypes and to recognize family resemblances as well.

Learning

Although we noted that one particular computer program that plays checkers improved its play by learning from its mistakes, it is also the case that a checkers-playing program is not able to learn how to diagnose illness more effectively. That is to say, the program's ability to learn is strictly limited to the narrow domain for which it has been designed. It is unable to learn outside that domain; it requires a new program designed for a new domain. Humans, on the other hand, obviously learn from experience across a broad range of domains. One question is whether or not human learning is, like Symbol-System AI, a matter of following rules. At least one consideration suggests that there is more to it than that. The human ability to learn in a very wide variety of areas suggests that if rules make that possible, they must be extraordinarily

13. See G. Kempermann and F. H. Gage, "New Nerve Cells for the Adult Brain," *Scientific American*, May 1999.

general. And it is precisely general rules of that sort that Symbol-System AI theorists have not been able to find and program. Recall the efforts to construct a General Problem-Solving machine—a machine that could deal with knowledge and problems across a wide variety of fields, much as we do. That project was scaled back and replaced by narrow "expert" programs.

Soft Constraints

It has probably become clear by now that one of the areas of disagreement among AI researchers concerns the role played by explicit rules in cognitive performance. At one extreme, the view is that rule following is essential to cognitive function; at the other extreme, the view is that it is unnecessary. But at least one middle ground also seems plausible. There appear to be cases of cognitive performance in which we do indeed follow rules quite explicitly. When you do math or logic problems, when you first learn how to ski, or when you are accessing a file on your computer, you are almost certainly following rather explicit rules—and often you do so quite consciously. As you become more familiar with the process, conscious rule following probably disappears. But one issue between Symbol-System theorists and Connectionists concerns the question of whether or not you are *always* following rules (albeit not always consciously) when you carry out any cognitive function.

More particularly, is our ability to handle "soft constraints" governed by symbol-level rules? "Soft" constraints occur when there is a series of constraints governing a situation, but not all of them need to be satisfied in order for the system to act. "Hard" constraints, on the other hand, allow no exceptions and cannot be overridden; if all the hard constraints are not honored, the system cannot continue its procedure. At a nontechnical, intuitive level, one can see everyday examples where we deal with hard and soft constraints. The situation generally involves some goal, something we want to accomplish. In order to reach that goal, some factors are absolutely essential; these are the *hard* constraints. Other factors are more negotiable; these are *soft*. We humans distinguish reasonably well between the two. We usually recognize which factors can be missing or somewhat degraded while still allowing us to accomplish the task, and which factors absolutely must be taken into account. A very simple example will illustrate the difference. Suppose you are trying to recognize a friend in an old photograph. Some of the hard constraints will include getting the correct sex, approximate age, and size. Some of the soft constraints might include such things as expectations about hair style, presence of glasses, style of clothing, other people in the picture. You are able to recognize the friend even if some of the soft constraints are not met. The trick, of course, is to be able to decide which constraints are negotiable in a given situation. Here one approaches all the problems associated with judging relevance. Trying to specify a set of explicit rules that can tell a system when it is permissable to ignore one or more constraints—and which constraints those are in each possible situation—would be an enormously complex task. It is a task we do not yet know how to accomplish.

The problem points again to the "frame" problem: One needs to know a great deal about how things are related, what things are essential to a situation and what things are negotiable, before one is in a position to know what can be safely ignored and what cannot. While human beings are very good at dealing with soft constraints, it seems that we don't do it simply by moving through a list of rules.

Memory

Connectionists see yet another weakness in Symbol-System AI. We speak easily of computer *memory*. If there is one plausible candidate for computer mental function, it might be thought that memory is it. But there are some significant differences between what we think of as memory and what computers have. First, Symbol-based computers have what is called *"location-addressable"* memory. That is, when you want to find something in the computer you normally have to tell it what drive to look in, what file to go to. Human memory, in contrast, is *"content-addressable."* That means that when you are trying to remember someone's name, for example, you don't have to specify the "address" in your brain at which the information is stored. Rather, you can call up other aspects of the person (other related *contents*)—she has red hair, used to be in my chemistry class, lives in New York, and so on. With luck, you may activate enough related material so that you will be able to call up the name. Instead of going to a particular drive or file, you go to related *content*. One other thing about computer memory distinguishes it from its human counterpart. Many theorists believe that what we do when we remember something is *selectively reconstruct* it. We don't simply call up a stored replica of the object or event as a computer does. We reconstruct it, and we do so by selecting some aspects for retrieval, omitting others, often adding to or embellishing the content. This is very likely related to the fact that we have interests and needs of our own that influence our selection of what we consider relevant or important to remember. The computer has no such needs or interests.

Serial versus Parallel Systems

Finally, Connectionists note that Symbol-based AI systems function *serially*, they perform just one operation at a time. They can perform an astonishingly large number of operations per second, but the fact is that they can do only one of them at a time. Hence the description, *serial* computer. Evidence strongly suggests that human cognitive functions are carried out in massively *parallel* ways. That is to say, our brains carry out multiple operations simultaneously. And these operations don't simply happen at the same time; they also affect one another. One of the pieces of evidence that is offered in support of our being parallel systems is called the "Hundred Step Argument." It goes like this:

1. It usually takes neurons just a couple of milliseconds (thousandths of a second) to fire.

2. But people can carry out some complex cognitive processes (like recognition) in about 100 milliseconds (about one-tenth of a second).

3. If the brain were functioning serially, it would only have time to carry out at most 100 steps to complete a complex cognitive process.

4. But even relatively simple cognitive processes in a serial computer require *thousands* of steps.

5. Parallel systems, in contrast, can be carrying out many steps simultaneously and would therefore be able to complete thousands of steps in 100 milliseconds.

6. Therefore, in order for the brain to carry out the complex cognitive processes that it does in such a short time, it seems that it must operate as a parallel system.

Furthermore, psychologists James McClelland, David Rumelhart, and Geoffrey Hinton—pioneers in the field of Connectionism—point out that people are very good at "perceiving objects in natural scenes and noting their relations, at understanding language and retrieving contextually appropriate information from memory, at making plans and carrying out contextually appropriate actions. . . ." And they note in connection with these abilities that "these tasks generally require the simultaneous consideration of many pieces of information or constraints. Each constraint may be imperfectly specified and ambiguous. Yet each can play a potentially decisive role in determining the outcome of the processing."[14] They believe that it is our capacity for *parallel* processing that allows us to accomplish these complex tasks.

All of these considerations taken together—our flexibility, our ability to handle ambiguity, the graceful degradation of brain function when the brain is damaged, our skill at pattern recognition, our ability to generalize with considerable ease, our ability to handle soft constraints, our ability to learn in a wide variety of domains, and the likelihood that we operate as parallel processing systems—have motivated some AI theorists to argue that Symbol-System AI has failed to produce adequate models for understanding *human* mental function. They argue that Connectionist systems can handle all the characteristics just mentioned and are, therefore, more plausible models for mental function—at least as we understand it in its most accessible form, our own.

Some defenders of Symbol-System AI, like Jerry Fodor and philosopher Zenon Pylyshyn, argue that the criticisms of Symbol-based systems are aimed at properties of the systems that are not intrinsic to those systems or are attributable to the architecture of current computers. The fact that the computers now in use function with central processing units and operate serially is, they say, unnecessary to Symbol systems. In fact, they claim that the systems do not even need explicit rules. Instead, they say, some functions can simply be hard-wired.

Structure of a Connectionist System

As I noted earlier, Connectionist systems are modeled, not on the serial digital computer, but on the *brain*. While they don't attempt to reproduce all the characteristics of brain function—at this point in history, they couldn't—they mimic some of the brain's most basic features.

A Connectionist system consists of a series of *units* or *nodes* that are linked with one another by way of excitatory, and usually also inhibitory, connections, somewhat like the neurons in the brain. For this reason, the Connectionist models are sometimes referred to as "neural networks." One layer of units can receive input; a second layer can produce output. Between the input layer and the output layer there are generally one or more "hidden" layers of units. These are hidden in the sense that they generally don't have access to anything outside the system. The information that they receive comes only from other units in the system. Input units are generally *activated* by input from outside, while hidden units and output units are normally activated by their

14. McClelland, Rumelhart, and Hinton, "The Appeal of Parallel Distributed Processing," in *Parallel Distributed Processing*, D. Rumelhart and J. McClelland, eds. (Cambridge, MA: MIT/Bradford, 1986), pp. 3–4.

connections to other units in the system. These connections between units have *weights* (or *strengths*). So the effect of one unit on another will be a function of the levels of activation and the weight of the connection between those units. (If you have studied any brain science you will notice again the general similarity with connections among neurons in the brain.)

A Connectionist system does not contain a set of binary representations that have been programmed into the system and stored there. It also contains no formal rules that would govern such representations. Instead, a "trainer" provides the system with some input, usually thought of as a "problem." At the start, the weights of the connections between units are set at arbitrary levels, and the system is allowed to process the input, using those levels. The output is at first quite random, as one would expect. The trainer then can readjust some of the weights in an effort to bring the output closer to the desired output, or the trainer can simply give the system feedback on the difference between its current output and the desired output, letting the system itself readjust its levels of activation and connection. After numerous trials (sometimes tens of thousands), the system will generally "learn" to produce the desired output. Notice that the *learning* simply amounts to alterations in weights between units until a better outcome is produced.

An example of a simple system might help. This one comes from work done by J. L. McClelland, D. E. Rumelhart, and G. E. Hinton, and is described in their classic work on Connectionism, *Parallel Distributed Processing*. They devised a system that could recognize a set of four-letter words—even when the input on a word is degraded. The system has units for portions of letters (e.g., the horizontal bars that appear in E or H or L, the vertical bars that appear in those letters as well as in M and N, the angled bars for letters like A, N, or Z). These units are connected in various ways to units for letters. Horizontal bars, for example, would have strong *excitatory* connections to letters like E, F, L, and the like, and would have *inhibitory* connections to letters like M, N, and the like. Finally, there are units for the four-letter words. And again, the connections between the letters and the words will be both excitatory and inhibitory. Connections between E and ABLE and TIME will be strong; between E and TRIP will be inhibitory. When the system encounters a degraded word in which one of the letters is partially blurred or blocked, the system can use its units for *portions* of letters to disambiguate the word. So, for example, when it encounters WOR_K_, it can evaluate the final letter as either R or K, and then can recognize that WORK is a word, while WORR does not occur in its list of words. Unlike most Symbol-based systems, what such a system illustrates is the

Connectionist claim that its systems exhibit the sort of flexibility that can handle some degree of ambiguity or degraded data.

The example is not entirely typical, however, because the designers gave all the units in the system a particular interpretation. Hidden units (those between input and output units) usually do their own work of filtering the input to them and generating their output without being given explicit interpretation by the trainer. The regularities that they respond to are sometimes referred to as "microfeatures," and are generally difficult to label. Nonetheless, the example is helpful in illustrating some of the important capabilities of Connectionist systems.

Some Comparisons and Contrasts

Given the differences in the physical organization of Connectionist and Symbol-based systems, what are some of the implications for AI? Consideration of the contrasts between the two types of systems will highlight some of the ways in which Connectionist systems can solve some of the problems that it attributed to Symbol-based systems.

Let's begin with *representations*. Both systems make use of representations, but the way they are generated and used by the two are different. Recall that in Symbol systems the representations are explicitly programmed, usually in binary notation, and are stored in memory for later retrieval and manipulation. In a Connectionist system, the trainer does not normally program explicit representations at some address, to be stored in the system for later retrieval. Instead, she sets starting weights among units and enters some data that activates the input units, which in turn activate the hidden units, which eventually activate output units. What *is* normally stored is the connection weights among units so that the representations can be reconstituted as needed. Recall that there is some evidence that we, too, reconstruct at least some (perhaps all) of our memories and mental images, rather than store them as complete pieces of data.

Furthermore, there need be no one "address" in the system at which that representation can be found. Connectionist representations come in two varieties: *local* and *distributed*. A representation is *local* when it is identified with one unit in the system. For example, if you wanted to keep track of a group of people and various of their associated characteristics, you might assign individual names to some units and specific characteristics to other units. Bob, Tom, Betty, and Alice would each get one unit, while *tall, short, New Yorker, Floridian, employed, unemployed*, and so forth, would each get a unit. When the system has been trained, the connections between each individual and his or her characteristics should be strong, while connections to inapplicable characteristics should be inhibitory. All the representations in such a system would be *local*, that is, there would be one complete item assigned to each unit.

On the other hand, representations can be *distributed*. Suppose you wanted to represent a certain group of animals. Instead of interpreting one unit as *dog*, another as *tabbycat*, another as *chimp*, you could distribute their representations by assigning different characteristics to units. One unit might represent *four-legged*, another *feline*, another *canine*, another *primate*, another *wild*, another *domesticated*, and so on. Then the representation for *dog* would arise from the connections among *canine*, *four-legged*, *domesticated*, and the like. There would be no single unit for *dog* itself. Similarly, *tabbycat* would involve *feline*, *four-legged*, *domesticated*. And *chimp* would normally involve *primate*, *wild*, and so forth. The representations for *dog*, *tabbycat*, and *chimp* would all be *distributed*.

Distributed representations highlight some attractive features of Connectionist systems. Because the system represents things by a *collection* of characteristics, and because many things share at least some of their characteristics, the system can isolate commonalities among things. That is, it can generalize. For example, both *dog* and *tabbycat* can be generalized as being *four-legged* and *domesticated* (unlike *chimp*). This allows the system to generate family resemblances, much as we do, and facilitates their capacity for pattern recognition.

Distributed representations also facilitate dealing with incomplete or degraded data. If the system receives as input a set of characteristics that is incomplete, it can sometimes produce an appropriate output because the connections among the given characteristics may either be strong enough to activate the rest of the relevant characteristics, or the system will give a response based on probabilities, given what it has been told. Related to this is the fact that the system has a version of content-addressable memory. Given some characteristics (some 'content') related to the target concept, it can often reconstitute the representation of the target concept. Connectionists argue that both humans and Connectionist systems exhibit both abilities. Recall that these abilities were features that Symbol systems lack. Although both Symbol and Connectionist systems employ representation, they generate, use, and store them in significantly different ways. It is because it makes considerable use of distributed representations and emphasizes the importance of parallel processing,[15] that Connectionism is also referred to as Parallel Distributed Processing, or PDP.

15. Note that this is in spite of the fact that current PDP systems are generally instantiated on the currently available serial computers.

What about *rules*? Obviously, there are rules of a sort in Connectionist systems. When the weight between units has a certain strength, one unit must activate the other. But those are not the sort of rules that are of interest to Symbol-based AI systems. Recall that Symbol systems use rules that govern the relations among *representations*. These are *symbol-level rules*, and they are often like rules of logic. It is this type of rule that Connectionist systems don't use. Processes in a Connectionist system are governed by input and by the weights of connections between units. There is no formal program, no central processing unit (CPU), nothing of an executive or what one might think of as a counterpart of a Self; everything is controlled by the weights of the connections, sometimes with feedback either among units or from the trainer to the system. But even that feedback does not make use of symbol-level rules. In other words, a Connectionist or PDP system can produce what appears to be rule-governed behavior without using rules. It also provides some indication of the ways in which groups of neurons might perform mental functions without directions from an executive Self.

More broadly, Andy Clark notes, "Where the Classicist [Symbol System theorist] thinks of mind as essentially static, recombinable *text*, the connectionist thinks of it as highly fluid environmentally coupled dynamic *process*. This shift of emphasis, I believe, constitutes connectionism's most fundamental contribution to shaping the future of cognitive science and the philosophy of mind."[16]

Criticisms of Connectionist AI

Connectionism, like Symbol-System AI, is not without its critics.

Internal Structure

Jerry Fodor and Zenon Pylyshyn[17] have argued that the most global problem with Connectionism is that its representations lack internal syntactic and semantic structure. What this means is that the system lacks the characteristics of a *language*. And recall that for Fodor, thought and mental processes have a linguistic structure. So, they argue, Connectionist systems lack the productivity, systematicity, and inferential coherence that language and thought require. Since the system is not governed by rules, it is incapable of mirroring the inferential

16. Andy Clark, "From Text to Process," in *The Future of the Cognitive Revolution*, D. M. Johnson and C. E. Erneling, eds. (Oxford: Oxford University Press, 1997), p. 185.

17. See their paper, "Connectionism and Cognitive Architecture: A Critical Analysis."

relationships among representations that are essential to the process of *reasoning*. And reasoning, they believe, is at the heart of mental functioning. Recall our earlier discussion of the various reasons that Fodor and others have given for thinking that an adequate model of mental states must be *linguistically* structured.

Associationism

On the view of some critics, what Connectionism really amounts to is simply another version of Associationism. On the classical Associationist view, ideas are related to one another by virtue of occurring together in experience, thereby becoming associated by the person experiencing them. Such ideas would not necessarily reflect real connections among the things they represent. They would merely be associated in the mind of the person in whom they happen to co-occur. Fodor and Pylyshyn argue that the representations in a Connectionist system have little more relationship to one another than this feature of occasional co-occurrence. Their point can be illustrated by the example of *systematicity* that Fodor uses. A Connectionist system can have a unit representing *John*, another for *loves*, and a third for *Mary*. But the system is unable to distinguish between "John loves Mary," and "Mary loves John."

Connectionists have offered replies to both sorts of criticisms. Bechtel and Abrahamsen argue that Connectionism is a good deal more than its classical Associationist predecessor. Among other things they note its use of distributed representations, of hidden units, "which function to encode microfeatures and enable complex computations on inputs," mathematical models of learning by association, supervised learning, and feedback mechanisms.[18]

As for the lack of internal structure among representations, many Connectionist theorists agree that their systems lack syntax. That is, they don't have the kind of internal structure that language has. But they argue that it is not necessarily true that mental processes are linguistically structured. They suggest that Symbol-System AI is taking a "top-down" approach to the mental, assuming that mental processes must be structured the same way that they appear in our conscious experience of thinking. But, they argue, that may be simply the final phase of the process and may be quite different in character from the unconscious processes that make it possible. Again Andy Clark comments: "Classicists [Symbol-System theorists] believe that thinking just is the manipulation of items having propositional or logical form; connectionists insist that this is just the icing on the cake and that thinking ('deep' thinking,

18. *Connectionism and the Mind*, p. 102.

rather than just sentence rehearsal) depends on the manipulation of quite different kinds of structure."[19]

In fact, some Connectionists argue that language and thought are not perfectly systematic or inferentially coherent, and that PDP systems can better account for this fact than idealized Symbol-based systems can. (Consider, they would say, some of the illogical and unsystematic thoughts you have had and comments you have heard.) They argue further that some of the apparent rule-governedness is really just an emerging property. That is, the system's behavior can be *described* as if it were rule-governed in spite of the fact that it isn't actually produced by following rules.

Some defenders of Connectionism argue that pattern recognition—a process that their systems can carry out quite well—may well be the most basic process that underlies our ability to reason. The ability to recognize *inferential patterns* does seem to be crucial to effective reasoning. These Connectionists suggest that pattern recognition, rather than linguistically structured reasoning, may be the most fundamental and essential aspect of mental functioning and that logical reasoning may be a later, emerging capability.

Tentative Conclusions

There are good reasons to think that neither Symbol-System AI nor Connectionist AI has yet produced a model of mental function that is completely adequate. According to one view, there is a global problem that still faces AI in both its Symbol-based and Connectionist forms. "Intelligence has to be motivated by purposes in the organism and goals picked up by the organism from an ongoing culture. If the minimum unit of analysis is that of a whole organism geared into a whole cultural world, neural nets as well as symbolically programmed computers still have a very long way to go."[20]

Several possibilities for the future remain open. Theorists may decide that we need some combination of the two types of systems, a combination that capitalizes on the strengths of both and avoids each of their weaknesses—if such a thing is possible. Or perhaps theorists will be able to exend the capabilities of Connectionist systems in such a way

19. Andy Clark, "Connectionism, Competence, and Explanation," in *The Philosophy of Artificial Intelligence*, M. Boden, ed., pp. 305–6.

20. Hubert Dreyfus and Stuart Dreyfus, "Making a Mind Versus Modelling the Brain," in *The Philosophy of Artificial Intelligence*, M. Boden, ed., p. 331.

that they will be able to exhibit some of the combinatorial properties that appear in conscious thinking. Or perhaps there is a third type of system, quite different from Symbol-based or Connectionist systems, yet to be created, that will provide an adequate model of mental function.

In the chapter on consciousness, I focused primarily on the consciousness of *living* systems. That discussion left a host of issues yet to be resolved: What can be said about consciousness in *nonliving* systems like computers and robots? Of course, if panpsychism is true, then presumably everything, including nonliving systems, would have some degree of consciousness. And if Epiphenomenalism is true, then perhaps it doesn't make much practical difference one way or the other because consciousness would have no causal role in the system anyway.

But suppose that neither panpsychism nor Epiphenomenalism is true. What are the prospects for a system like a computer or robot being conscious? If, as William James suggested, one of the primary functions of consciousness is to provide the system with flexibility that is not pre-programmed, then it looks as if rigid Symbol systems, governed by inflexible rules, would not be good candidates for consciousness. And if consciousness is indeed a product of electro-chemical events in the brain, then perhaps future computers would need some biochemical additions to their electrical components in order to produce consciousness. On the other hand, if consciousness does not emerge from neuro-physiology, but from highly structured mental processes (whatever their physical basis), then perhaps some future computers and robots will be capable of conscious states. For the present, given the gaps in our current understanding of the nature and function of consciousness, we can do little more than speculate on the possibilities for nonliving systems like computers and robots.

Finally, at this point in history, what kind of answer can we give to our opening question: *Is it possible in principle for a nonliving system like a computer or robot to be capable of any mental functions (processes, capacities)?*

Perhaps no *non*living system will exactly model human mental functions. Ours, and presumably those of any other mentally endowed living system, are closely connected with our needs and interests as *living* systems. Our mental processes play a large role in keeping us alive and well. That means that a good deal of the information that we actively seek, and the relationship that it has to our behavior, is a function of our interests and needs, our efforts to provide for our continued life and well-being. Nonliving systems obviously do not share that need to maintain life and well-being. Nonetheless, it may be possible to create systems capable of their own type of mental functions—and perhaps to a very limited degree we have already done so.

Issues for Discussion

1. Is it important that a model for mental functions be capable of emotions? Do you think that Symbol-based AI systems could be capable of emotions? Explain your answer.

2. Is there any sense in which a computer might be said to have a Self? Explain your answer.

3. If AI is possible—on the Classical model, on the Connectionist model, or perhaps some yet-to-be-discovered alternative model—do you think that the possibility of AI strengthens the plausibility of any of the theories of mind discussed in Chapter 1? Explain your answer.

4. Are there any reasons for thinking that *human* mental function, and therefore the human *brain*, should provide the most basic model for understanding mental function in general? Or is it just a case of chauvinism? Give reasons for your answer.

5. Do you think that humans are best understood as machines? Explain your answer.

6. Do you think that some AI systems already have some mental functions? Give reasons for your answer.

7. a. Do you think that it is possible to behave as if you understand something when you really don't?

   b. Do you think that it is possible to think or feel that you understand something when you really don't?

   c. Do you think that Turing's *behavioral* criteria or Searle's *experiential* criteria are the most reliable criteria for determining the presence of understanding—or do you think that we need to use both? Explain.

8. If pattern recognition, rather than linguistically structured reasoning, turned out to be the most fundamental aspect of mental functioning, what implications might that have for the issue of nonhuman animals' mental capabilities?

9. Do you think that a computer or robot could be conscious? Explain your answer.

Suggested Research Projects

a. Look in Joseph Weizenbaum's book, *Computer Power and Human Reason*, for a description of his *Eliza* program. What does the program do, and what were Weizenbaum's concerns about the program?

b. Read Chapter 2, "Some Dazzling Exhibits," in Jack Copeland's book, *Artificial Intelligence*, and make a brief summary of five of the programs he discusses. What apparently intelligent abilities do these programs suggest that computers might have?

c. Read Chapter 9, "Are We Computers?," in Jack Copeland's book, *Artificial Intelligence*. What are some similarities he notes between brains and computers? What are some differences?

d. Read Chapter 7, "Machines and Selves," in Todd Moody's book, *Philosophy and Artificial Intelligence*. What claims does the author make about the possible relations between machines and Selves? Do you agree with his claims? Explain your view.

e. Read the article by L. A. Cooper and R. N. Shepard, "Chronometric Studies of the Rotation of Mental Images," in *Visual Information Processing*, W. G. Chase, ed. (New York: Academic Press, 1973). Explain the evidence that the authors offer that mental images play a role in some mental processing. Do you think that their data present a problem for Symbol-System AI? Explain.

*f. Prepare a brief summary of Marvin Minsky's book, *The Society of Mind*. What does he mean by *society* of mind? Do you find in his views any implications for either form of AI? Explain.

g. In Howard Gardner's book, *Frames of Mind: The Theory of Multiple Intelligences*, how many types of intelligence does he describe? What are they? Do you think his view has any implications for AI? Explain.

7

How Do We Link Behavior to Mental States?

Several times in previous chapters I have pointed out that we have no direct access to the mental states of others. This fact became especially obvious in the case of nonhuman animals. What we do have access to is their behavior. And we generally use that behavior as some indication of the mental states that we think caused it. But that raises a question about how we make that move from observed behavior to unobserved mental states.

You regularly explain and predict the behavior of other people on the basis of the beliefs, desires, fears, expectations, and so forth, that you attribute to them. How do you do that? In spite of the fact that you don't have access to those alleged beliefs and other mental states, you seem to have little difficulty in understanding why people generally behave in ways that they do. How is this possible? What allows us to make the link between behavior and mental states?

Philosophers have traditionally referred to this as the *problem of other minds*. But as you will see, there are even some questions about our knowledge of our own minds.

From a practical point of view, the ability to make such a link is extremely useful. Given our social nature, from an evolutionary point of view it is adaptive to be able to attribute mental states to others. It provides us with some rational account of their behavior, allows us to predict that behavior with some degree of reliability so that we can respond to it in appropriate ways.

But how have we come to see behavior as an indicator of mental states? Notice that it does not function that way in every case. When your computer communicates with you, either in writing or orally, that does not automatically indicate to you that it has mental states. Or when a spider behaves in certain ways, few people are inclined to say that its behavior is guided by mental states. So how is it that we rather readily attribute mental states to some systems but not to all, based on their behavior? As with most philosophical questions, this one has received a number of different answers. Let's consider some of the leading contenders.

Argument from Analogy

One of the oldest philosophical answers to the *problem of other minds* rests on an argument from analogy. Like all arguments based on analogy, this one depends on recognizing certain similarities between two things. For example, one might use analogy to say that airplanes are like birds in that both of them have wings and can fly. But in spite of the similarities between them, there are of course glaring dissimilarities. Planes don't mate, build nests, lay eggs, and so forth. Birds don't have pilots, metal flaps, tons of jet fuel. In a word, every analogy implies both similarities and differences. An analogy is said to "limp" to the extent that the differences are more significant than the noted similarities. An *argument* based on analogy, then, is going to have some weaknesses built into it. Not only does analogy itself assume differences, but an argument from analogy generally goes one step beyond the noting of obvious similarities. On the basis of *observed* similarities, it argues for a further but *unobserved* similarity. This is the case when the argument is used to justify our claims about mental states in other human beings.

In its simplest form the argument runs like this: This individual is similar to me in its physical characteristics and in many of its behaviors. In my own case, my behaviors are guided by my mental states. So it is reasonable to believe that similar behaviors in this other individual are likewise guided by its mental states. For example, when I am angry I am likely to stamp my feet or say something in an agitated voice or shake my fist. When I see another individual behave in similar ways, I argue by analogy that it is likely that she is angry. I argue from the observed similarity in our bodies and behavior to an unobserved similarity in our mental states as causes of our respective behaviors.

Strengths and Weaknesses of the Argument from Analogy

The Argument from Analogy has a certain intuitive appeal. It seems obvious to us that the behaviors of others are often similar to our own; we believe that we understand the mental states that motivate or guide our own behavior; so it seems reasonable to conclude to the presence of relevantly similar mental states as motivating or guiding the behavior of others.

Keep in mind, too, that our title question is simply, How *do* we link behavior to mental states? The question is not, What is the *best* way to link it? So, of course, it is possible that we do in fact use this method in attributing mental states to others. But as an argument intended to *justify* our linking of behavior and mental states, it has some significant problems.

In spite of its appeal, the argument faces all the weaknesses associated with any analogy. It always "limps" to some extent. That is to say, in spite of the similarities that we share, we inevitably also have differences—adult/child, male/female, cultural and linguistic differences, and the like. One of the difficulties attached to concluding much of significance from an analogy is that the differences may be more telling than the similarities, as they probably are in the case of birds and airplanes. In the case of humans, however, the argument relies on the assumption that our psychological and behavioral similarities do outweigh our differences.

The particular case of attributing mental states to others carries further difficulties. I am analogizing on the basis of one case—the connection between *my own* mental states and behavior—and I am using that one case to generalize to others. It is always possible that my own case is unique or at least atypical or abnormal. Using it as a basis to judge all other individual cases is risky.

Appeals to my own case highlight one further issue, namely a reliance on introspection and on my ability to know what I need to know about my own mental states in order to see how they are connected with my behavior. Assumptions about this kind of self-knowledge are fraught with problems. Recall that Descartes believed that we could access and understand our own mental states simply by introspecting them. However, investigations, particularly in psychology and neuroscience, have called his view into doubt. It is now widely agreed that introspection cannot be counted on as a completely reliable guide in coming to understand our mental states.

For some philosophers, these doubts about introspection have been sufficient reason to place our knowledge of our own minds on the same footing with our knowledge of other minds—a matter of fallible inferences at best. Owen Flanagan, on the other hand, has argued for a more cautious approach.[1] He distinguishes four elements that could be candidates for our knowledge of our own minds: mental *processes*, mental *content*, the *causes* of our mental states, and the simple fact that we *have* mental states at all. Flanagan argues that experiments in cognitive science provide strong evidence that we can be mistaken about our mental processes, our mental content, and the causes of our mental states. This is not to say that we are never correct in our claims about any of the three, but it does mean that we lack the kind of infallible

1. *The Science of the Mind* (Cambridge, MA: MIT/Bradford, 1984, 2nd ed. 1991), Chapter 6, pp. 193–200.

introspective access to them that a Cartesian viewpoint seems to assume. Consider each of them briefly.

The clearest case in which introspection is not to be fully trusted concerns our knowledge of our own mental *processes*. What mental processes, for example, allow us to recognize a face? What processes allow us to bind together the data from vision, hearing, and touch, in order to perceive a telephone? What processes allow us suddenly to remember a name that yesterday we were trying, unsuccessfully, to remember? If answers to questions like these are going to be forthcoming at all, they will not come from introspection, but from scientific investigations.

The *contents* of our mental states may seem to be guaranteed to introspection. And in many cases, maybe most, we do seem to be directly aware of what we are thinking about, wanting, fearing, and so forth. But there are hidden factors even with content. First, there is the problem of unconscious content. Remember that not all mental states are conscious. The content of unconscious mental states would not, by definition, be available to introspection. Flanagan offers a somewhat different challenge: Articulate the content of all your beliefs. As he notes, it cannot be done. While you can very likely articulate the content of your currently active, conscious beliefs, there is a virtually endless series of other beliefs that you hold and that do not simply appear to your introspection. Even with some of one's conscious, current beliefs there can arise questions about how reliable is introspection of the *full* content of those beliefs. Consider a person who is racist or sexist but who is unwilling to admit his prejudice explicitly even to himself. The content of his belief about a person of a different race or sex may seem to him to be nothing more than a justified belief that the particular person is inept. In reality, the full content of the belief may involve a wholly negative generalization about people in that group. This is a classic case of self-deception, where one does not allow oneself to access and acknowledge the full content of one's own beliefs.

The issue of knowledge of the *causes* of our mental states is a bit more complex. Mental processes and content are internal to the person, while the causes of one's mental states can be both internal or external. Some of the internal causes can be unconscious, and as such, they would not be open to introspection. For causes that originate outside of us, the case is no better. In a classic experiment by psychologists Timothy Wilson and Richard Nisbett,[2] fifty-two people passing an exhibit in a

---

2. "The Accuracy of Verbal Reports about the Effects of Stimuli on Evaluations and Behavior," *Social Psychology* (1978), 41(2):123–4.

store volunteered to make a judgment on the respective quality of four pairs of nylon stockings. The stockings were arranged in a row and labeled A, B, C, and D (left to right). In reality, all four pairs were identical. Nonetheless, fifty of the fifty-two individuals selected one pair as being of the best quality. Of particular interest for our purposes is the fact that 71 percent of the participants judged that one of the two pairs on the *right* side of the exhibit was the best-quality stocking (31 percent at C, and 40 percent at D). The reasons they gave for their judgment included such things as the sheerness, the workmanship, elasticity, and so forth. When asked if spatial position played any role in their judgment, they all denied that it did. Given the fact that the stockings were all identical, it seems clear that the participants were mistaken about the factors that caused their judgment. (Only two people, of the fifty-two, said that they believed the stockings were identical.)

Likewise, from the chapter on emotions, recall the experiment done by Schachter and Singer. If the subjects had been asked what caused their subsequent feelings of anger or happiness, it is likely that they would have given a variety of answers—for some it would seem that the shot (of adrenaline or the placebo) caused their feelings, for others it might seem that the cause was the angry or happy person they were with, for still others it might seem that it was some unrelated event like a letter from home, or a good grade in a recent test, or the weather.

So it seems that our knowledge of all three factors—our own mental *processes*, the *content* of our mental states, and the *causes* of our mental states—turns out to be much less reliable than a Cartesian view might suggest. To that extent, our knowledge of our own minds has some of the same limitations that attach to our knowledge of other minds. But what about our knowledge of the link between our own mental states and our behavior? This would be an important piece of knowledge if the Argument from Analogy is to go through. Here, too, there are problems.

As David Hume pointed out over two centuries ago, our knowledge of causal relations is always vulnerable. We do not have direct experience of the *necessary connection* between events that is an essential aspect of causality. We rely, instead, on various other types of correlations. But none of these guarantee the presence of a causal relation. If they did, we would have recognized the cause of various diseases long ago. So our knowledge of causal relations in any context is likely to be fallible. Two other considerations are relevant. I noted earlier the significant role that unconscious mental events can play. That role includes the capacity to cause our behavior. Our knowledge of these unconscious mental events and their relation to our behavior will come from

third-person investigations (if it comes at all), not from our own introspection. Secondly, as John Stuart Mill pointed out, most events have
multiple causes, but we have a tendency to focus on just one of them as
the explanation of the event in question. To the extent that we do that
in relation to explanations of our own behavior, our account of its
causes is likely to be incomplete at best.

At this point, in spite of the fact that we have some *fallible* knowledge of our own mental states and their possible relations to our behavior, it might seem as if we can be *certain* about almost nothing in
relation to them. But as I mentioned earlier, Flanagan selected *four*
candidates for knowledge of our minds. The fourth is the fact that I
have a mind. As Descartes argued, the one thing that I can be certain
about is the fact that I am thinking, that I have mental states. In that
respect at least, my *knowledge* that I have a mind differs importantly
from my *belief* in the minds of others.

Nonetheless, since the Argument from Analogy begins not only
from the assumption that I *have* a mind but also that I know and understand my own mental states and their connection with my behavior,
worries about the reliability of this latter type of knowledge raise a problem for the argument. The conclusions I reach about how my own
mental states are related to my behavior may not be warranted. I may
simply have misunderstood the nature and function of my own mental
states and their relation to my behavior. Recall our earlier discussion of
the centuries-long reliance on the "four humors" and their alleged role
in explaining behavior. It seems that many people were systematically
mistaken in their beliefs about what explained their behavior. Although
it seems unlikely to us that we are similarly mistaken, introspection by
itself provides no guarantees that we have a completely correct understanding of the nature of our mental states and their role in causing our
behavior. Hence, using myself as a model and concluding that others
function as I do may only compound my misunderstanding. In a sense,
the *problem of other minds* becomes at least to some extent the *problem
of all minds*, including my own.

Further, even if one accepts the Argument from Analogy as plausible, it severely limits the cases to which it might apply. Based as it is on
certain types of relevant similarities, it could eliminate some cases from
consideration. People with severe mental illness or retardation may not
exhibit behavior that is significantly similar to mine. And when physical
similarity diminishes, the cases become even less clear. We might be
inclined to attribute mental states to other primates, but as physiology
alters, how far will analogy carry us? Four-legged animals? Creatures
with no legs? Individuals with no physiology at all, made of aluminum

or plastic? Some theorists have argued that the analogy is valid only in cases where the other individual uses a *language* that has a recognizable syntax and semantics. But that restriction places extraordinary limitations on the scope of the Argument from Analogy. On the other hand, if language use is the decisive criterion, that might make a talking computer appear to be a more plausible candidate for mental states than are other primates or human infants.

Problems with the Argument from Analogy have motivated theorists to look for a better alternative. Two leading candidates have emerged. But first, let's explore some background on their development.

Chimps and False Beliefs: Background to Alternative Theories

Perhaps ironically, the question of how we manage to link behavior and mental states received new impetus from some experiments with a chimpanzee. The experiments were reported in a 1978 journal article by psychologist David Premack and primatologist Guy Woodruff, "Does the Chimpanzee Have a Theory of Mind?"[3] Recall that in the chapter on mental evolution, we explored some evidence for the claim that at least some nonhuman animals *have* some mental states. Premack and Woodruff assumed that chimps do have such states, and they pushed the issue one step further. They asked, Do some nonhuman animals (e.g., chimps) *attribute mental states to others*? In their words, do chimps have a "theory of mind"? Since their research has led to the development of the two competing accounts of how *we* come to attribute mental states to others and link those mental states with their behavior, it will be useful to say a bit about that research.

In an effort to answer their title question, Premack and Woodruff devised a series of tests for a fourteen-year-old female chimp, named Sarah. As a start, they made a series of videotapes of one of Sarah's trainers facing a problem situation. There were tapes of various problem situations—for example, reaching for bananas that were out of reach. After seeing the videotape, Sarah was then shown a pair of photographs, one in which the trainer solves his problem (for example, by stepping on a box or using a stick to reach the fruit), and one photo showing the trainer doing something that did not solve his problem. The hope was that if Sarah chose the picture with the solution to the problem, that might indicate that she had some understanding of the

3. *Behavioral and Brain Sciences*, 1(4):515–26.

trainer's *intention* or *purpose*, as well as a sense of what would satisfy it. In other words, it might indicate that she was attributing certain mental states to the trainer, that she had a theory of mind. Sarah picked out the correct solution in twenty-one out of twenty-four trials.

At first glance the results seem impressive. But Premack and Woodruff noted that Sarah's behavior lent itself to more than one interpretation. Either she has a theory of mind that allows her to attribute mental states to the trainer, or she is operating from *empathy*—that is, she puts herself in the place of the trainer and chooses the solution that *she* would use.

In an effort to distinguish between these two interpretations, they devised a further experiment. They reasoned that the *empathy* interpretation would be supported if the identity of the trainer had no effect on Sarah's choices of a solution. Presumably, she would select a solution that *she* would use, not one that the trainer might intend. On the other hand, if the identity of the trainer did make a difference, Premack and Woodruff believed that that would indicate that Sarah was not acting from empathy but was focused on the trainer and *his* purpose or intention.

The experiment was structured like the earlier one, with videos of problem-to-be-solved, and photographs that included one with the solution. But this time two trainers were used for two different sets of videos, one trainer whom Sarah liked, and one she appeared to dislike. As it turned out, the identity of the trainer in the video did indeed seem to make a difference. Sarah rather consistently chose a good solution for the trainer she liked and a poor solution for the trainer she disliked. But the experiment still did not provide decisive evidence that she was operating with a theory of mind. It could be the case, for example, that Sarah was choosing the photo that represented what *she* wanted to happen to the respective trainers.

Premack and Woodruff designed a number of other tests in the hope of obtaining clearer evidence of just what Sarah was doing. In the end, they suggested that perhaps she was capable of attributing desires, purposes, or motivations to others, but perhaps not cognitive states like beliefs. In fact, in a later paper Premack notes that reliable evidence that chimps have a theory of mind is "painfully thin."[4]

Nevertheless, perhaps one of the most important consequences of Premack's and Woodruff's paper is that it has set a group of philosophers

4. "'Does the Chimpanzee Have a Theory of Mind?' Revisited," in *Machiavellian Intelligence*, R. W. Byrne and A. Whiten, eds. (Oxford: Clarendon, 1988), p. 176.

and psychologists in search of an answer to the question whether *human beings* attribute mental states to others by way of a theory of mind or by way of some variation on empathy. Commentaries on the paper, especially those made by three philosophers—Jonathan Bennett, Daniel Dennett, and Gilbert Harman—were particularly instrumental in giving direction to future debates.

Some of the commentaries raised a question about the authors' suggestion that Sarah gave evidence of recognizing purposes, desires, and the like, but perhaps did not show that she attributed cognitive states like beliefs. Bennett and Harman both argued that one cannot attribute desires without also attributing beliefs. (Recall that one of the objections leveled against Behaviorism was that behavioral definitions of desires presupposed the presence of beliefs, and vice versa.)

Two responses to this concern have emerged. On the one hand, Premack and Woodruff argue that *perception* is enough to generate desires and purposes, and Sarah clearly perceives what is going on. According to most philosophical theories, perception generates perceptual *beliefs*. On this view, if there is perception, there would normally be beliefs. But while it may be the case that perception does in fact generate beliefs, it is possible that the chimps are not aware of those states as beliefs and do not attribute such states to others. Their theory of mind, if they have one, may simply be a naive approximation to the mature and fully developed theory that defenders of Folk Psychology postulate. To claim that a chimp has a "theory of mind" may not entail that it has a completely adequate theory.

A second and related sort of response argues that there is an early version of desire or purpose that is not closely tied to representational cognitive states like beliefs. On this view, very young children (and perhaps other primates) develop an understanding of desire in terms of motor possibilities. As psychologists Alison Gopnik and Henry Wellman put it, "desire and perception can be, and at first are, understood in non-representational terms. Desires at first are conceived simply as drives towards objects. . . . very young children [two-year-olds] seem to treat desire and perception as fairly simple causal links between the mind and the world. Given that an agent desires an object, the agent will act to obtain it."[5]

But the philosophers raised a second concern, and it has shaped much of the debate that has ensued since the 1980s. Jonathan Bennett noted that it was difficult to know just what Sarah was really up to.

5. "Why the Child's Theory of Mind Really *Is* a Theory," in *Folk Psychology*, Martin Davies and Tony Stone, eds. (Oxford: Blackwell, 1995), p. 237.

What does she think her task is? Does she think she is supposed to predict what the trainer will do? Does she think she is supposed to show what she wants? Or is she really attributing certain mental states to the trainer? He suggested that further experiments need to focus more clearly on Sarah's beliefs, and particularly on her beliefs *about* beliefs — that is, they need to test for evidence that Sarah has beliefs about the *trainer's* beliefs.

Daniel Dennett and Gilbert Harman suggested a possible test that might reveal whether or not Sarah is genuinely attributing beliefs to the trainer. Variations on it have come to be known as the *"false belief tests."* Although there are a number of variations, one generic version looks like this: Place some object in an opaque container in the presence of a trainer while Sarah watches; later, while the trainer is distracted, move the object to a second opaque container; if Sarah expects the trainer to look in the container where the object was originally placed, that would seem to provide evidence for Sarah's having a belief about the trainer's (false) belief.

What would make a false belief test particularly instructive in Sarah's situation is that it could distinguish between the cases in which Sarah is just showing what she would do or prefer, or in which she is simply showing what *she* wants the trainer to do, and the case in which she recognizes that the belief of the trainer is different from her own and is the belief that will dictate his behavior. The *false* belief plays a crucial role. If Sarah and her trainer have the *same* belief, it is virtually impossible to know which belief is motivating Sarah. But if she sees where the object actually is (and presumably has a true belief), and she has observed that the trainer has not seen that it was moved (and thus has a false belief), then it should be possible to tell which belief explains her behavior. The trick, of course, is to design an experiment that will show clearly that Sarah recognizes a false belief and can attribute it to the trainer. That goal has proved elusive.

However, developmental psychologists quickly saw the relevance of designing such a test for young children, to find out when they develop their understanding of beliefs and when they develop their ability to attribute beliefs to others. In particular, evidence for the ability to attribute a *false* belief to another would show clearly that the child was not simply showing what he wants or thinks. He would be in a position to distinguish his own *true* belief from the *false* belief that he would attribute to the other. And, of course, the advantage of working with children rather than chimps is that the children can *say* what they are thinking and expecting.

In 1983 psychologists Heinz Wimmer and Josef Perner devised just such a test.[6] Using puppets, they showed children the following scenario: One puppet, Maxi, puts some chocolate in a box and goes out to play. While he is out, and unknown to him, his puppet-mother takes the chocolate out of the box and puts it in the cupboard. The children were then asked where Maxi would look for his chocolate when he comes back into the house. Older children (usually five years and older) answered correctly that Maxi would look in the box (where he had put the chocolate and where he *falsely* believes that it still is). But the three- and four-year-olds answered that he would look in the cupboard (where *they* know that the chocolate actually is).

The conclusion that the experimenters drew was that children do not develop an understanding of false belief until they are about five years old. The younger children seem to assume that Maxi knows just what they themselves know, in spite of the fact that Maxi did not see what they saw. That is, they apparently attribute their own beliefs to Maxi.

Since the publication of Premack's and Woodruff's article, along with the commentaries on it, a number of philosophers and psychologists have renewed the search for an adequate explanation of how *we* manage to attribute mental states to others on the basis of their behavior. Two of the accounts that were offered for Sarah's behavior—that she has a "theory of mind" or that she is behaving on the basis of some version of empathy—have given rise to two competing theories of how *we* attribute mental states: the Theory-theory and the Simulation theory. As we shall see, both of these theories have tried to explain, among other things, the results of the false belief tests in order to show that their account of mental attribution is the correct one.

Let's look first at the defense for a Theory-theory approach.

The Theory-Theory of Mental Attribution

This account of our ability to explain and predict behavior by attributing mental states to others is called, somewhat paradoxically, the "Theory-theory" or "Theory of Mind theory." The redundancy is not accidental. According to this theory, we attribute mental states to others because we have a *theory* that correlates certain types of observable behavior with certain types of unobservable mental states.

6. "Beliefs about Beliefs: Representation and Constraining Function of Wrong Beliefs in Young Children's Understanding of Deception," *Cognition*, 13 (1983): 103–28.

Note on Terminology: Although the term 'theory' is used in a number of different ways, sometimes just to indicate a viewpoint or a speculative account of something, the scientific notion of a theory is more precise. It generally postulates a set of *unobservable* entities, as well as laws that govern the interactions among those entities, in order to explain and/or predict the behavior of certain *observable* phenomena. Because they are dependent to some degree on the theory, these unobservables are often referred to as *theoretical* entities and are given their meanings in terms of their role in the theory. On some slightly less formal accounts, a theory could be any structured body of information, or a model that is used to simplify or systematize data.

When Theory-theorists explain how we are able to attribute mental states to others and to explain and predict their behavior by appealing to these mental states, they claim that we make use of a *theory of mind*— most commonly construed as *Folk Psychological* theory. While there has been considerable debate about which notion of *theory* is being appealed to when one speaks of a theory of mind, the dominant view seems to be that it is reasonably close to the scientific notion of a theory. On this view, the theory of mind has some of the characteristics of a scientific theory, but not all of them. On the one hand, it is generally characterized as postulating unobservable mental states like beliefs, desires, regrets, fears, and so forth, and some laws or principles (or at least "rules of thumb") that govern their interactions as well as their causal relations with environmental input and with observable behaviors. On the other hand, the theory of mind is not normally the subject of ongoing laboratory experiments as many scientific theories are. One philosopher, David Lewis, has characterized it as a "term-introducing" theory.

Making use of this roughly scientific sort of theory, with its reference to theoretical entities and causal laws, one might link behavior and mental states by saying, for example, that a *belief* that it is raining was probably *caused* by some perceptual input, and when it is coupled with a *desire* to remain dry, it will likely lead to *behavior* like carrying an umbrella [unless some other factors intervene]. But notice that generalizations of this sort, while reasonably reliable, are not the result of scientific experiments. Hence the name *Folk* Psychology, to indicate their less formal character.

Folk Psychology has two very important characteristics. First, it is not new; it is thousands of years old. One can find clear evidence of it in the writings of the philosophers in ancient Greece. Second, it is a "commonsense" sort of theory, often compared with other informal theories such as *Folk Physics*. Folk Physics includes the "rules of thumb" that allow us to deal in practical and useful ways with the physical world. We have a pretty good idea of how to avoid falling off cliffs, how to handle heavy objects, and so forth. According to Theory-theorists, we likewise have pretty good ideas about how to connect the beliefs and desires that we and other people have, with ensuing behavior.

Some examples of Folk Psychological *predictions*:

- Charlie *believes* that the Cubs will beat the Mets; he *wants* to see that game; so Charlie will do what he can to get to the game.

- Alice *wants* to go to graduate school in mathematics; she *believes* that in order to do that she must pass her course in Calculus; so Alice will make every effort to pass her course in Calculus.

Some examples of Folk Psychological *explanations*:

- Ellen *believes* that running is good for one's health; she *wants* to do something good for her own health; that is why Ellen has started jogging every morning.

- Brian *wants* to run for political office; he *believes* that he needs to raise a good deal of money in order to do that; that is why he has been out fundraising.

But when one offers these predictions and explanations in Folk Psychological terms, one needs to add a *ceteris paribus* clause. The phrase *ceteris paribus* translates as "other things being equal." So, for example, Charlie will do what he can to get to the game *unless* there are some mitigating factors (i.e., "other things" are not "equal"). Charlie may not have enough money to go to the game; he may have another engagement that cannot be canceled; he may prefer to see the game on television. Ellen may have the belief and desire that correlate running with good health, but she may have started jogging every morning because an attractive young man in the neighborhood is out jogging every morning.

These *ceteris paribus* additions obviously loosen the tight connection between the mental states that are postulated as causes of the behavior and the ensuing behavior. There may be any number of mitigating circumstances that we are unaware of when we predict or explain the behavior of others. Folk Physics, like Folk Psychology, also requires *ceteris paribus* clauses.

Sources of Folk Psychological Theory

You undoubtedly recognize the sort of examples of Folk Psychological reasoning that I have mentioned. The theory is very old and very familiar to most of us. But where did we get it? As I said, it is not the result of careful experiments. Several suggestions have been offered. According to one account we have *learned* the theory. Paul Churchland put it this way: "All of us learn that [Folk Psychological] framework (at mother's knee, as we learn our language), and in so doing we acquire the common-sense conception of what conscious intelligence is."[7] Opponents of such a view argue that this cannot be right. While most of us can mouth a few platitudes linking beliefs and desires with behavior, it has proved extraordinarily difficult to clearly articulate the laws that are supposed to function in Folk Psychology. There is little reason, they argue, to believe that our mothers were able to teach us what most philosophers find difficult to formulate with any precision.

However, some supporters of the view that we learn Folk Psychology from others might appeal to the philosophy of Ludwig Wittgenstein. Wittgenstein argued that one cannot come to understand the meaning of mental terms simply by introspecting one's own mental states. In addition to the problems associated with the reliability of introspection, Wittgenstein pointed to another issue. The problem, as he saw it, would be that one would have no way of knowing if the sense that one gave to one's own mental terms had any relation to the sense that others were giving to their mental terms. In every case we would be appealing to something private, unsharable. That, he argued, would make meaningful communication about mental states impossible. We must, he said, learn the meaning of mental terms from the way those terms are used in our society. If he is right, that would mean that we must learn the meaning of the terms that function in Folk Psychology, even if we are not explicitly taught the theory itself, "at our mother's knee."

But many defenders of Theory-theory have taken a somewhat different tack. They argue that very young children learn language without having their parents list the rules of grammar for them. In recent years it has been widely accepted that children have a "language aquisition mechanism" that allows them to learn the language they are exposed to and to be constrained by its underlying grammar—all without being taught that grammar and without being able to articulate it themselves. The analogy with Folk Psychology would suggest that there is no need for mother to articulate its laws any more than she does for language.

7. *Matter and Consciousness* (Cambridge, MA: MIT/Bradford, 1988), p. 59.

On this particular view, the child comes with some innate learning mechanism that allows him to acquire a theory of mind. But there are still other alternatives available.

A second proposal about how we acquire Folk Psychology is that we construct it for ourselves bit by bit as we mature. On this view children gradually construct a theory about the relation between behavior and mental states, revising and improving the theory in light of their experiences. Psychologists Alison Gopnik and Henry Wellman put it this way: "We believe that the child's understanding of mind is helpfully construed as a theory, and that changes in understanding may be thought of as theory changes. But we believe this because such an account provides the best explanation for the currently available developmental evidence."[8]

While it might at first seem implausible that children construct a theory of mind somewhat the way scientists construct theories, Gopnik and Wellman offer some evidence from developmental psychology in support of that claim. Their general strategy is to lay out the characteristics of theories and theory formation and then to argue that the developmental stages that children go through parallel theory formation about mental states. They give some examples of how scientific theories change. First, recalcitrant evidence is ignored, then it is incorporated in a peripheral way, and finally revisions in the original theory attempt to incorporate that recalcitrant evidence centrally. They argue that children's developing theory of mind should be expected to go through analogous changes if they are constructing a theory, and they claim that the data show that they do. They first ignore data that do not fit with their initial theory of mind, then they accommodate the data in a somewhat superficial way, and then they gradually alter their theory of mind until it accords with their experiences in reasonably adequate ways.

But this suggestion, too, has met with opposition. Critics note that it is "miraculous" that all children seem to arrive at precisely the same theory—a feat that adults rarely do when generating scientific theories about how the world works. Further, some argue that we lack precise models for how scientific theories actually develop—sometimes following a hunch, sometimes good luck, often building on what others have already done. This, they say, offers a poor analogy for understanding children's acquisition of a (fairly uniform) theory of mind quite early in life.

A third view about how we acquire our theory of mind has been defended by Jerry Fodor. He argues that the theory must be *innate*, and he has offered at least three reasons for thinking that this must be so.

8. "Why the Child's Theory of Mind Really *Is* a Theory," pp. 232–3.

First, the use of mental states to explain and predict behavior seems to be universal; second, even very young children can explain behavior by reference to mental states; and third, the other proposals about how children acquire this ability all appear implausible.[9] One version of the innateness view, defended by psychologist Alan Leslie, suggests that what is innate is a specialized theory of mind module. This innate mechanism includes a representational system and is "specialized by adaptive evolution for the task of interpreting agents' behavior in terms of propositional attitudes [i.e., mental states like beliefs and desires]."[10]

Early critics of Theory-theory argued that the view itself is implausible on the grounds that most people have no awareness of having such a theory and would be hard pressed to articulate any of its laws in spite of the fact that they are alleged to make mental attributions in accordance with those laws. Theory-theorists respond, however, that there is no reason to assume that either the theory itself or our use of it must be conscious. They analogize the situation to our use of language, with its syntax. When we speak, we are normally not conscious of the grammar that governs language use. Nonetheless, we are able to be guided by it. Similarly, there is no reason to assume that the theory of mind and its laws must be accessible to conscious awareness in order to guide our mental attributions. (Recall the point made in the chapter on consciousness, that not all mental states and processes are conscious.) The widely accepted view of Theory-theorists is that Folk Psychology is a *tacit* theory—that is, it is not normally used in a conscious way, but it can be articulated to some extent and made conscious on occasion, much like the grammar of our language.

Meaning of Mental Concepts

I noted earlier that the Argument from Analogy assumes that one has an introspective understanding of the nature of one's own mental states. We have seen that recent work in psychology and neuroscience has challenged that assumption. But if we don't learn about the nature and function of mental states simply through introspection, the question then becomes: What is the source of our understanding of those mental states and of the concepts that apply to them? Theory-theory offers a response.

9. *Psychosemantics* (Cambridge, MA: MIT/Bradford), pp. 132–3.

10. "Knowledge and Ability in 'Theory of Mind': One-Eyed Overview of a Debate," in *Mental Simulation*, M. Davies and T. Stone, eds. (Oxford: Blackwell, 1995), p. 140.

One of the common characteristics of scientific theories is that the theoretical (unobservable) entities that are postulated by the theory are also *defined* by their role in that theory. Folk Psychology, as an informal theory, does not make such definitions explicit. However, in recent years certain versions of Functionalism have tried to offer explicit definitions of mental states in terms of their causal relations with other mental states, with input, and with behavior. Some defenders of Functionalism have also defended a Folk Psychological theory of mental attribution. This alliance has generated more explicit theoretical definitions of belief, desire, etc., than our ordinary use of Folk Psychology had provided. For example, a Functionalist might define 'belief' in terms of its causal relations with certain types of input—usually of a perceptual sort—its causal relations with certain other mental states (including inferential relations with other beliefs), and its causal relations to certain types of behavior.

If this approach is right, then the theory provides one general set of definitions of mental states that would apply quite generally, both to my own case and to the cases of others. This would seem to entail that once a child has grasped the meaning of some mental concepts, there should be no difference in his ability to attribute them to himself or to others. As we shall see in the next section, there is some dispute about whether or not this is the case.

Philosopher Robert Gordon objects to the view that the meaning of mental concepts is determined by their role in a theory of mind. He agrees with the generally accepted view that quite young children are able to understand the meaning of many mental concepts, but he says that the view that their understanding would depend on having a grasp of their role in a theory of mind is implausible: "mastery of its [Folk Psychology's] concepts would seem to demand a highly developed theoretical intellect and a methodological sophistication rivaling that of modern-day cognitive scientists. That is an awful lot to impute to the four-year-old, or to our savage ancestors."[11]

Defenders of Theory-theory, like philosophers Stephen Stich and Shaun Nichols, respond by appealing to the analogy with language. They argue that children don't formulate theories the way scientists do. But they note that children learn language even sooner than they learn Folk Psychology, and they all learn much the same grammar. Similar things can be said about their learning of "Folk Physics"—the ability to predict the behavior of ordinary objects. It is plausible to suppose, they

11. "Folk Psychology as Simulation," in *Folk Psychology*, M. Davies and T. Stone, eds., p. 71.

argue, that natural selection has equipped children with either innate knowledge structures or with special-purpose learning mechanisms that assist them in these three crucial areas.[12]

Furthermore, a defender of the Theory-theory might argue that people can *use* mental concepts appropriately even if they cannot explicitly *define* them and are unaware of the theory that gives them their technical meaning. Perhaps the ability to use a concept in practical contexts, and the ability to understand others when they use it in such contexts, should be adequate to indicate an understanding of the meaning of the concept. Some concepts, like 'bachelor', perhaps require some understanding of their definition. But understanding other concepts, like 'funny' or 'dog' or 'heat', don't seem to require an ability to provide theoretical definitions. So the defender of Theory-theory might argue that the fact that children, and even many adults, cannot provide theoretical definitions of mental terms may not count as a significant objection. Their ability to use these terms appropriately in practical contexts is evidence of a reasonable understanding of mental concepts.

Developmental Data: False Beliefs and Autism

Recall that in our discussion of Premack's and Woodruff's experiments with the chimp Sarah there was some difficulty being sure just what Sarah was really up to. Some philosophers suggested that one might be able to find out if Sarah was really attributing mental states to others if there was a way to clearly distinguish between what Sarah believed about something and what she believed that her trainer believed. If Sarah's behavior indicated that she recognized the difference between the two and could predict the trainer's behavior based on *his* belief rather than on her own, that would provide pretty clear evidence that she was attributing mental states to him. This was the insight that gave birth to the false belief test. When used with children, the tests indicated that they develop an understanding of false beliefs in others when they are about five years of age.

On the face of it, the results of the false belief test looked as if they presented a problem for Theory-theorists. If children learn the theory of mind from adults, or if it is innate, it seems that once they have mastered the concept of belief, they should have no difficulty in attributing beliefs to others, even false beliefs. However, the experiments showed that until about five years of age children do have difficulty attributing false beliefs under certain circumstances.

12. "Folk Psychology: Simulation or Tacit Theory?" in *Folk Psychology*, M. Davies and T. Stone, eds., pp. 136–7.

Theorists like Gopnik and Wellman, however, who claimed that children formulate the theory for themselves on the basis of their experience, had a quick response: The children's theory is still in the process of formation, with recalcitrant data, revisions in progress, and so on, until about the age of five. Hence, the children's inability to ascribe false beliefs to others before that time is not surprising. Their understanding of belief as a representational state, one that could misrepresent as well as accurately represent, is not yet fully formed.

Jerry Fodor offers a different solution to the apparent problem caused by false belief tests. He argues that even very young children have a concept of belief, including false belief. As support, he recounts an instance of the "belief explanation task." According to one variation of the test, a young child is told that Mary is looking for her kitten. The kitten is under the chair, but Mary is looking under the piano. The child is then asked why Mary is looking under the piano. Even some young children respond that Mary *thinks* (believes) that the kitten is under the piano.[13] This, Fodor argues, is evidence that at least some very young children have a concept of false belief and can attribute it to others. However, he hypothesizes that they often take a simpler route when predicting another's behavior. They predict what is likely to satisfy desires, without taking beliefs into consideration. For example, some children respond to the question about Mary by saying simply that she *wants* to find her kitten. Gradually, he suggests, they learn that this heuristic shortcut doesn't always work, that it leads to mistaken explanations, and they begin to make reference to both beliefs and desires. On Fodor's view, young children have just the same theory of mind that adults have, but they don't make full use of its resources from the start.[14]

As we have seen, the false belief tests were designed to see if individuals are capable of attributing mental states to other people, particularly when those mental states are different from their own. Some psychologists had begun to suspect that *autistic* children might not be capable of such mental attribution.

To test the possibility that autism might be linked with the inability to attribute mental states to others (see box on page 241), Simon Baron-Cohen, Alan Leslie, and Uta Frith designed a series of experiments

13. K. Bartsch and H. M. Wellman, "Young Children's Attribution of Action to Beliefs and Desires," *Child Development*, 60 (1989):946–64.

14. "A Theory of the Child's Theory of Mind," in *Mental Simulation*, M. Davies and T. Stone, eds., pp. 109–22; originally published in *Cognition*, 44 (1992).

modeled on the false belief tests.[15] Three different groups of children were involved in the experiments: normal four and five year olds, Down's syndrome children with a mental age of five, and autistic children with a mental age of nine years. The results were dramatic. Both the normal and the Down's syndrome children were able to do quite well on the false belief test. The autistic children, on the other hand, did quite poorly, answering mostly like the normal three year olds. That is, many were unable to attribute false beliefs to others. The psychologists concluded that this inability, in spite of their advanced mental ages, was evidence that they lack a theory of mind.

Autism: Autism is a syndrome, generally appearing in early childhood, that can carry a fairly diverse set of symptoms. Three characteristics are most often associated with it: deficits in communicative skills, in social reciprocity, and in spontaneous pretend-play. In addition, some autistic individuals show abnormalities in sensory or perceptual capacities, some have language-learning difficulties, some engage in obsessive behaviors, and some appear to be mentally retarded to some degree.[16] Several different theories have been proposed to explain the syndrome. According to one account, the autistic person is overwhelmed by an excessive sensitivity to sensory stimulation and is therefore unable to respond appropriately to it. More recently, some psychologists have argued that individuals with autism suffer from "mindblindness." That is to say, they lack the ability to attribute mental states to others, and are therefore quite unable to understand other people's behavior.[17]

To further test their findings, they devised another series of tests in which a similar group of three different sets of children—normal, Down's syndrome, and autistic—were tested. This time they used nonverbal tests involving picture sequencing. All of the children did well when the pictures dealt with mechanical situations involving physical causality (e.g., a child running and falling over a stone), indicating that

15. "Does the Autistic Child Have a 'Theory of Mind'?" *Cognition*, 21(1985): 37–46.

16. Cf. Jill Boucher, "What Could Possibly Explain Autism?" in *Theories of Theories of Mind*, P. Carruthers and P. Smith, eds. (Cambridge: Cambridge University Press, 1996).

17. See Simon Baron-Cohen, *Mindblindness* (Cambridge, MA: MIT/Bradford, 1995); and Uta Frith, "Autism," *Scientific American*, June 1993.

the autistic children were not lacking in general intelligence. They understood Folk Physics. But the autistic children were again unable to properly sequence pictures that involved false beliefs. The psychologists again concluded that at least one of the deficits of autistic children is that they lack a theory of mind, and they are unable to attribute certain types of mental states to others.

As we shall see, opponents of the Theory-theory will offer somewhat different explanations of both the false belief tests and the experiments with autistic children.

Strengths and Weaknesses of the Theory-Theory

Our very familiarity with some of the platitudes associated with Folk Psychology seems to give the Theory-theory an initial intuitive appeal.

However, a more significant advantage of the theory is that it holds some promise of being able to provide explicit definitions of mental terms, particularly when linked with a Functionalist account of the mental (although as some critics have argued, even these Functionalist definitions continue to have their problems).

Further, it appeals to a type of theoretical explanation that is currently in widespread and rather successful use in cognitive science. While this provides no guarantee that Theory-theory is right, it puts the view in some impressive company. Unlike some versions of its chief competitor, it manages to avoid virtually all of the objections that have been leveled against the Argument from Analogy.

Finally, the view gains some of its plausibility from analogies with the linguistic case. The latter is widely thought to be a well-confirmed case of innate, tacit, knowledge structures that underlie certain of our critical cognitive capacities. That fact lends a certain degree of credibility to the Theory-theory's claims to have a similar character.

Opponents of the Theory-theory point to several problems with it. Philosopher Alvin Goldman cites three of them. For one thing, he says, the theory is vague. Recall my comments on the *ceteris paribus* clauses that must be attached to our predictions and explanations. These possible exceptions to the rule cannot be spelled out in any detail, making it seem to some that the rules are not serious theoretical rules at all but simply rough approximations. On Goldman's view, they leave too much to be accounted for. Further, he notes that the laws of Folk Psychology make no distinction between *dispositional* and *occurrent* mental states—for example, between a long-term but now inactive desire one may have, and a current and active one. The two could be expected to be governed by somewhat different rules and have somewhat different effects on behavior. Finally, he challenges the notion that the theory is really as universal as some have claimed it to be.[18]

For those who see Folk Psychology as an *acquired* theory—acquired either by learning or by a process of theory formation—some philosophers have argued that young children are not yet sophisticated enough to learn or formulate such a theory, let alone to make reasonable use of it in predicting and explaining behavior.

Simulation Theory of Mental Attribution

Recall that there were at least two plausible interpretations of the chimp Sarah's behavior: Either she had a theory of mind, or she was operating from *empathy*. In the latter case, she would be seeing herself in the situation of the other (the trainer). The *empathy* interpretation of her behavior has developed into the Simulation theory of mental attribution.

In our discussion of the Theory-theory approach to mental attribution, it became clear that there are some variations in the views held by its defenders. Some believe that the theory is learned, some that it is constructed, and some that it is innate. In addition, some see the theory of mind on rather close analogy with scientific theories, while others see it as less formal than that.

Simulation theory also has its variations. One view, introduced by Robert Gordon, is sometimes referred to by him as "radical simulation." A second version of Simulation theory, defended by Alvin Goldman and to some extent by psychologist Paul Harris, is sometimes referred to by Goldman as "Complex Simulation theory." A third variation, first defended by Jane Heal, might be called a "hybrid" version. Let's look first at Gordon's account.

In his 1986 paper, "Folk Psychology and Simulation," Gordon explains his view by describing a series of psychological facts that he believes lead quite naturally to the Simulation theory of mental attribution.

- I am extremely reliable in predicting my own behavior.

- These predictions are often the outcome of practical reasoning that leads to a decision.

18. "Interpretation Psychologized," in *Folk Psychology*, M. Davies and T. Stone, eds., pp. 79–80.

- They are not the outcome of the application of a theory and its laws to my behavior; I don't know all of my mental states and the laws that are supposed to govern them well enough to base my predictions on such a theory; and the application of a theory would not account for the high degree of reliability and confidence that attend my predictions about my behavior.

- I can even predict my behavior in hypothetical situations by engaging in a kind of *simulated* practical reasoning or *pretend-play*; in the process, I can take the system "off-line" so that my pretend decisions do not issue in behavior; so, for example, I can simulate what I would do if I heard an unexpected noise in the basement.

- One type of hypothetical *self*-prediction can involve simulating what one would do if one were in *someone else's* situation.

- In order to predict the behavior of the *other* person, one would need to make appropriate adjustments in relation to differences between oneself and that other.

- Hypothetico-practical reasoning involves pretending that one is in some hypothetical situation and reasoning about how one would behave.

- When one uses such a method to predict or explain the behavior of another person, one can formulate a hypothesis about that person's behavior and then test it by watching further reactions and behavior of various sorts.

- Predictions, even after testing, will not be guaranteed to be correct, but they can increasingly approximate the behavior of the other.

Gordon characterizes this sort of theory—based on practical reasoning, motivation, and emotion—as using a "hot" methodology, and he contrasts it with what he calls the "cold" methodology of Theory-theory, which operates with a purely intellectual application of a theory.

Gordon notes that a Simulation theory can look very much like a close relative of the old Argument from Analogy, and he is at pains to dispel the opinion that his account has all the problems associated with that argument. To this end, he makes three moves intended to explicitly distance his view from the analogical argument. He claims that his account does not involve an analogical *inference* from one's own case to that of another person. Further, he does not mean to rely on *introspective* ascriptions of mental states to himself. And finally, he denies that his account assumes that one is already in possession (by introspection) of the mental concepts that one ascribes to another. On Gordon's view, any Simulation theory that does not distance itself from the Argument from Analogy in these ways will be problematic.[19]

In an effort to avoid the claim that his view requires one to make an *inference* from oneself to the other (as the Argument from Analogy does), Gordon argues that in simulation, one does not simulate *oneself* in the situation of the other. On the contrary, one simulates or pretends to *be* that other. One does not first imagine what one would do if one were *oneself* in John's place—that move would presumably then require one to make an inference from one's own case to the case of John. This, in turn, would likely involve some appeal to psychological *theory* in order to justify that inference. Gordon, of course, is arguing against the need to appeal to such a theory. In contrast, he says that one simulates *being* John, with whatever adjustments are needed in order to allow for significant differences between him and me, and one comes to a *pretend decision* about what John would do. He characterizes the process in the following way: "To simulate [another] in his situation requires an egocentric shift, a recentering of my egocentric map on [that other]. He becomes in my imagination the referent of the first person pronoun 'I'. . . . Such recentering is the prelude to transforming myself in imagination into [the other] much as actors become the characters they play" (p. 55).

Gordon uses the analogy of an actress who is able to play the part of a number of different characters. She does not, he says, have lists of theoretical knowledge about those characters in her mind; rather, she has a "set of operations . . . [a] set of changes or adjustments" that she makes as she enters the role. Further, she does not have a code of information about herself that she must introspect. "She needs no inventory of *her own* mental states, processes, and tendencies."[20] That is to say, the actress does not begin by introspecting her own mental states and then make some sort of move to the mental states of the character she will play. She simply "re-centers" herself and pretends to *be* that character. Thus, on Gordon's account of simulation, one does not rely on intro-

19. "Simulation without Introspection or Inference from Me to You," in *Mental Simulation*, M. Davies and T. Stone, eds., pp. 53–4.

20. "Reply to Stich and Nichols," in *Folk Psychology*, M. Davies and T. Stone, eds., p. 179.

spection or on making inferences from oneself to others. His view, he argues, is not an update of the Argument from Analogy.

We shall return in the next subsection to Gordon's third effort to distance his view from that argument—namely, his account of mental concepts. But first it might be useful to pause and consider how Alvin Goldman's version of Simulation theory differs from Gordon's on these first two issues.

The first of these differences concerns the process of simulation itself. While Gordon believes that one simulates *the other*, much as an actor assumes the part of a character, Goldman sees the process as using *oneself* as a model for the other. Goldman describes his view of simulation in the following way: "The initial step, of course, is to imagine being 'in the shoes' of the agent, e.g., in the situation of [the agent]. This means pretending to have the same initial desires, beliefs, or other mental states that the attributor's background information suggests the agent has. The next step is to feed these pretend states into some inferential mechanism, or other cognitive mechanism, and allow that mechanism to generate further mental states as outputs by its normal operating procedure. . . . In short, you let your own psychological mechanism serve as a 'model' of his."[21]

If Goldman's version is right, one imagines *oneself* in the position of the other, tries to imagine what one would do if one were in that situation, and lets one's "inferential mechanism" predict the behavioral outcome. Because he sees the process as using *oneself* as a model for the other, Goldman sees it as involving an *inference* from one's own case to the case of the other. So on both of these counts, Goldman's version of Simulation theory is closer to the Argument from Analogy than is Gordon's.

It may be difficult to say, from an *experiential* point of view, what the precise difference is between pretending to *be* the other (Gordon's view) and imagining *oneself* in the situation of the other (Goldman's). Does an actress transform herself into the character, or does she imagine herself in the situation of the character? But consider some of the *theoretical*, rather than the experiential differences in the two views.

As we saw in the discussion of the Argument from Analogy, the role played by introspection is problematic. Goldman's account of the Simulation theory, as well as that of Paul Harris, seems to require some role for introspection. Gordon, on the other hand, argues that introspection is not required. Instead, he says, we can execute what he calls an "*ascent*

21. "Empathy, Mind, and Morals," in *Mental Simulation*, M. Davies and T. Stone, eds., p. 189.

routine." It runs like this: In order to articulate my beliefs, I don't need to look into my mind, try to find some state that has the "feel" of a belief, and then put it into language. Rather, I make statements about how I see things in the world, how I take things to be. So, I might say, "The snow will come early this year." Or, I might *ascend* to a more Folk Psychological version of the same thing: "I *believe* that the snow will come early this year." Or when asked, "Do you think that the Cubs will win the World Series this year?" I might reply, "Yes, I do." Or I might *ascend* and say, "I *believe* that they will win it this year." In *both* cases I am articulating a belief, and in neither case do I introspect my mental states to look for and recognize that belief. Gordon notes that this capacity to articulate how they see things arises in very young children before they have developed the ability to introspect or to recognize beliefs by their phenomenological "feel" (if indeed beliefs have any sort of "feel").

On Gordon's view, when I articulate my own beliefs I am saying how I see the world; when I simulate another, I put myself in her place, and say (with as much accuracy as I can) how she sees some aspect of her world. "Rather than rehearse the well-known objections to introspection, I have argued that ascent routines, coupled with our capacity for recentering our egocentric maps, enable us directly, rather than by inference from our own case, to identify the mental states of others."[22]

Gordon's *ascent routine,* as well as his insistence that simulation involves transforming oneself in imagination into the other person, avoids on his view any need to appeal to introspection or to make an inference from his own mental states to those of another—all problems associated with the Argument from Analogy. This, then, is one of the significant theoretical implications of Gordon's insistence, against views like Goldman's, that one does not use *oneself* as a model for the other. If we can imaginatively "transform" ourselves into the other, there will be no need to make an inference to what the other would do; we are (metaphorically) already "there."

Goldman, on the other hand, acknowledges the similarity of his view with the Argument from Analogy. However, he suggests that the use of simulation does not entail a conscious belief in certain premises of the argument and an inference based on those premises. Rather, he sees the use of the analogy as a function of certain "mechanisms, or routines, that are built into the cognitive architecture."[23] This suggests

22. "Simulation without Introspection," in *Mental Simulation,* M. Davies and T. Stone, eds., pp. 60, 63.

23. "Interpretation Psychologized," in *Folk Psychology,* M. Davies and T. Stone, eds., p. 93.

a certain innate tendency to analogize others to ourselves in place of a self-consciously constructed theoretical argument to an analogy. As I suggested earlier, in spite of problems with analogies, there is no guarantee that we don't make use of them in mental attribution. Similarly, the fact that introspection has problems does not entail that we don't rely on it to some extent.

The use of inference, however, may indicate a need to appeal to some sort of theory to justify the inference (unless such an inference could be unconscious and automatic). This points to one other area in which Goldman's view appears to be less "radical" than Gordon's. It concerns the role that theory might play in conjunction with simulation. Goldman claims that explicit or implicit simulation is the *fundamental* method that we use when we attribute mental states to others. But he does not insist that simulation is the only method that can be used. He believes that particularly as we mature, we develop information about certain types of behavioral regularities in other individuals; we learn by induction how some behaviors are most likely to follow certain types of stimuli. Given this occasional reliance on generalizations and rules of thumb, Goldman concludes, "We might call this the complex variant of the simulation approach. It converges somewhat toward the folk-theory theory (though the exact degree of convergence depends on the nature of the inductively based knowledge structures it posits)."[24] So for Goldman, some combination of simulation with theory is possible. On the other side, in more recent papers, several Theory-theorists have in fact suggested that perhaps Theory-theory can accommodate *some* use of simulation, but it would occur only in certain special types of cases.

Paul Harris agrees that simulation and some sort of theory are probably both used in mental attribution, but like Goldman he believes that simulation plays a foundational role. He sees adults as probably using both theory and simulation in various contexts, but he argues that children first acquire a theory of mind by a process of simulation.[25]

Harris offers a couple of examples showing how each of the two views might be used. He notes that a clinical psychologist treating an individual with schizophrenia need not simulate the individual's schizophrenic mental states in order to diagnose the disorder. *Theory* will be useful here.

24. "Interpretation Psychologized," in *Folk Psychology,* M. Davies and T. Stone, eds., p. 88.
25. "From Simulation to Folk Psychology," in *Folk Psychology,* M. Davies and T. Stone, eds., p. 211.

To illustrate the role played by *simulation*, he asks you to imagine that you are given a set of sentences that have been studied by others and determined to be grammatical or not. You are asked to predict how most people had judged the sentences. He notes that it is unlikely that you call up some theory of grammar in order to predict. Rather, it is highly likely that you look at the sentences, decide if they seem grammatical or not to you, and then predict a similar judgment on the part of most other people. That is, you simulate.

Simulation theory, like Theory-theory, has its critics. One objection to Simulation theory, raised by Daniel Dennett, is that it *must* make use of some sort of theory. Dennett says that if one were to simulate a suspension bridge, one could only do so by making some use of a theory about how bridges behave under various conditions. In like fashion, he reasons, if we simulate others we must be making use of some sort of theory about them. Goldman responds by distinguishing between the simulation of inanimate objects like bridges or weather and the simulation of a living organism who is reasonably like oneself. In the former case, he says, Dennett is right; we do need to make use of some sort of theory. But in the latter case no such theory is required. He specifies two conditions that must be met if a simulation does not need to appeal to a theory:

> This can happen if (1) the *process* that drives the simulation is the same as (or relevantly similar to) the process that drives the system, and (2) the initial states of the simulating agent are the same as, or relevantly similar to, those of the target system. [This is achieved by pretending to be in the same, or roughly the same, initial states.] . . . It is not necessary that the simulating agent have a theory of what the routine is, or how it works. In short, successful simulation can be *process-driven*.[26]

One simulates objects by a *theory-driven* approach; one simulates other living organisms, especially conspecifics, by a *process-driven* approach.

A second objection, raised by philosophers Stephen Stich and Shaun Nichols, points out one characteristic that differentiates Theory-theory from Simulation theory, a characteristic that might be used to determine which of the two theories is correct. They call it *cognitive penetrability*. The idea is this: A process like predicting someone's behavior is *cognitively penetrable* if one's knowledge about mental states and their relationships can affect the prediction; the process is

26. "Interpretation Psychologized," in *Folk Psychology*, M. Davies and T. Stone, eds., p. 85.

cognitively impenetrable if one's knowledge about mental states and their relations has no effect on the prediction. Stich and Nichols believe that predictions of behavior *are* cognitively penetrable; that is, the predictions are influenced by one's knowledge of Folk Psychology. Simulation theory, on the other hand, is not guided by the knowledge of any theory but by pretending to be in another person's situation. Simulation is *process-driven* not *theory-driven*, as Goldman has insisted. All of this, on the view of Stich and Nichols, has some practical, testable consequences.

According to them, mistaken predictions about others' behavior are easily explained by a faulty or incomplete theory; in the case of simulation, it should not matter if one does not know something about how mental states and behavior are related because one simply runs one's own system, and if there is something unexpected or unknown about the workings of that system it will still influence the predictions of the other's behavior: "If there is some quirk in the human decision-making system, something quite unknown to most people that leads the system to behave in an unexpected way under certain circumstances, the accuracy of predictions based on simulations should not be adversely affected. If you provide the system with the right pretend input, it should simulate (and thus predict) the unexpected output."[27]

In a variety of experiments it has been shown that people's behavior under certain circumstances is surprising, would not have been predicted by them, but is remarkably consistent across groups. Recall the experiment in which people were invited to judge which pair of nylon stockings was of the highest quality. In spite of the fact that the pairs were identical, most of the participants consistently chose items from the right-hand side of the collection as being of the best quality. When asked to explain their choice, they insisted that the item they selected had some distinguishing characteristic—greater sheerness, elasticity, and the like. But in fact, the items did not differ in these respects. The experiments suggest that there is some *unconscious* tendency to select items from the right-hand side of collections (sometimes followed by confabulated reasons for having done so).

Stich and Nichols argue that this apparent anomaly can be explained by Theory-theorists simply as a gap or a bit of misinformation in their theory. Folk Psychology does not include an item about preference for the right side of collections. (Theory-theorists have never argued that Folk Psychology is complete or wholly accurate—just that it is usually fairly reliable.) Given an adjustment to the theory, they can

27. "Folk Psychology: Simulation or Tacit Theory?" in *Folk Psychology*, M. Davies and T. Stone, eds., p. 150.

then predict such behavior accurately. Simulation theorists, on the other hand, have a problem. If simulation is indeed the process by which we predict the behavior of others, then when we simulate, we should predict that the others will choose from the right side of collections. The unconscious bias toward the right ought to operate in the simulator just as it does in the others. The fact that it is unconscious should not make any difference. Since Simulation is driven by process and not by knowledge of theory, the process ought to return a prediction of right-side choice.

Simulationists have responded by saying that in order to accurately reproduce this experimental situation, simulators would have to have precisely the same inputs and internal processes as the test subjects. But under those circumstances they would no longer be *simulating* others, they would merely be replacing them in the experiment. Simulation involves imaginative or pretended placement of oneself in the place of another. Imagination and pretense never replicate *all* the relevant circumstances that have influenced the behavior of another. Hence, one might fail to predict the right-side bias because, for example, one was not in actual visual contact with the collection of items.

Meaning of Mental Concepts

An adequate account of how we attribute mental states to others should also explain how we have come to understand what those states are. Goldman himself raises this as an apparent difficulty for the Simulation theory. He says that he believes that the theory is incapable of explaining how we arrive at an understanding of mental state concepts, and that Simulation theory must *assume* a prior understanding of those concepts. For some theorists this constitutes a serious shortcoming of the theory. Goldman does, however, suggest a way of handling the problem: "The time is ripe to reconsider the prospects of the first-person approach to the understanding of mental concepts. It has always seemed plausible, prior to philosophical theorizing, that our naive understanding of mental concepts should prominently involve introspective and not merely causal/relational elements."[28]

Gordon, on the other hand, believes that Simulation theory *can* provide an account of the meaning of mental concepts. Recall his appeal to what he calls the *ascent routine*, as a way of avoiding any appeal to introspection. Gordon argues that this same ascent routine provides his

28. "Interpretation Psychologized," in *Folk Psychology*, M. Davies and T. Stone, eds., p. 94.

view with one further advantage that also distances it further from the Argument from Analogy: it elucidates the meaning of certain mental concepts, independent of any appeal to introspection. On Gordon's version of the Simulation theory, "to attribute a belief to another person is to make an assertion, to state something as a fact, *within the context of practical simulation.* Acquisition of the capacity to attribute beliefs is acquisition of the capacity to make assertions in such a context."[29] That is to say, I can attribute a belief to another person by pretending to be that person and stating how she sees some situation. So, on Gordon's view, I don't appeal to a theory for my understanding of belief, and I don't appeal to introspection. I learn the meaning of mental concepts by acquiring the ability to execute an ascent routine and by acquiring the capacities for simulation.

Developmental Data: False Beliefs and Autism

How does Simulation explain the problem that very young children have in attributing false beliefs? When asked where Maxi will look for his chocolate, three and four year olds standardly answer that he will look in the cupboard (where his mother put it after he went out to play). They seem to assume that Maxi knows what they know. Gordon suggests that the inability to ascribe false beliefs to others like Maxi probably arises from the child's inability to move beyond her egocentric viewpoint. So the child ascribes *her own* belief to Maxi. She assumes that everyone sees the world as she sees it. By about the age of five, she develops a more flexible ability to see the world from the point of view of another. Paul Harris sees the development of a child's ability to attribute mental states, even false beliefs, to others, as being dependent on the increasing flexibility of the child's imagination.[30]

Simulationists argue, too, that if the capacity to attribute false belief to another depends on the ability to *pretend* or to place oneself imaginatively in another's place, this fact might explain some aspects of autism. Autistic children rarely engage in pretend-play. And recall that in false belief tests, autistic children did notably worse than normal or even Down's syndrome children. They appear to be unable to put themseves in the place of others, to see the world from another's viewpoint. For Simulationists, this deficit in pretend-play and imaginative flexibility

29. "Folk Psychology as Simulation," in *Folk Psychology*, M. Davies and T. Stone, eds., p. 68.

30. "From Simulation to Folk Psychology," in *Folk Psychology*, M. Davies and T. Stone, eds., pp. 214–5.

would explain their deficit in attributing false beliefs. More generally, the inability to place oneself in another's place might also explain the tendency of autistic children to treat other people as objects, rather than as subjects with mental states.

Goldman acknowledges that the experiments with autistic children are not yet decisive between Simulation and Theory-theory. Nevertheless, he offers two stories from psychologist Uta Frith's dealings with autistic youngsters, both of which he believes are best explained by a failure at simulation, rather than by an absence of a theory of mind. In the first situation, a helpful young autistic man is at home while his mother is baking. She asks her son to go out and get her some *cloves*. He leaves and then a few minutes later he returns with a bag full of women's *clothes*. Goldman notes that the boy understood that his mother *wanted* something, but he had a completely absurd notion of what that was. He was unable to simulate what one might want when one is baking.

The second story involved a ten-year-old autistic girl. When she went to have a blood test, the nurse said, "Give me your hand; it won't hurt." The girl was terrified. She apparently thought that the nurse was asking her to cut off her hand and give it to her. When she was told to put out her finger, she calmed down. But again, Goldman notes that the girl had a bizarre understanding of what the nurse *wanted*. If she were capable of simulation, he argues, she would have been able to interpret the request in a reasonable way.

Stich and Nichols reply that both cases could perhaps be understood *behavioristically*. That is, both autistic individuals may have understood simply that they were being told to *do* something. It is possible, they say, that the two did not understand anything at all about what someone else *wanted*.

There is at least one other version of the Simulation theory: the Hybrid version. We have seen that some supporters of Simulation, like Goldman and Harris, are quite willing to accept a mild hybrid account that *allows* for both Simulation and some appeal to Theory.

But some philosophers, like Jane Heal, have argued that there is reason to think that both Simulation and Theory are *required*. "I shall suggest that simulation must be central as far as dealing with the contents of others' mental states is concerned but is much less clearly of relevance in dealing with non-content. Thus philosophers and psychologists should not oppose simulation to theory, but should rather ask what is the appropriate realm of each and how they interact."[31] She distinguishes

31. "Simulation, Theory, and Content," in *Theories of Theories of Mind*, P. Carruthers and P. Smith, eds., p. 75.

content from *non-content* where the latter includes propositional attitudes like believing, desiring, as well as the qualitative character of sensation and perception. Content, of course, includes *what* one believes or desires—for example, believing *that the economy is healthy*, desiring *that we find a solution for homelessness*. While non-content may be accounted for by Theory-theory, she argues that content requires Simulation. Part of the reason for that is the fact that we lack any theory of relevance. As a consequence, a theory won't tell us what sorts of content will be relevant to what other sorts of content or to what type of behavior. (Recall our discussion, in the previous chapter, of the enormous difficulties that theories in Artificial Intelligence have faced because of our inability to formulate rules that could determine relevance.) So on this hybrid account, neither Theory alone nor Simulation alone can provide an adequate story about mental attribution. Both are required.

Strengths and Weaknesses of the Simulation Theory

Recall that one of Goldman's criticisms of Theory-theory is that it is vague. He points out that the *ceteris paribus* clauses that must be appended to any plausible attempt to articulate the laws of the theory leave the theory less than clear. Gordon turns this issue into one of the strengths of the Simulation theory: "*in the context of practical simulation*, the unspecifiable constraints on *one's own* practical reasoning would enable one to delimit the application of these rules."[32] In other words, we know from our own experience, not from some theory, what sorts of *ceteris paribus* conditions are likely to be relevant.

Goldman argues that yet another strength of simulation is that it can account for mental attributions that allow for failures in logic and rationality.[33] One reason that we don't use stringent norms of rationality, he says, is that we are aware of our own failures in these areas. That awareness allows us to see our fallible selves in the place of the other, and to simulate the ability to think in inconsistent or illogical ways. In other words, Simulation better explains my ability to predict or explain these failures of rationality in others.

Goldman also argues that Simulation helps to explain how it is that I can gauge what sorts of allusions you will understand when I converse with you, or which of my jokes you are likely to find funny. In neither case, he says, do we have a theory that applies. Instead these situations

---

32. "Folk Psychology as Simulation," in *Folk Psychology*, M. Davies and T. Stone, eds., p. 67.

33. "Interpretation Psychologized," reprinted in *Folk Psychology*, M. Davies and T. Stone, eds.

depend on our ability to simulate the viewpoint of another.

Gordon, who has done a good deal of work on the philosophy of emotions, argues that Simulation theory is better able to make use of *emotions* in predicting and explaining behavior. He notes that experimental evidence indicates that when one imitates the facial expression of another, that mere act of physical mimicry can activate the emotion expressed by the other person's face. This suggests that simulating the emotional expression of another may give one a richer access to at least some of the mental states motivating the behavior than would a "cold" theoretical approach.

Goldman makes a related claim. He argues that empathy provides significant support for Simulation theory. When one feels empathy toward someone else, it is unlikely that one's reaction is guided by theories about emotions, or about empathy. Rather, the reaction appears to be process-driven—that is, a matter of role-taking, of simulation. Similar things can be said for the emotions one might feel when seeing a play or movie or reading a novel. Emotive and sexual responses seem not to arise from theories about how these work but from putting oneself in the imagined place of another. These examples don't prove that Simulation is used in all cases of mental attribution, but they enhance its plausibility in a certain range of cases.

One of the persistent criticisms of Simulation theory is that it is circular. It must assume an understanding of the very mental concepts whose attribution it tries to explain—without being able to explain how such an understanding arises. Philosopher Gary Fuller argues that there are at least two areas that appear to be problematic for Gordon's radical version of Simulation theory: When I simulate the beliefs, and so forth, of another, I cannot simulate just any old mental states, I must simulate the appropriate one; when I attribute the final state to the other, again, I must attribute the appropriate one—not just any one that happens to come to mind. On Fuller's view, it seems that in both cases some concept of the required state or states would have to be understood.[34] In response to Gordon's account of the *ascent routine*, an objector might insist that Gordon knew just how to pick out what would count as a belief rather than a desire. Is it possible that he is making tacit use of some bit of theory?

For now at least, the issue of the role of introspection in Simulation, and an adequate account of how we come to understand the mental concepts we use in Simulation, remain problematic for Simulationists.

---

34. "Simulation and Psychological Concepts," in *Mental Simulation*, M. Davies and T. Stone, eds., pp. 25–8.

Some Comparisons and Contrasts

Theory-theory and Simulation theory arose as more satisfactory alternatives to the Argument from Analogy. But the debate continues about which of the two theories is the more plausible alternative. Here are a few of the areas of dispute that await further investigation.

- First, is our capacity for mental attribution driven by theory or by imaginative process, or by some combination of both?

- Second, is autism best explained as a failure of imaginative flexibility, as Simulationists argue, or by an absence of (or weakness in) the theory of mind, as Theory-theorists contend?

- Third, is the developmental data in young children, including their changing performance on false belief tests, best explained as the gradual acquisition or maturation of a theory of mind or as the gradual development of the imaginative ability to put oneself in the place of another?

- Fourth, is our understanding of mental concepts best explained by grasping their role in theory (Theory-theorists) or by some version of an *ascent routine* (Gordon), or by introspection (Harris, and perhaps Goldman)?

- Fifth, are there significant differences in children's abilities to attribute mental states to themselves and to others? If so, are these best explained by an incomplete understanding of theory (Gopnik and Wellman), by a failure to make full use of the theory (Fodor), or by an inability to put themselves imaginatively in the place of others (Simulationists)?

Some Tentative Conclusions

The debate about how we are able to explain and predict the behavior of others by attributing mental states to them is far from over. At this point in time, the Theory-theory appears to be the dominant view among both philosophers and psychologists. Nonetheless, the Simulation theory has some strong supporters.

In fact, as the debate has continued, some philosophers and psychologists on both sides of that debate are beginning to suggest that a full explanation of our ability to attribute mental states, and to explain and predict behavior in light of them, will probably need to appeal to both Theory and some form of Simulation. Their respective accounts differ on how and when such a combination might work. But there does seem to be at least some movement toward more hybrid accounts.

So the answer to our title question, How do we link behavior to mental states?—like so many other questions relating to mental states—awaits further investigation.

Issues for Discussion

1. If one attributes mental states to nonhuman animals, would Theory-theory or Simulation theory be a more useful approach? Explain.

2. Which of the three theories of mental attribution, Argument from Analogy, Theory-theory, or Simulation theory strikes you as the most plausible? Give careful reasons for your answer.

3. Some psychologists have argued that children develop some understanding of *desire* before they develop a fully representational theory of mental states like beliefs. If true, might this have any relevance to the claim that language-using primates sign almost entirely in terms of wants and desires and rarely in terms of beliefs? Explain.

4. Can you design an experiment for the chimp Sarah that would indicate that she can attribute beliefs to other individuals where those beliefs are different from her own? Describe how you would go about it.

5. Do any of the theories of mental attribution defeat the thought experiments concerning zombies, which we discussed in the chapter on consciousness? Explain your answer.

6. Which, if any, of the theories of mental attribution would be useful in attributing mental states to computers and robots? Explain.

7. If nonhuman animals like chimps do attribute mental states to others, do you think that it is more likely that they do so by using a theory of mind or by some version of empathy/simulation? Explain.

Suggested Research Projects

a. It is sometimes claimed that when nonhuman animals engage in *deception*, that is evidence that they attribute mental states to others. Read R. W. Byrne and A. Whiten, "Computation and Mindreading in Primate Tactical Deception," in *Natural Theories of Mind*, A. Whiten, ed. (Oxford: Blackwell, 1991). Why do they distinguish between *strategic* and *tactical* deception? What conclusion do they reach about deception and mental attribution in primates?

b. Read R. Nisbett and T. Wilson, "Telling More than We Can Know: Verbal Reports on Mental Processes," *Psychological Review*, 84(3):231–59. (1) What conclusions do they draw about introspection? (2) Describe several of the experiments that they discuss. (3) How do the experiments support their conclusions about introspection?

c. What is solipsism? How is it relevant to the problem of other minds? Are the arguments in defense of solipsism self-defeating? Explain your answer.

d. The Existentialist philosopher Jean-Paul Sartre has claimed that we know about the existence of other minds (or "subjects of experience" or the "for-itself"), not by way of reasoned arguments, but by way of particular types of *feelings* we experience in the presence of the Other's gaze. He uses shame as an example. Read the section on "the Look" in his book, *Being and Nothingness*. Briefly describe his account of the situation in which the look or gaze of another arouses just such a feeling that one is in the presence of another mind. Do you think that his claim is right? Do you think that there are other feelings that provide evidence of our knowledge that there are other minds? Explain your answer.

Some Additional Resources

In putting together additional bibliographic information, I thought it would be more useful to readers if I divided the material into seven groups — one group for each of the seven chapters. Hence, works connected with theories of mind are in the first section, those on consciousness in the second section, and so on. See also Some Resource Materials on page 13.

1. Theories of Mind (and closely related topics)

Armstrong, D. 1968. A *Materialist Theory of Mind*. London: Routledge & Kegan Paul.

———. 1980. *The Nature of Mind*. Ithaca, NY: Cornell University Press.

Bechtel, W. 1988. *Philosophy of Mind*. Hillsdale, NJ: Erlbaum.

Biro, J., and R. Shahan, eds. 1982. *Mind, Brain, and Function*. Norman, OK: University of Oklahoma Press.

Blakemore, C., and S. Greenfield, eds. 1987. *Mindwaves*. Oxford: Blackwell.

Block, N., ed. 1980–81. *Readings in Philosophy of Psychology*. 2 vols. Cambridge, MA: Harvard University Press.

Broad, C. D. 1951. *The Mind and Its Place in Nature*. New York: Humanities.

Calvin, W. 1990. *The Ascent of Mind*. New York: Bantam.

Calvin, W., and G. Ojemann. 1994. *Conversations with Neil's Brain*. Reading, MA: Addison-Wesley Publishers.

Churchland, Patricia S. 1986. *Neurophilosophy*. Cambridge, MA: MIT/Bradford.

Churchland, Patricia S., and T. Sejnowski. 1992. *The Computational Brain*. Cambridge, MA: MIT/Bradford.

Churchland, Paul M. 1988. *Matter and Consciousness*. Cambridge, MA: MIT/Bradford.

———. 1989. *A Neurocomputational Perspective*. Cambridge, MA: MIT/Bradford.

———. 1995. *The Engine of Reason, the Seat of the Soul*. Cambridge, MA: MIT/Bradford.

Crick, F. 1994. *The Astonishing Hypothesis: The Scientific Search for the Soul.* New York: Simon & Schuster.

Dennett, D. 1978. *Brainstorms.* Cambridge, MA: MIT/Bradford.

——. 1987. *The Intentional Stance.* Cambridge, MA: MIT/Bradford.

——. 1996. *Kinds of Minds.* New York: Basic Books.

Descartes, R. 2000. *Philosophical Essays and Correspondence,* Roger Ariew, ed. Indianapolis: Hackett Publishing Company.

Dretske, F. 1995. *Naturalizing the Mind.* Cambridge, MA: MIT/Bradford.

Edelman, G. 1992. *Bright Air, Brilliant Fire: On the Matter of the Mind.* New York: Basic Books.

Flanagan, O. 1991. *The Science of the Mind.* 2nd ed. Cambridge, MA: MIT/Bradford.

Fodor, J. 1975. *The Language of Thought.* Cambridge, MA: Harvard University Press.

——. 1981. *Representations.* Cambridge, MA: MIT/Bradford.

——. 1983. *The Modularity of Mind.* Cambridge, MA: MIT/Bradford.

Gardner, H. 1985. *The Mind's New Science.* New York: Basic Books.

Godfrey-Smith, P. 1996. *Complexity and the Function of Mind in Nature.* Cambridge: Cambridge University Press.

Graham, G. 1993. *Philosophy of Mind: An Introduction.* Oxford: Blackwell.

Gregory, R. 1987. *The Oxford Companion to the Mind.* Oxford: Oxford University Press.

Guttenplan, S., ed., 1994. *A Companion to the Philosophy of Mind.* Oxford: Blackwell.

Hannan, B. 1994. *Subjectivity and Reduction: An Introduction to the Mind-Body Problem.* Boulder, CO: Westview Press.

Haugeland, J. 1997. *Mind Design II.* Rev. ed. Cambridge, MA: MIT/Bradford.

Heil, J. 1992. *The Nature of True Minds.* Cambridge: Cambridge University Press.

——. 1998. *Philosophy of Mind.* London: Routledge.

Hirschfeld, L., and S. Gelman, eds. 1994. *Mapping the Mind: Domain Specificity in Cognition and Culture.* Cambridge: Cambridge University Press.

Humphrey, N. 1992. *A History of the Mind.* New York: HarperCollins.

Jacquette, D. 1994. *Philosophy of Mind.* Englewood Cliffs, NJ: Prentice-Hall.

Johnson, M. 1987. *The Body in the Mind.* Cambridge: Cambridge University Press.

Kenny A. 1989. *The Metaphysics of Mind.* Oxford: Oxford University Press.

Kim, J. 1993. *Supervenience and Mind.* Cambridge: Cambridge University Press.

——. 1996. *Philosophy of Mind.* Boulder, CO: Westview Press.

Longair, M., ed. 1997. *Roger Penrose: The Large, the Small and the Human Mind.* Cambridge: Cambridge University Press.

Lycan, W., ed. 1990. *Mind and Cognition.* Oxford: Blackwell.

Lyons, W. 1986. *The Disappearance of Introspection.* Cambridge, MA: MIT/Bradford.

MacDonald, C. 1991. *Mind-Body Identity Theories*. London: Routledge.

McGinn, C. 1982. *The Character of Mind*. Oxford: Oxford University Press.

Minsky, M. 1985. *The Society of Mind*. New York: Simon & Schuster.

Nagel, T. 1986. *The View from Nowhere*. Oxford: Oxford University Press.

Piaget, J. 1971. *Biology and Knowledge*. Edinburgh: University of Edinburgh.

Pinker, S. 1997. *How the Mind Works*. New York: Norton.

Priest, S. 1991. *Theories of the Mind*. Boston: Houghton Mifflin.

Putnam, H. 1975. *Mind, Language, and Reality*. Cambridge: Cambridge University Press.

Rey, G. 1997. *Contemporary Philosophy of Mind*. Oxford: Blackwell.

Rosenthal, D., ed. 1991. *The Nature of Mind*. Oxford: Oxford University Press.

Russell, B. 1921. *The Analysis of Mind*. London: Allen & Unwin.

Ryle, G. 1949. *The Concept of Mind*. New York: Harper & Row.

Searle, J. 1992. *The Rediscovery of the Mind*. Cambridge, MA: MIT/Bradford.

Smith, P., and O. Jones. 1986. *The Philosophy of Mind*. Cambridge: Cambridge University Press.

Sober, E. 1985. "Panglossian Functionalism and the Philosophy of Mind," *Synthèse*, 64:165–93.

Sterelny, K. 1990. *The Representational Theory of Mind*. Oxford: Blackwell.

Varela, F., E. Thompson, and E. Rosch. 1991. *The Embodied Mind*. Cambridge, MA: MIT/Bradford.

2. Consciousness

Aquila, R. 1990. "Consciousness as Higher-Order Thought: Two Objections," *American Philosophical Quarterly*, 27:81–7.

Baars, B. 1988. *A Cognitive Theory of Consciousness*. New York: Cambridge University Press.

———. 1997. *In the Theater of Consciousness*. New York: Oxford University Press.

Block, N. 1995. "On a Confusion about the Function of Consciousness," *Behavioral and Brain Sciences*, 18:227–87.

Block, N., O. Flanagan, and G. Guzeldere, eds. 1997. *The Nature of Consciousness*. Cambridge, MA: MIT/Bradford.

Byrne, A. 1997. "Some Like It HOT: Consciousness and Higher-Order Thoughts," *Philosophical Studies*, 86(2):103–29.

Chalmers, D. 1996. *The Conscious Mind*. New York: Oxford University Press.

Churchland, Patricia S. 1983. "Consciousness: The Transmutation of a Concept," *Pacific Philosophical Quarterly*, 64:80–95.

Crick, F., and C. Koch. 1992. "The Problem of Consciousness," *Scientific American*, (September):153–9.

Damasio, A. 1999. *The Feeling of What Happens: Body and Emotion in the Making of Consciousness*. New York: Harcourt Brace.

Davies, M., and G. Humphreys, eds. 1993. *Consciousness*. Oxford: Blackwell.

Dennett, D. 1982. "How to Study Human Consciousness Empirically, or, Nothing Comes to Mind," *Synthèse*, 53:159–80.

———. 1991. *Consciousness Explained*. New York: Little, Brown.

Dretske, F. 1993. "Conscious Experience," *Mind*, 102:263–83.

———. 1997. "What Good Is Consciousness?" *Canadian Journal of Philosophy*, 27(1):1–15.

Flanagan, O. 1992. *Consciousness Reconsidered*. Cambridge, MA: MIT/Bradford.

———. 1995. "Zombies and the Function of Consciousness," *Journal of Consciousness Studies*, 2:313–21.

Gennaro, R. 1993. "Brute Experience and the Higher-Order Thought Theory of Consciousness," *Philosophical Papers*, 22:51–69.

Globus, G., G. Maxwell, and I. Savodnik, eds. 1976. *Consciousness and the Brain*. New York: Plenum Press.

Hameroff, S., A. Kaszniak, and A. Scott, eds. 1996. *Toward a Science of Consciousness*. Cambridge, MA: MIT/Bradford.

Hannay, A. 1991. "Consciousness and the Experience of Freedom," in *John Searle and His Critics*, E. Lepore and R. Van Gulick, eds. Oxford: Blackwell.

Hardcastle, V. 1995. *Locating Consciousness*. Amsterdam: John Benjamins.

Humphrey, N. 1984. *Consciousness Regained*. Oxford: Oxford University Press.

Jackendoff, R. 1987. *Consciousness and the Computational Mind*. Cambridge, MA: MIT/Bradford.

James, W. 1904. "Does Consciousness Exist?" *Journal of Philosophy*, vol. 1(18), reprinted in *Essays in Radical Empiricism* (1912).

Jamieson, D., and M. Bekoff. 1992. "Carruthers on Nonconscious Experience," *Analysis*, 52:23–8.

Jaynes, J. 1976. *The Origin of Consciousness in the Breakdown of the Bicameral Mind*. Boston: Houghton Mifflin.

Kihlstrom, J. 1987. "The Cognitive Unconscious," *Science*, 237:1445–52.

Levine, J. 1997. "Recent Work on Consciousness," *American Philosophical Quarterly*, 34(4):379–404.

Lycan, W. 1987. *Consciousness*. Cambridge, MA: MIT/Bradford.

———. 1997. *Consciousness and Experience*. Cambridge, MA: MIT/Bradford.

Marcel, A. J., and E. Bisiach, eds. 1988. *Consciousness in Contemporary Science*. Oxford: Clarendon.

McGinn, C. 1991. *The Problem of Consciousness*. Oxford: Blackwell.

Nagel, T. 1974. "What Is It Like to Be a Bat?" *Philosophical Review*, 83:435–50.

Natsoulas, T. 1978. "Consciousness," *American Psychologist*, 33:906–14.

Penfield, W. 1975. *The Mystery of the Mind: A Critical Study of Consciousness and the Human Brain*. Princeton: Princeton University Press.

Penrose, R. 1994. *Shadows of the Mind: A Search for the Missing Science of Consciousness*. Oxford: Oxford University Press.

Rey, G. 1983. "A Reason for Doubting the Existence of Consciousness," in *Consciousness and Self-Regulation*, R. Davidson, G. Schwartz, and D. Shapiro, eds., vol. 3. New York: Plenum.

Rosenthal, D. 1986. "Two Concepts of Consciousness," *Philosophical Studies*, 3:329–59.

——. 1993. "Higher-Order Thoughts and the Appendage Theory of Consciousness," *Philosophical Psychology*, 6:155–67.

Schachter, D. 1989. "On the Relation between Memory and Consciousness: Dissociable Interactions and Conscious Experience," in *Varieties of Memory and Consciousness: Essays in Honour of Endel Tulving*, H. Roedinger and F. Craik, eds. Hillsdale, NJ: Erlbaum.

Seager, W. 1994. "Dretske on HOT Theories of Consciousness," *Analysis*, 54:270–6.

Searle, J. 1990. "Consciousness, Explanatory Inversion, and Cognitive Science," *Behavioral and Brain Sciences*, 13:585–95.

Shear, J., ed. 1995–97. *Explaining Consciousness—The 'Hard Problem'*. Cambridge, MA: MIT/Bradford.

Sperry, R. 1969. "A Modified Concept of Consciousness," *Psychological Review*, 76:532–36.

Tye, M. 1995. *Ten Problems of Consciousness*. Cambridge, MA: MIT/Bradford.

Van Gulick, R. 1989. "What Difference Does Consciousness Make?" *Philosophical Topics*, 17:211–30.

Villanueva, E. ed. 1991. *Consciousness*. First volume of *Philosophical Issues*. Atascadero, CA: Ridgeview.

Weiskrantz, L. 1997. *Consciousness Lost and Found*. Oxford: Oxford University Press.

. . . and *The Journal of Consciousness Studies*

3. Emotions

Arnold, M. 1960. *Emotion and Personality*. 2 vols. New York: Columbia University Press.

——. 1968. *The Nature of Emotion*. Baltimore: Penguin.

Arnold, M., ed. 1970. *Feelings and Emotions*. New York: Academic Press.

Damasio, A. 1994. *Descartes' Error: Emotion, Reason, and the Human Brain*. New York: Putnam.

Darwin, C. 1872/1998. *The Expression of the Emotions in Man and Animals*. New York: Oxford University Press.

DeSousa, R. 1987. *The Rationality of Emotions*. Cambridge, MA: MIT/Bradford.

Ekman, P. 1992. "An Argument for Basic Emotions," *Cognition and Emotion*, 6:169–200.

Gordon, R. 1969. "Emotions and Knowledge," *Journal of Philosophy*, 66:408–13.

Gordon, R. 1973. "Judgmental Emotions," *Analysis*, 34:40–8.

——. 1974. "The Aboutness of Emotions," *American Philosophical Quarterly*, 11:27–36.

——. 1980. "Fear," *The Philosophical Review*, 89:560–78.

——. 1986. "The Passivity of Emotions," *The Philosophical Review*, 95: 339–60.

——. 1987. *The Structure of Emotions*. Cambridge: Cambridge University Press.

Greenspan, P. 1988. *Emotions and Reasons*. New York: Routledge.

Griffiths, P. 1997. *What Emotions Really Are*. Chicago: University of Chicago Press.

Harre, R. 1986. *The Social Construction of Emotions*. New York: Blackwell.

Izard, C. 1992. "Basic Emotions, Relations among Emotions, and Emotion-Cognition Relations," *Psychological Review*, 99:561–5.

Izard, C., J. Kagan, and R. Zajonc, eds. 1984. *Emotions, Cognition, and Behavior*. Cambridge: Cambridge University Press.

James, W. 1890/1981. "The Emotions," in *The Principles of Psychology*. Cambridge, MA: Harvard University Press.

Kenny, A. 1963. *Action, Emotion, and Will*. London: Routledge & Kegan Paul.

Kitayama, S., and H. Marcus, eds. 1994. *Emotion and Culture*. Washington, DC: American Psychological Association.

LeDoux, J. 1989. "Cognitive-Emotional Interactions in the Brain," *Cognition and Emotion*, 3:267–89.

——. 1993. "Emotional Memory Systems in the Brain," *Behavioural Brain Research*, 58:69–79.

——. 1994. "Emotion, Memory and the Brain," *Scientific American*, 270:32–9.

——. 1996. *The Emotional Brain*. New York: Simon & Schuster.

LeDoux, J., and W. Hirst, eds. 1986. *Mind and Brain*. Part IV: Emotion. Cambridge: Cambridge University Press.

Lyons, W. 1980. *Emotion*. Cambridge: Cambridge University Press.

Mandler, G. 1975. *Mind and Emotion*. New York: Wiley.

Ortony, A., G. Clore, and A. Collins. 1988. *The Cognitive Structure of Emotions*. Cambridge: Cambridge University Press.

Rorty, A., ed. 1980. *Explaining Emotions*. Berkeley: University of California Press.

Shaffer, J. 1983. "An Assessment of Emotion," *American Philosophical Quarterly*, 20:161–73.

Schachter, S., and J. Singer. 1962. "Cognitive, Social, and Physiological Determinants of Emotional States," *Psychological Review*, 69(5):379–99.

Solomon, R. 1977. "The Rationality of the Emotions," *Southwestern Journal of Philosophy*, 8:105–14.

——. 1977. "The Logic of Emotions," *Nous*, 11:41–9.

——. 1993. *The Passions: Emotions and the Meaning of Life*. Indianapolis: Hackett.

Solomon, R., and C. Calhoun, eds. 1984. *What Is an Emotion?* Oxford: Oxford University Press.

Watson, J. B. 1919. *Psychology from the Standpoint of a Behaviorist.* Philadelphia: Lippincott.

Zajonc, R. 1980. "Feeling and Thinking: Preferences Need No Inferences," *American Psychologist*, 35(2):151–75.

4. Mental Evolution

Allen, C., and M. Bekoff. 1997. *Species of Mind.* Cambridge, MA: MIT/Bradford.

Barkow, J., L. Cosmides, and J. Tooby. 1992. *The Adapted Mind: Evolutionary Psychology and the Generation of Culture.* Oxford: Oxford University Press.

Bekoff, M., and D. Jamieson, eds. 1996. *Readings in Animal Cognition.* Cambridge, MA: MIT/Bradford.

Beninger, R., S. Kendall, and C. Vanderwolf. 1974. "The Ability of Rats to Discriminate Their Own Behaviors," *Canadian Journal of Psychology*, 28:79–91.

Blakemore, C., and S. Greenfield, eds. 1987. *Mindwaves.* Oxford: Blackwell.

Boesch, C. 1991. "Teaching among Wild Chimpanzees," *Animal Behavior*, 41:530–2.

Boesch, C., and H. Boesch. 1993. "Diversity of Tool-use and Tool-making in Wild Chimpanzees," in *The Use of Tools by Human and Non-human Primates*, A. Berthelet and J. Chavaillon, eds. Oxford: Clarendon Press.

Bonner, J. 1980. *The Evolution of Culture in Animals.* Princeton: Princeton University Press.

Bowler, P. 1984. *Evolution: The History of an Idea.* Berkeley: University of California Press.

Byrne, R. 1995. *The Thinking Ape: Evolutionary Origins of Intelligence.* Oxford: Oxford University Press.

Byrne, R., and A. Whiten. 1992. "Cognitive Evolution in Primates: Evidence from Tactical Deception," *Man* (new series), 27:609–27.

———, eds. 1988. *Machiavellian Intelligence: Social Expertise and the Evolution of Intellect in Monkeys, Apes, and Humans.* Oxford: Clarendon Press.

Cairns-Smith, A. G. 1996. *Evolving the Mind.* Cambridge: Cambridge University Press.

Carey, S., and R. Gelman, eds. 1991. *Epigenesis of Mind: Studies in Biology and Culture.* Hillsdale, NJ: Erlbaum.

Cheney, D., and R. Seyfarth. 1990. *How Monkeys See the World.* Chicago: University of Chicago Press.

Corballis, M. 1991. *The Lopsided Ape: Evolution of the Generative Mind.* Oxford: Oxford University Press.

Cummins, D., and C. Allen, eds. 1998. *The Evolution of Mind.* Oxford: Oxford University Press.

Darwin, C. 1859/1964. *On the Origin of Species.* Cambridge, MA: Harvard University Press.

———. 1871/1981. *The Descent of Man and Selection in Relation to Sex.* Princeton: Princeton University Press.

———. 1974. *Metaphysics, Materialism, and the Evolution of Mind.* Early Writings of Charles Darwin [M and N Notebooks], transcribed and annotated by P. Barrett. Chicago: University of Chicago Press.

Dawkins, R. 1976. *The Selfish Gene.* Oxford: Oxford University Press.

———. 1996. *Climbing Mount Improbable.* New York: W.W. Norton.

Desmond, A., and J. Moore. 1991. *Darwin: The Life of a Tormented Evolutionist.* New York: Time Warner.

de Waal, F. 1982. *Chimpanzee Politics.* London: Jonathan Cape.

———. 1996. *Good Natured. The Origins of Right and Wrong in Human and Other Animals.* Cambridge, MA: Harvard University Press.

Donald, M. 1991. *Origins of the Modern Mind.* Cambridge, MA: Harvard University Press.

Edelman, G. 1987. *Neural Darwinism: The Theory of Neuronal Group Selection.* New York: Basic Books.

Gallup, G. 1977. "Self-Recognition in Primates: A Comparative Approach to the Bi-directional Properties of Consciousness," *American Psychologist,* 32:329–38.

Gibson, K., and T. Ingold, eds. 1993. *Tools, Language and Cognition in Human Evolution.* Cambridge: Cambridge University Press.

Gould, S. 1973. *Ever Since Darwin.* New York: Norton.

———. 1980. *The Panda's Thumb.* New York: Norton.

———. 1985. *The Flamingo's Smile.* New York: Norton.

Griffin, D. 1984. *Animal Thinking.* Cambridge, MA: Harvard University Press.

———. 1986. *The Question of Animal Awareness: Evolutionary Continuity of Mental Experience.* New York: Rockefeller University Press.

———. 1992. *Animal Minds.* Chicago: University of Chicago Press.

Kitcher, P. 1982. *Abusing Science: The Case against Creationism.* Cambridge, MA: MIT/Bradford.

Lumsden, C., and E. Wilson. 1983. *Promethean Fire: Reflections on the Origin of Mind.* Cambridge, MA: Harvard University Press.

Midgely, M. 1978. *Man and Beast: The Roots of Human Nature.* Ithaca, NY: Cornell University Press.

Mithen, S. 1996. *The Prehistory of the Mind: The Cognitive Origins of Art, Religion, and Science.* London: Thames and Hudson.

Povenelli, D. 1993. "Reconstructing the Evolution of the Mind," *American Psychologist,* 48:493–509.

Premack, A., and D. Premack. 1972. "Teaching Language to an Ape," *Scientific American,* 227:92–9.

Richards, R. 1987. *Darwin and the Emergence of Evolutionary Theories of Mind and Behavior*. Chicago: University of Chicago Press.

Ruse, M., ed. 1996. *But Is It Science? The Philosophical Question in the Creation-Evolution Controversy*. Amherst, NY: Prometheus.

Sober, E. 1981. "The Evolution of Rationality," *Synthèse*, 46:95–120.

Tomasello, M., and J. Call. 1997. *Primate Cognition*. New York: Oxford.

Vauclair, J. 1996. *Animal Cognition: An Introduction to Modern Comparative Psychology*. Cambridge, MA: Harvard University Press.

Wallace, A. R. 1870. *Contributions to the Theory of Natural Selection*. London: Macmillan.

Wilson, E. O. 1998. *Consilience*. New York: Knopf.

5. Self

Allen, D., ed. 1997. *Culture and Self: Philosophical and Religious Perspectives, East and West*. Boulder, CO: Westview Press.

Bermudez, J., A. Marcel, and N. Eilan, eds. 1995. *The Body and the Self*. Cambridge, MA: MIT/Bradford.

Dennett, D. 1978. "Where Am I?" in *Brainstorms*. Montgomery, VT: Bradford.

Elster, J., ed. 1986. *The Multiple Self*. Cambridge: Cambridge University Press.

Ferguson, A. 1997. "Moral Responsibility and Social Change: A New Theory of Self," *Hypatia*, 12(3):116–41.

Flanagan, O. 1996. *Self-Expressions: Mind, Morals, and the Meaning of Life*. New York: Oxford University Press.

Gazzaniga, M. 1970. *The Bisected Brain*. New York: Appleton-Century-Crofts.

———. 1985. *The Social Brain: Discovering the Networks of the Mind*. New York: Basic Books.

Hofstadter, D., and D. Dennett, eds. 1981. *The Mind's I: Fantasies and Reflections on Self and Soul*. New York: Basic Books.

Hume, D. 1739/1973. *A Treatise of Human Nature*. Oxford: Oxford University Press.

Kant, I. 1781/1996. *Critique of Pure Reason*. Werner S. Pluhar, trans. Indianapolis: Hackett.

Locke, J. 1690/1996. *An Essay Concerning Human Understanding*. vol. 1. Indianapolis: Hackett.

Mead, G. 1934. *Mind, Self, and Society*. Chicago: University of Chicago Press.

Meyers, D., ed. 1997. *Feminists Rethink the Self*. Boulder, CO: Westview Press.

Parfit, D. 1984. *Reasons and Persons*. New York: Oxford University Press.

Perry, J. 1978. *A Dialogue on Personal Identity and Immortality*. Indianapolis: Hackett.

Pettit, P., and J. McDowell. 1986. *Subject, Thought, and Context*. Oxford: Clarendon.

Ramachandran, V., and S. Blakeslee. 1998. *Phantoms in the Brain*. New York: Morrow.

Rorty, A., ed. 1976. *The Identities of Persons*. Berkeley: University of California Press.

Sacks, O. 1987. *The Man Who Mistook His Wife for a Hat*. New York: Harper.

Schechtman, M. 1996. *The Constitution of Selves*. Ithaca, NY: Cornell University Press.

Scheffler, I. 1982. *Science and Subjectivity*. Indianapolis: Hackett.

Shaffer, J. 1966. "Persons and their Bodies," *Philosophical Review*, 25:59–77.

Taylor, C. 1989. *Sources of the Self*. Cambridge, MA: Harvard University Press.

Wiggins, D. 1987. "The Person as Object of Science, as Subject of Experience, and as Locus of Value," in *Persons and Personality*, A. Peacocke and G. Gillett, eds. Oxford: Blackwell.

Wilkes, K. 1988. *Real People*. Oxford: Clarendon.

Williams, B. 1973. *Problems of the Self*. Cambridge: Cambridge University Press.

Vesey, G. 1974. *Personal Identity*. Ithaca, NY: Cornell University Press.

6. Artificial Intelligence

Bechtel, W., and A. Abrahamsen. 1991. *Connectionism and the Mind*. Oxford: Blackwell.

Boden, M. 1981. *Minds and Mechanisms*. Ithaca, NY: Cornell University Press.

——. 1987. *Artificial Intelligence and Natural Man*. 2nd ed. London: MIT Press.

——. 1988. *Computer Models of the Mind*. Cambridge: Cambridge University Press.

——. 1990. *The Creative Mind: Myths and Mechanisms*. London: Weidenfeld and Nicolson.

——, ed. 1990. *The Philosophy of Artificial Intelligence*. New York: Oxford University Press.

Clark, A., and P. Millican, eds. 1996. *Connectionism, Concepts, and Folk Psychology*. Oxford: Clarendon.

Copeland, J. 1993. *Artificial Intelligence: A Philosophical Introduction*. Oxford: Blackwell.

Dreyfus, H. 1972/1992. *What Computers Still Can't Do*. Cambridge, MA: MIT/Bradford.

Fodor, J., and Z. Pylyshyn. 1988. "Connectionism and Cognitive Architecture: A Critical Analysis," *Cognition*, 28:3–71.

Franklin, S. 1995. *Artificial Minds*. Cambridge, MA: MIT/Bradford.

Gardner, H. 1983. *Frames of Mind: The Theory of Multiple Intelligences*. New York: Basic Books.

——. 1993. *Multiple Intelligences: The Theory in Practice*. New York: Basic Books.

Graubard, S., ed. 1988. *The Artificial Intelligence Debate*. Cambridge, MA: MIT/Bradford.

Gunderson, K. 1971. *Mentality and Machines*. Minneapolis: University of Minnesota Press.

Haugeland, J. 1985. *Artificial Intelligence: The Very Idea*. Cambridge, MA: MIT/Bradford.

———, ed. 1997. *Mind Design II: Philosophy, Psychology, Artificial Intelligence*. Cambridge, MA: MIT/Bradford.

Hookway, C., ed. 1984. *Minds, Machines, and Evolution*. Cambridge: Cambridge University Press.

Horgan, T., and J. Tienson. 1989. "Representations without Rules," *Philosophical Topics*, 17:147–74.

———. 1996. *Connectionism and the Philosophy of Psychology*. Cambridge, MA: MIT/Bradford.

Johnson, D. M., and C. E. Erneling, eds. 1997. *The Future of the Cognitive Revolution*. Oxford: Oxford University Press.

de La Mettrie, J. 1748/1912. *Man a Machine*. LaSalle, IL: Open Court.

Moody, T. 1993. *Philosophy and Artificial Intelligence*. Englewood Cliffs, NJ: Prentice-Hall.

Penrose, R. 1989. *The Emperor's New Mind: Concerning Computers, Minds, and the Laws of Physics*. Oxford: Oxford University Press.

Ringle, M., ed. 1979. *Philosophical Perspectives on Artificial Intelligence*. Atlantic Highlands, NJ: Humanities Press.

Rumelhart, D., and J. McClelland, eds. 1986. *Parallel Distributed Processing*. 2 vols., Cambridge, MA: MIT/Bradford.

Schank, R. 1984. *The Cognitive Computer*. Reading, MA: Addison-Wesley.

Searle, J. 1984. *Minds, Brains, and Science*. Cambridge, MA: Harvard University Press.

Simon, H. 1981. *The Sciences of the Artificial*. 2nd ed., Cambridge, MA: MIT/Bradford.

Smolensky, P. 1987. "The Constituent Structure of Connectionist Mental States: A Reply to Fodor and Pylyshyn," *Southern Journal of Philosophy*, 26 Supplement, published as *Connectionism and the Philosophy of Mind*, T. Horgan and J. Tienson, eds.

Tienson, J. 1987. "An Introduction to Connectionism," *Southern Journal of Philosophy*, 26 Supplement, published as *Connectionism and the Philosophy of Mind*, T. Horgan and J. Tienson, eds.

Van Gelder, T. 1990. "Compositionality: A Connectionist Variation of a Classical Theme," *Cognitive Science*, 14:355–84.

Weizenbaum, J. 1976. *Computer Power and Human Reason*. San Francisco: Freeman.

7. Behavior and Mental States

Baron-Cohen, S. 1995. *Mindblindness: An Essay on Autism and Theory of Mind*. Cambridge, MA: MIT/Bradford.

Baron-Cohen, S., A. Leslie, and U. Frith. 1985. "Does the Autistic Child Have a 'Theory of Mind'?" *Cognition*, 21:37–46.

Bartsch, K., and H. Wellman. 1989. "Young Children's Attribution of Action to Beliefs and Desires," *Child Development*, 60:946–64.

Carruthers, P., and P. Smith, eds. 1996. *Theories of Theories of Mind*. Cambridge: Cambridge University Press.

Davies, M., and T. Stone, eds. 1995. *Folk Psychology*. Oxford: Blackwell.

———. 1995. *Mental Simulation*. Oxford: Blackwell.

Fodor, J. 1987. *Psychosemantics*. Cambridge, MA: MIT/Bradford.

Gopnik, A., and H. Wellman. 1992. "Why the Child's Theory of Mind Really *Is* a Theory," *Mind and Language*, 7; reprinted in *Folk Psychology*, M. Davies and T. Stone, eds.

Graham, G., and G. Stephens, eds. *Philosophical Psychopathology*. Cambridge, MA: MIT/Bradford.

Premack, D. 1988. "Does the Chimpanzee Have a Theory of Mind? Revisited," in *Machiavellian Intelligence*, R. Byrne and A. Whiten, eds., Oxford: Clarendon, pp.160–79.

Premack, D., and G. Woodruff. 1978. "Does the Chimpanzee Have a Theory of Mind?" *Behavioral and Brain Sciences*, 1(4):515–26.

Whiten, A., ed. 1991. *Natural Theories of Mind: Evolution, Development and Simulation of Everyday Mindreading*. Oxford: Blackwell.

Wilson, T., and R. Nisbett. 1978. "The Accuracy of Verbal Reports about the Effects of Stimuli on Evaluations and Behavior," *Social Psychology*, 41(2):118–31.

Wimmer, H., and J. Perner. 1983. "Beliefs about Beliefs: Representation and Constraining Function of Wrong Beliefs in Young Children's Understanding of Deception," *Cognition*, 13:103–28.

Index

(Page numbers in **bold type** indicate the place
where the item is first defined or explained.)

Abrahamsen, Adele, 195, 217
absent qualia argument, 43, **44–5**
Allport, Alan, 67, 69
American Sign Language, 38, 139, 144
amnesic syndrome, 15, 66, **166**
Analogy, Argument from, 223–4, 226–8,
    237, 242, 244, 246–8, 252, 256
animal minds, 136–45
"animal spirits" (*see* Descartes, René)
anosognosia, **173**
anthropomorphism, **143**, 144–5, 146
aphasia, 15, **83**, 85, 194
Aristotle, 4, 96, 97, 109–10, 115, 121
Armon-Jones, Claire, 117
Armstrong, David, 40–1, 43, 66, 72–5
Artificial Intelligence (*see also* Symbol
    Systems *and* Connectionism/
    PDP), 55–6, 191
ascent routine, **246–7**, 251, 252, 255, 256
asomatognosias, **173**
Associationism, 217
assumptions, 50, **51**
asymmetry argument, 6–9, 15, 17, 29,
    30, 35
Augustine, 55
autism, **241**, 242, 252, 253, 256
autonomy of psychology, 43
autotopagnosia, **173**

Baars, Bernard, 85–7
Balint's Syndrome, **205**
Baron-Cohen, Simon, 240
Bechtel, William, 195, 217
Behaviorism, 14, 17–20, 21, 23, 40, 99,
    106–9, 154, 165, 179, 230
    Linguistic (Logical), 14, 17, 19
    Metaphysical, 17, 18, 51, 155
    Methodological (Psychological), 17,
        18, 19, 155
Bennett, Jonathan, 230
Bergson, Henri, 190

binary notation, 81, 192, 213, 214
binding problem, 88
blindsight, 15, **44**
Block, Ned, 20, 43
Bonner, John, 150
brain scans, **101**
Brentano, Franz, 30
Buddha, 169–70
Byrne, Alex, 79

category mistake (*see also* Ryle,
    Gilbert), 14
causality, 168–9, 226
Causal Theory of Mind, 40–1
Central State Identity Theory (*see*
    Identity Theory)
ceteris paribus clauses, **234**, 242, 254
Chalmers, David, 34, 79–82, 152
"Chinese Room" argument, 198–9
Churchland, Patricia, 19, 26–9, 66, 67
Churchland, Paul, 9, 27, 29, 235
Clark, Andy, 216, 217
co-evolution of theories, 28
cognitive closure, 89
cognitive penetrability, **249–50**
combinatorial explosion, **201**
commissurotomy, **60**
computers, serial vs. parallel, 211, 215
conceptual analysis, 100
contrastive analysis, 86
Connectionism (or Parallel Distributed
    Processing—PDP), 205–16
consciousness, 20, 30, 33, 47, 52, 54–93,
    107, 127, 151–2, 159–63, 165,
    173, 185, 203
    biological naturalism, 87–8
    criteria for attributing, 56
    Eliminativism, 89–90
    functions of, 90–93
    global workspace theory, 85–7
    Higher-Order theories, 71–9, 86

Multiple Drafts theory, 82–5
nonphysical property theories, 69–71
    (Descartes); 79–82
    (Chalmers)
synchronous neural oscillations,
    88–9
the "Mysteria," 89
constraints, hard vs. soft, 209–10
Copeland, Jack, 195
Corballis, Michael, 102
Craik, Kenneth, 91–2
Crick, Francis, 88–9
Cummins, Robert, 46
"Cyc," 201

Damasio, Antonio, 173, 186
Darwin, Charles, 121–3, 132–3, 134,
    138, 148, 178
definitions (*see also* necessary and
    sufficient conditions)
    compositional vs. functional, 39–40
de La Mettrie, Julien, 189
Dennett, Daniel, 45, 82–5, 87, 146,
    202–3, 230–1, 249
Descartes, René, 2–11, 33, 58, 139, 143–
    5, 148, 153, 160–2, 178, 189,
    224, 227
    on "animal spirits," 10
    on *cogito ergo sum*, 160–1
    on consciousness, 69–71
    on emotions, 99, 102–4, 105, 115,
        118, 121–3, 127
    on mind as mental substance, 2–3
    on Self, 159–62
Dewey, John, 200
dispositional vs. occurrent mental states,
    111, 242
domain-specific claims, 25, 47
Donald, Merlin, 150
dreams, 56, 57, 66, 67
Dretske, Fred, 73–4, 77–8
Dreyfus, Hubert, 199–203
Dualism, **2**, 21, 36, 58, 88, 145, 165
    Property Dualism, 33–36, 79–80,
        127, 152, 156, 191
    Substance Dualism, 2–11, 14, 22,
        35, 102–3, 127, 154, 156, 160

élan vital, 190
Eliminativism, **26–7**, 89–90

emergent properties, **33**, 34, 87, 152,
    218
emotions, 45, 47, 52, 96–128, 143, 185,
    199, 203, 244, 255
    Behavioral view, 106–9, 125, 127
    Cognitive view, 109–20
    functions of, 121–3
    Physiological/Feeling view, 102–5,
        111, 124
empiricism, **165**, 166, 169, 178
Epiphenomenalism, 35, **36**, 44, 59, 80,
    127, 219
evaluation of theories, 49–53, 126, 131,
    154
evolution (*see also* natural selection), 10,
    30, 76, 104, 122, 131–3, 178, 237
    of brain, 135, 155
    mental, 131–56, 186
    and Self, 184–6
explanatory gap, 59, 88
extension vs. intension of a term, **100**
extraterrestrial intelligence (ETI), 38,
    191

false belief test, 231–2, 239, 240–2, 252,
    256
Family Resemblance, **67**, 75, 120, 208
Flanagan, Owen, 69, 82, 89, 224–7
fMRI (*see also* brain scans), **101**
Fodor, Jerry, 20, 40, 42, 193–5, 212, 216,
    217, 236, 240, 256
Folk Psychology, 27, 230, 233–8, 242,
    243, 250
"frame" problem, 207, 210
free will, **5–6**, 7, 29
Frith, Uta, 240, 253
Fuller, Gary, 255
Functionalism, 38–48, 156, 165, 195,
    238, 242
    Homuncular, 45–6, 74, 83
    Machine, 41–5, 51, 128, 195
    Teleological, 46, 74, 128

Goldman, Alvin, 242, 243, 246–51,
    253–6
Gopnik, Alison, 230, 236, 240, 256
Gordon, Robert, 238, 243–6, 251–2,
    254–6

Harmon, Gilbert, 230, 231

Harris, Paul, 243, 246, 248, 252, 253, 256
Heal, Jane, 243, 253
Heidegger, Martin, 199
hemi-neglect, 15, 19
hemispherectomy, 194
higher-order mental states, 71
Hinton, Geoffrey, 211, 213
Hobbes, Thomas, 21, 195
homunculus, 45, 74, 83
Hume, David, 99, 161
    on causality, 168–9, 226
    on Self, 166–9, 174, 176, 178
humors (four), 27, 227
Humphrey, Nicholas, 62, 92, 142
Hundred Step argument, 211

Identity Theory, 23, 26, 27, 40
images (see representations, mental)
immortality, 2, 4–5, 6, 9, 29, 161
information, mathematical notion of, 81
instrumentalism, 145–6
intentionality, 30, 105, 115, 119, 194
interaction problem (mind/body), 10, 19, 22, 29
introspection, 8, 9, 17, 57, 58, 93, 100, 101, 103, 107, 169, 224, 225, 227, 251–2, 255
Inverted Spectrum argument, 43–4

Jackson, Frank, 29, 34
James, William, 17, 90–1, 105, 111, 113, 120
    on emotions, 99, 104
    on Self, 175–8, 184
Janet, Pierre, 102
Johnson-Laird, Philip, 204

Kant, Immanuel, 170–1
Kluver-Bucy Syndrome, 205
Koch, Christof, 88
Kosslyn, Stephen, 205

La Belle Indifférence, 102
language of thought (LOT), 194
LeDoux, Joseph, 113–5, 122
Leibniz, Gottfried, 195
Lenat, Doug, 201
Leslie, Alan, 237, 240
Lewis, David, 40, 233

Locke, John, 166, 176
    on Self, 162–4, 178
Lycan, William, 45, 46, 72, 73–5, 77, 79
Lyons, William, 112–3

MacIntyre, Alasdair, 182–3
materialism, 21, 22
McClelland, James, 211, 213
McGinn, Colin, 89
Mead, George Herbert, 179–81
memory, 56–7, 67, 164–5, 168, 184, 214
    content-addressable vs. location-addressable, 210, 215
mental dissociations, 15, 189
metaphysical issues, 6
Meyers, Diana, 184
Mill, John Stuart, 227
Minsky, Marvin, 85, 151, 190
multiple realizability, 39

Nagel, Thomas, 29, 152
natural selection, 36, 132–3, 147, 148–54
necessary and sufficient conditions, 65, 66–9, 75, 98, 120, 208
neurogenesis, 208
Nichols, Shaun, 238, 249–50, 253
Nisbett, Richard, 225

other minds, problem of, 222–3, 227

Panksepp, Jaak, 185
panpsychism, 55, 80, 219
Parallel Distributed Processing (see Connectionism)
parallel processing systems (see computers, serial vs. parallel)
Parfit, Derek, 165–6, 174–5
pattern recognition, 207, 218
Perner, Josef, 231
PET scans (see also brain scans), 101
phantom limb, 7, 8, 160
Physicalism, 21–31, 42, 48, 75, 155
    Eliminative, 26–7, 155
    Nonreductive, 28–9, 34, 42, 155
    Reductive, 27–8, 155
    Token, 24, 25–6, 27, 42, 43, 155
    Type, 24–5, 27, 38, 43, 155
Pinker, Steven, 63
Place, U. T., 23

Plato, 2, 159
Premack, David, 228–30
prosopagnosia, 15, **23**, 62
Prototype theory, **68**, 75, 120, 208
Putnam, Hilary, 40
Pylyshyn, Zenon, 212, 216, 217

qualia, **31**, 43–5, 47, 62, 63, 127

Ramachandran, V. S., 8
rationality, 96–8, 123–5, 254
reductio ad absurdum argument, 82
relevance, problems determining, 200–
    3, 210, 254
representations, mental, 199–200, 206
    analog vs. digital, **204**
    images, 199, 204, 205, 214
    linguistic, 192–5, 204, 216
    local vs. distributed, **214–5**, 217
Representations and Rules Theory, 191–
    5, 199
Rey, Georges, 89–90
Rosch, Eleanor, 68
Rosenthal, David, 72, 73, 75–7, 78
Rumelhart, David, 211, 213
Russell, Bertrand, 152, 195
Ryle, Gilbert, 11, 14–6, 19, 64

Samuel, Arthur, 196
Schachter, Stanley, 110–2, 114, 226
Schechtman, Marya, 182
Searle, John, 34, 87–8, 198–9
Self, 45, 62, 64, 74, 92, 159–186, 216
    bodily (at least) theory, 171–4
    Bundle theory, 166–9
    multidimensional theory, 175–8
    Narrative theory, 182–3
    Nonphysical theory, 159–62
    Psychological theory, 162–6
    Reciprocal theory, 181–2
    Social Construct theory, 178–82
    Transcendental theory, 170–1
self-consciousness, 64
serial computers (*see* computers, serial
    vs. parallel)
Shannon, Claude, 81
Simulation theory (of mental
    attribution), 243–54
Singer, Jerome, 110–2, 114, 226

Skinner, B. F., 18, 19, 107–8, 179
Smart, J. J. C., 23
Sober, Elliott, 46
Social Constructionism, 116–9, 120,
    178–80
Sociobiology, 150–1
Solomon, Robert, 115–6, 120, 122
soul, **4**, 148
    in Aristotle, 4, 109
    in Descartes, 4, 102, 103, 122, 160
Spinoza, Benedict de, 99
split-brain syndrome, 15, **60**, 61, 66, 85,
    87, 164
Stich, Stephen, 238, 249–50, 253
substance, 2, **3**, 4, 14, 33, 35, 160–3, 177
supervenience, 79, 81
Symbol-System theories, 191–9

theory, **233**, 236, 238, 248, 253–5
theory of mind (*see also* Folk
    Psychology), 92, 142, 228–30,
    232–3, 236–7
Theory-theory (of mental attribution),
    232–42
thought experiment, 44, **172**, 171–4
transcendental questions, **170**
Turing, Alan, 41, 197
Turing machine, 41–2
Turing test, 197–9
type/token distinction, **24**

visual agnosia, **62**
vitalism, **190**

Wallace, Alfred Russel, 148–53
Watson, John, 17–9, 99, 106–7, 179
ways of knowing mind and body (*see*
    asymmetry argument)
Wellman, Henry, 230, 236, 240, 256
Whitehead, Alfred North, 195
Williams, Bernard, 171–4
Wilson, Timothy, 225
Wimmer, Heinz, 231
Wittgenstein, Ludwig
    on Family Resemblance, 67, 120
    on mental concepts, 235
Woodruff, Guy, 228–30

zombies, **44**, 45, 58, 59, 79, 90, 173